Readings from the Disciplines
Research Models for Writers

Christine A. Hult
Utah State University

Allyn and Bacon
Boston London Toronto Sydney Tokyo Singapore

Copyright © 1997 by Allyn & Bacon
A Viacom Company
160 Gould Street
Needham Heights, Massachusetts 02194

Internet: www.abacon.com
America Online: keyword: College Online

All rights reserved. No part of the material protected by this copyright may be reproduced or utilized in any form or by any means, electronic or mechanical, including photocopying, recording, or by any information storage and retrieval system, without the written permission of the copyright owner.

ISBN 0-205-26916-8

Printed in the United States of America

10 9 8 7 6 5 4 3 2 1   02 01 00 99 98 97

CONTENTS

Preface 6

PART ONE : 7

READINGS FROM THE SCIENCES & TECHNOLOGY 7

Using Academic Integrity To Teach Engineering Ethics 8
    P. Aarne Vesilind
    JOURNAL OF ENGINEERING EDUCATION

Interactions Between Coyotes and Red Foxes in Yellowstone National Park, Wyoming 19
    Eric M. Gese, Timm E. Storrs, and Scott Grothe
    JOURNAL OF MAMMALOGY

Values & Biology Education 30
    James R. Nichols
    THE AMERICAN BIOLOGY TEACHER

Emissaries to the Stars: The Astronomers of Ancient Maya 38
    Anthony F. Aveni
    MERCURY

Editorial: Is Physics Multicultural? 45
    Don S. Lemons
    AMERICAN JOURNAL OF PHYSICS

TABLE OF CONTENTS

PART TWO: 48

READINGS FROM THE SOCIAL SCIENCES 48

The Immediate Effects of Homicidal, Suicidal, and Nonviolent Heavy Metal and Rap Songs on the Moods of College Students 49
    Mary E. Ballard and Steven Coates
    YOUTH & SOCIETY

Take Your Partners: A Description of a Student Social System in a Secondary School Dance Class 69
    Peter A. Hastie and Andrew Pickwell
    JOURNAL OF TEACHING IN PHYSICAL EDUCATION

Being a Grandmother in the Tewa World 93
    Sue-Ellen Jacobs
    AMERICAN INDIAN CULTURE & RESEARCH JOURNAL

Trading Arms for Hostages? How the Government and Print Media "Spin" Portrayals of the United States' Policy Toward Iran 109
    William J. Brown and Richard C. Vincent
    POLITICAL COMMUNICATION

Doing Sociology: Connecting the Classroom Experience with a Multiethnic School District 129
    Jose Calderon and Betty Farrell
    TEACHING SOCIOLOGY

PART THREE: 144

READINGS FROM THE HUMANITIES AND ARTS 144

What's Wrong with Telling the Truth? An Analysis of Gossip 145
    Margaret G. Holland
    AMERICAN PHILOSOPHICAL QUARTERLY

"Put a Pretty Face On It": Stevie Smith and Anti-Semitism 166
    Catherine A. Civello
    RE: ARTS & LETTERS

Maturation of Tribal Governments During the Atomic Age 182
    Marjane Ambler
    HALCYON

Yes, It's True: Zimbabweans Love Dolly Parton 194
    Jonathan Zilberg
    JOURNAL OF POPULAR CULTURE

Moving from First-Stage to Second-Stage Multiculturalism in the Art Classroom 210
    John A. Stinespring
    ART EDUCATION

Playing it Safe 218
    Britt Allen
    TEACHING MUSIC

PREFACE

In this reader, you will find articles written by scholars in their fields that were first published in professional journals. These articles will serve you well as models for your own research papers and reports in your college classes. The articles are engaging and accessible, with topics ranging from coyotes and foxes in Yellowstone to the social system of a high school dance class. Because these articles were chosen exclusively from professional journals, they will help you to become familiar with the types of academic writing you will encounter throughout your college experience and into your chosen career.

This reader is designed to be used independently or with a research guide or handbook. The purpose of this reader is to provide you with professional journal articles as models for your own research. *Readings from the Disciplines* introduces you to the types of writing typically found in the professional journals from various fields. It will be an important learning tool for you, because it provides you with real writing from your discipline in an accessible form. In this way, you will become familiar with the types of articles and the formats those articles are presented in from various academic fields.

Readings from the Disciplines is divided into three parts: I. Readings from the Sciences and Technology, II. Readings from the Social Sciences, and III. Readings from the Humanities and Arts. Each article is presented in its entirety as it was originally printed in the professional journal. Following the article are discussion questions to encourage you to look for features of the article such as the effectiveness of its argument, the author's thesis or tone, the article's organization or structure, and so on. You are also encouraged to make connections between the articles and your own experience as a beginning scholar.

1

Readings from the Sciences and Technology

The sciences hold an authoritative position in modern society and have been enormously successful at formulating and testing theories related to the natural and physical world. Scientific insights and methods have also been carried over to fields of applied science and technology, such as computer science and engineering. Writing in the sciences tends to be of two general types: 1) reports of original research or 2) reviews or speculative articles on more general bodies of information. The readings selected for Part I exemplify both kinds of scientific writing.

The article by Gese, Storrs & Grothe from the *Journal of Mammalogy* illustrates type one: a straightforward report of original research. These wildlife biologists studied animal behaviors in the field and they report their findings in the form of a journal article. The sections of the report also typify this kind of scientific writing: Abstract, Materials & Methods, Results, Discussion, Acknowledgments, and Literature Cited.

The remaining articles broadly illustrate type two, although they vary from a scholarly argument favoring ethics in engineering education to a more informal discussion of Mayan astronomy. The range of readings is intended to illustrate for you the range of writing found in the sciences and technology. Both Vesilind and Nichols argue for curricular reform in their disciplines: Vesilind for inclusion of ethics in engineering education and Nichols for inclusion of values in biology education. Aveni describes in a colorful and lively way the astronomers of ancient Maya. His article is geared toward a less specialized audience with the purpose of entertaining as well as informing on his topic. The final piece is an editorial from a physics journal which attempts to place the field of physics into the larger university discussion of multiculturalism.

All of the articles included in Part One are reproduced in their entirety from the journals in which they were originally published, by permission of the publisher and/or author(s).

Using Academic Integrity To Teach Engineering Ethics

P. Aarne Vesilind, Duke University

ABSTRACT

Ethics can be taught by using case studies to which students can relate. Since all students appreciate and understand problems of academic dishonesty, the nature of ethical problems in academics can be used to illustrate ethical problems encountered in professional engineering. If students can be sensitized to the value of ethical behavior while in school, they will carry this understanding over to their profession. The purpose of this paper is to suggest that academic integrity can be used to introduce the basic concepts of professional engineering ethics. A videotape and instructor's manual using this pedagogical technique is described.

I. ACADEMIC INTEGRITY

Although most engineering educators and practitioners agree that engineering ethics should be included in the engineering curriculum, this is often difficult to achieve. First, most engineering schools do not have faculty who are qualified to teach professional ethics, and second, teaching engineering ethics in its abstract is ineffective since students have difficulty recognizing the significance of ethical problems in engineering. Students cannot identify with the problems facing the practicing engineer since they have never been in that role. They have never had a client, for example, so how can they appreciate the problems of client confidentiality? Pedagogically, students respond best to material with which they are somewhat familiar. It only makes sense, therefore, to begin teaching ethics using problems that students understand and can relate to. The most ubiquitous and familiar ethical problem facing students is cheating on school work.

Copyright 1996 by the American Society for Engineering Education. Reprinted with permission from ASSE *Journal of Engineering Education* (January 1996, pp. 41-44).

The objective of this paper is to show how academic integrity can be used to illustrate the concept of professional ethics. It should be possible to sensitize students to future ethical problems they might encounter during their professional careers by relating academic dishonesty to professional engineering ethics.

The moral development and maturation of college students is rapid during their college years, and the quality of the education they receive can influence their professional conduct following graduation.[1] Derek Bok has eloquently discussed this moral development of students and called for the revival of moral education in the American universities.[2] As evidenced by the work of Heath, universities and colleges have a major influence on the moral development of students.[3] It therefore seems imperative that universities provide the courses, teachers and atmosphere for students' moral development.

The American university, in addition to its role as the purveyor of knowledge, is supposed to be a place where the students develop and mature intellectually in multiple dimensions. Chickering suggests that the college experience should include "developing intellectual competence; learning to manage emotions; developing and establishing autonomy, establishing identity, developing interpersonal relationships; developing a sense of purpose; and developing integrity."[4]

Heath studied the maturation of students and postulated that the college was influential in what he considered the important facets of human development: "To become a more mature person is to grow intellectually, to form guiding values, to become knowledgeable about oneself, and to develop social, interpersonal skills."[5] At the conclusion of his study of college graduates he was apparently surprised that "the college's distinctive, most salient, enduring effect was to permanently alter the character, the values, and the motives of many men."[3]

And yet, there is no doubt that academic dishonesty is a serious problem in American higher education. Numerous surveys have confirmed that a vast majority of college students cheat at least once during their time in college, and one fourth are regular cheaters. Some studies show that academic dishonesty has increased markedly in the past decades (see for example the 1979 Carnegie Council study, reference 6). There is little doubt that the level of cheating is very high, as measured by numerous surveys.[7-21]

Engineering students are just as likely to cheat as other students, and in some studies engineering students have been found to have a higher than average incidence of cheating. In a recent study, McCabe et al[22] show a breakdown by intended profession (Table 1), and engineering is high in the ranking of students cheating.

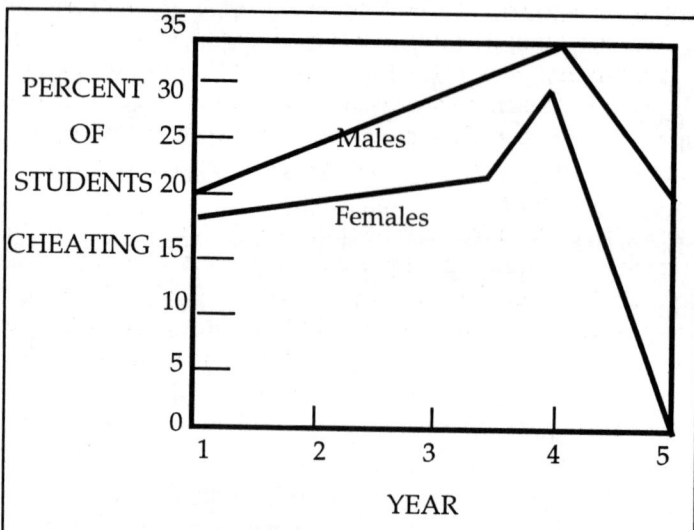

Figure 1. Incidence of cheating among engineering students at Drexel University Data by Nguyen et. al, courtesy of Professor William Zuspan (Emeritus), Department of Civil Engineering, Drexel University, Philadelphia, PA (18)

Intended Career	Percent of students who cheated at least once
Business	76%
Engineering	71%
Medicine	68%
Public Service	66%
Arts	64%
Law	63%
Education	57%

Table 1. Frequency of cheating, by intended major.(22)

Year	Percent of engineering students copying on term papers or assignments at least once
Freshman	26.1
Sophomore	58.6
Junior	70.9
Senior	59.7

Table 2. Academic dishonesty by engineering students.(23)

Interestingly, Nguyen and colleagues,[18] in a student project at Drexel University, found that cheating incidence for engineering students rose steadily from the first year to the fourth year, and then dropped off dramatically. They found that not a single female engineer interviewed had cheated during the senior year. Their study did not have statistical significance, but the results are nevertheless interesting. A summary of their results is illustrated in Figure 1.

The variability in cheating with year in college was also studied by Harp and Taietz who also found a parabolic relationship in cheating (Table 2).[23] The authors did not speculate on why the dropoff in cheating might occur for engineers during the senior year, but one explanation for the reduction in academic dishonesty during the senior year might be the students' moral development. Herch, Paolitto and Reimer cite an unreferenced study of college students that found that the level of moral development (as defined by the Kohlberg scale)* has an effect on academic integrity. They found that of those students who scored at level 3 and 4 on the moral development scale, 40% had cheated, whereas only 11% of the students who scored 5 or 6 cheated.[24]**

It seems reasonable to conclude that students do experience moral development during their schooling, that this process can be enhanced and strengthened, and that the results of such development will have a lasting effect on the students' professional lives. The key is to relate this development to professional engineering. In fact, this is not difficult, since many of the values involved in academic integrity apply equally well to professional engineering ethics. Since we know that engineering students tend to cheat as often as other students and that such cheating seems to be pervasive, it might be useful to take advantage of this and to use academic integrity as a bridge to the understanding of professional ethics.

II. THE BRIDGE FROM ACADEMIC INTEGRITY TO ENGINEERING ETHICS

There appears to be a direct link between academic integrity and professional engineering ethics. Consider the following scenarios to illustrate that similar values are involved in ethical problems commonly encountered by students and by professional engineers.

---

*The Kohlberg scale of moral develoment ranges from 1 where the individual has no sense of moral reasoning, to 6, the highest level of moral reasoning. See Kohlberg, L. *The Philosphy of Moral Development* vol. 1, Harper and Row, New York, 1971.

**There is some question about the validity of this study. None of Kohlberg's students in the original study ever reached level 6 in reasoning.

Loyalty to Friends and Deception

A.) Student A develops a foolproof way of cheating on a mechanics examination, and shows one of his friends (student B) what he intends to do. Student B does not want to participate in the scheme, and wants to stop student A from cheating. Should student B tell the professor what he knows in order to prevent the cheating from ever occurring?

B.) This scenario can be related to the problem many engineers face when they know that a colleague is planning to engage in unethical conduct. If engineer A decides to give himself a raise by padding his travel account, and tells engineer B about his plans, the alternative courses of action can range from doing nothing to alerting the accounting department and possibly preventing his friend from getting into trouble.

Confidentiality and Loyalty

A.) A homework problem in structural analysis is to be solved using a computer program. Student A writes a program that cuts down the computation time, but still requires further programming. She is asked by her friends to share the program with them. They try to convince her that this is simply a computational tool and has no bearing on their understanding of the problem. They appeal to her as a friend to help them. Should she share her work, and if one of her colleagues uses it, should it be cited?

B.) Engineer A has just started work for a company when her boss asks the engineer for information on the jobs conducted by the previous employer, suggesting that there is nothing sacred about such information and that sharing it would make engineer A more valuable to her new firm.

Plagiarism

A.) A student in an engineering project class uses a writing tutor to help him with the final report. What are the student's obligations to cite the assistance? At what point does assistance become unethical?

B.) An engineer, in writing a final report for a client, plagiarizes his own work that he did for another client. He does not acknowledge the original source, even though he receives compensation for the initial writing.

III. APPLICATION OF THEORY TO PRACTICE

Supported in part by funds from the National Science Foundation, the concept of using academic integrity to teach professional engineering ethics has been incorporated into a videotape and instructor's manual designed for classroom use. This videotape contains four scenarios illustrating problems in academic integrity—problems with which all students are familiar. The actors are Duke University students and the video is professionally directed and produced. In all four scenarios, the decision is left unresolved so as to provide maximum opportunity for classroom discussion.

The principles highlighted in all four scenarios are also basic principles in professional engineering. The instructor's manual which accompanies this videotape contains material that bridges these ethical issues to professional engineering. Also included are engineering case studies that parallel the videotape presentation. The cases presented on the videotape are:

The Take-Home Exam:
An engineering student discovers that a take-home examination has been copied from an old textbook. He decides to use the information, telling of his discovery to only one friend. The friend, out of loyalty, tells her roommate of the book in the library. After the examination has been graded, some of the students find out and complain to the professor.

The main themes in this scenario are loyalty, trust and the confidentiality of information. A secondary theme with which students identify is the credibility of the professoriate, or in a wider sense, the credibility of any organization that purports to hold regulatory or licensure power.
The four themes—loyalty, trust, confidentiality, and credibility—are key elements of engineering professional practice. In the American Society of Civil Engineers (ASCE) Code of Ethics, the operative section that relates to the themes of loyalty, trust and confidentiality is Fundamental Canon No. 4: "Engineers shall act in professional matters for each employer or clients as faithful agents or trustees, and shall avoid conflicts of interest."

When in Rome:
An engineering student discovers that two students from overseas are copying a term paper out of a book. He confronts them, and discovers that they do not believe that what they are doing is wrong. They argue that if copying material out of a book (without attribution) is acceptable in their countries, why isn't it just as acceptable here? The first student is placed in a dilemma of whether or not to tell the professor.

The central theme here is the question of the relativity of ethics. Can something be right in one society, and wrong somewhere else? Is copying material out of a book and handing it in as a paper to be graded acceptable in one country, and not another? Should United States engineers be allowed to pay bribes while doing work in countries where bribery is the normal way of doing business? In the United States, bribery for securing work is prohibited in the ASCE Code of Ethics. Under Fundamental Canon 5, the first guideline reads: "Engineers shall not give, solicit or receive either directly or indirectly, any commission, political contribution, or a gift or other consideration in order to secure work..."

Laboratory Efficiency:
Two engineering students decide to increase their mechanics laboratory grades by using old data. The teaching assistant catches them and reports the incident to the professor, who does not want to pursue the issue. The teaching assistant must decide if she will report the incident to the judiciary board.

The central theme is deceitfulness. Once a group of people agree to a proper way of conducting themselves, to secretly not follow the rules is deceitful and morally wrong. The reaction of the professor is also unprofessional. The professor should understand that she has a duty to act as an ethical role model.

The core value in engineering is truthfulness. Only by adhering to the most stringent principles of truthfulness can large and even small engineering projects be successfully completed. Sometimes being truthful is difficult, especially if it results in damage to one's career. Yet if one is not truthful this will be discovered in due time and one's effectiveness as an engineer in a cooperative environment is jeopardized.

The applicable statement in the ASCE Code of Ethics is: "Engineers shall issue public statements only in an objective and truthful manner."

Love Thy Neighbor:
Two engineering students in a chemistry laboratory notice that one of their colleagues is sabotaging another student's experiment. They confront the student and discover that she sees nothing wrong with cheating if this will help her get accepted to medical school. The students wonder if it is their responsibility to be concerned with the qualify of people entering the professions.

This scenario, based unfortunately on too many real experiences, shows the lengths to which some students will go to get good grades so that they can enter the professions. Engineers recognize that all professionals are responsible for the integrity of their professions. Society yields certain powers to the professions, and expects ethical behavior in service of the public in return, and professionals have a moral responsibility to police their own profession and to dismiss those who do not adhere to the code of ethical conduct. In the ASCE Code of Ethics, the third Fundamental Principle states that engineers should "strive to increase the competence and prestige of the engineering profession."

IV. CONCLUSIONS

In teaching professional engineering ethics, I share the frustration with other instructors in that it is difficult to measure just what the students have learned. All I can really hope to do is to sensitize students to ethical reasoning and to introduce them to the concept of engineering ethics. The teaching of ethics is greatly facilitated by the use of the bridge idea as incorporated in the videotape, *Academic Integrity: A Bridge to Professional Ethics*. Class discussions following the showing of the videotape have been both protracted and spirited. I hope that students realize that there are no right answers in ethics but that some answers are clearly better than others, and that the best answers are the ones that can be most vigorously defended.

ACKNOWLEDGMENT

Much of the work reported in this paper was done when the author was a National Science Foundation Fellow at the Center for the Study of Professional and Applied Ethics at Dartmouth College, Hanover, NH. Appreciation is expressed to Dr. Rachelle Hollander of the NSF and to Dr. Deni Elliott of Dartmouth College for their support and encouragement. This project was funded through a grant from the National Science Foundation, Curriculum and Course Development Program, award number 9354670. Dr. Charmers Sechrist was the Program Officer.

The videotape, *Academic Integrity: A Bridge to Professional Ethics*, and the Instructor's Manual are available for $50 from the Center for Applied Ethics, School of Engineering, Duke University, Durham, NC 27708-0290.

REFERENCES

1. Morrill, R. L., *Teaching Values in College*, Jossey-Bass Publishers, San Francisco, 1980.
2. Bok, D. *Beyond the Ivory Tower*, Harvard University Press, Cambridge MA, 1982.
3. Heath, D. "Prescription for Collegiate Survival: Return to Liberally Educate Today's Youth" Presented at the annual meeting of the Association of America's Colleges, New Orleans, 1977, as quoted in reference 1.
4. Chickering, A. W. *Education and Identity*, Jossey-Bass Publishers, San Francisco, 1969.
5. Heath, D. *Growing Up in College: Liberal Education and Maturity*, Jossey-Bass Publishers, San Francisco, 1968.
6. Carnegie Council on Policy Studies in Higher Education *Fair Practices in Higher Education: Rights and Responsibilities of Students and Their Colleges in a Period of Intensified Competition for Enrollment*, Jossey-Bass Publishers, San Francisco, 1979.
7. Cole, S. "Background Paper on the Stanford Honor Code" Stanford University, 1981.
8. Barnett, D. C. and J. C. Dalton, "Why College Students Cheat" *Journal of College Student Personnel*, vol. 22, no. 6, 1981, pp. 545-551.
9. Nuss, E. M., "Academic Integrity: Comparing Faculty and Student Attitudes" *Improving College and University Teaching* vol. 32, no. 3, 1984, pp. 140-144.
10. Hawley, C. S., "The Thieves of Academe: Plagiarism in the University System" *Improving College and University Teaching* vol. 32, no. 1, 1984, pp. 35-39.
11. Baird, J. S., "Current Trends in College Cheating" *Psychology in the Schools* vol. 17, 1980, pp. 515-520.
12. McCabe, D. L., "The Influence of Situational Ethics on Cheating Among College Students" *Sociological Inquiry*, (forthcoming).
13. McCabe, D. L., "Selected Results: Fall 1991 Faculty Survey' presented at the Academic Integrity Conference, Rutgers University, 5-7 March 1992.
14. Singhal, A. C. , "Factors in Student Dishonesty" *Psychological Reports*, vol. 51, 1982, pp. 775-780.
15. Kibler, W. L., "Addressing Academic Dishonesty from a Student Development Perspective" presented at the Academic Integrity

Conference, Rutgers University, Newark, NJ, 5-7 March 1992.

16. Balik, D., "Academic Integrity at Macalister College" presented at the Academic Integrity Conference, Rutgers University, Newark, NJ, 5-7 March 1992.

17. Pegg, J., C. Russo and J. Valent (1986) "College Cheating Survey" Drexel University (unpublished), 1986.

18. Nguyen, H. et. al., "Cheating at Drexel" Drexel University (unpublished), 1987.

19. Michaels, J. W. and T. Miethe, "Applying Theories of Deviance to Academic Cheating" *Social Science Quarterly*, vol. 70, 1989, pp. 870-885.

20. Haines, V. J., G. M. Diekhoff, E. E. Labeff and R. E. Clark, "College Cheating: Immaturity, Lack of Commitment and the Neutralizing Attitude" *Research in Higher Education*, vol. 25 , no. 4, 1986, pp. 342-354.

21. Heatherington, E. M. and S. E. Feldman, "College Cheating as a Function of Subject and Situational Variables" *Journal of Educational Psychology*, vol. 55, no. 4, 1964, pp. 212-218.

22. McCabe, D. L., J. M. Dukerich and J. E. Dutton, "Context, Values and Moral Dilemmas: Comparing the Choices of Business and Law School Students" *Journal of Business Ethics* vol. 10, 1991, pp. 951-960.

23. Harp, J. and P. Taietz, "Academic Integrity and Social Structure: A Study of Cheating Among College Students" *Social Problems*, vol. 32, no. 1, 1966, pp. 365-373.

24. Hersch, R. H., D. P. Paolitto, and J. Reimer, *Promoting Moral Growth from Piaget to Kohlberg*, Longman Inc., New York, 1979.

P. Aarne Vesilind is a professor of engineering in the Department of Civil and Environmental Engineering at Duke University.

P. AARNE VESILIND

QUESTIONS FOR DISCUSSION

1. This article points to a problem facing students: cheating on school work. What evidence does this article use to show that "academic dishonesty is a serious problem in American higher education"?

2. The author discusses ethical principles through four scenarios. Briefly outline the scenarios and the principles that correspond to each one.

3. What solutions does the author offer to the problem posed? What do you think about these solutions? How effective would they be in your college?

4. Is cheating a problem on your campus? What forms does cheating take? What kind of stand against cheating does your college take?

5. Recall any instances of cheating about which you are aware and discuss these with your classmates. Offer any solutions that might help the situation.

6. What are the implications of cheating in school for cheating on the job? Do you think it follows that those who cheat in school will necessarily be unethical in their work? If we teach ethics in school, will that help to decrease the amount of unethical behavior on the job?

7. Notice the documentation format for this article. What kind of documentation is this author using?

Interactions Between Coyotes and Red Foxes in Yellowstone National Park, Wyoming

Eric M. Gese, Timm E. Storrs, and Scott Grothe

Department of Wildlife Ecology, University of Wisconsin, Madison, WI 53706 (EMG). Present address: United States Department of Agriculture, Denver Wildlife Research Center, Utah State University, Logan, UT 84322-5295; Department of Animal Ecology, Iowa State University, Ames, IA 50011 (TES); Biology Department, Montana State University, Bozeman, MT 59717 (SC)

ABSTRACT

Interactions between coyotes (*Canis latrans*) and red foxes (*Vulpes vulpes*) indicate that coyotes often tolerate foxes, and yet at other times, are aggressive and kill foxes. The frequency and context in which coyotes are aggressive or tolerant of foxes are unknown. We observed 66 interactions between coyotes and red foxes in Yellowstone National Park, Wyoming, from February 1991 to April 1993. Foxes were deterred, displaced, or tolerated by coyotes in 17, 30, and 53% of the encounters, respectively. Deterrence and displacement of foxes by coyotes occurred at a similar frequency in the absence and presence of an ungulate carcass. Tolerance of foxes by coyotes occurred most frequently in the absence of a carcass. A group of coyotes feeding or resting at a carcass was a deterrent to approaching foxes. Key words: *Canis latrans*, coyote, *Vulpes vulpes*, red fox, displacement, deterrence, tolerance

From the *Journal of Mammalogy* (1996, Vol. 77.2, pp. 377-382). Reprinted by permission of the authors and publisher.

Coyotes (*Canis latrans*) and red foxes (*Vulpes vulpes*) are distributed widely throughout North America (Nowak, 1991). Where the two canids occur sympatrically, territories of foxes tend to be on the periphery or outside of territories of coyotes, indicating spatial avoidance (Harrison et al., 1989; Major and Sherburne, 1987; Sargeant et al., 1987; Voigt and Earle, 1983). Interference competition was suggested as the cause of spatial segregation between coyotes and foxes. Few observations of interspecific encounters between coyotes and red foxes exist. Dekker (1983) reported nine instances of coyotes chasing red foxes in central Alberta. Sargeant and Allen (1989) received 42 accounts of interactions between coyotes and red foxes, in which 30 described aggression by coyotes toward red foxes, but only four described tolerance. Seventeen encounters were of foxes killed by coyotes while the fox was in a trap or snare. While accounts of encounters between coyotes and foxes described types of interactions that occurred, frequency of interactions and context of occurrence were unknown.

We observed 66 interactions between free-ranging coyotes and foxes during late winter 1991-1993 in Yellowstone National Park. We examined number and behavior of the animals involved, distance between individuals, duration of interaction, social status of the coyote, and presence or absence of an ungulate carcass and the effect on the outcome of interactions between coyotes and red foxes.

MATERIALS AND METHODS

Observations were made in the Lamar River Valley, Yellowstone National Park, Wyoming (44°52'N, 110°11'E; elevation ca. 2,000 m) as part of a study that examined foraging and use of carcasses by coyotes. Habitats on the study area included forest, grassland, upland sage, sage-grassland, riparian, mesic meadow, and mesic shrub-meadow (modified from descriptions by Despain, 1990). We identified (by radiocollar, intraperitoneal implant, or unique pelage characteristics) 23, 34, and 41 coyotes from five resident packs in the study area during the winters of 1990-1991, 1991-1992, and 1992-1993, respectively and two, two, and seven foxes during the same winters, respectively.

Interactions were observed with a spotting scope of 15-30x magnification from a vehicle or vantage points on hills overlooking the valley. Observations occurred throughout the valley, but were within the boundaries of territories of the five resident packs of coyotes. For an encounter to be counted, the distance between a coyote and fox had to be <500m, and one of the individuals had to notice the presence of the other species. For each encounter, we recorded number of foxes and coyotes involved, behavior of foxes and coyotes immediately preceding the interaction, estimated distance between individuals at initiation of an interaction, duration of interaction, presence or absence of an ungulate carcass (elk, *Cervus elaphus*, or mule deer, *Odocoileus hemionus*), social status (if known) of coyotes, and outcome of interaction. Categories of behavior included traveling, resting, hunting small mammals, and feeding on a carcass (Bekoff and Wells, 1981). If a group of coyotes was involved, estimated distance was the distance between the fox and closest coyote in the group. We examined the social status of the coyote for interactions when only one coyote was involved. Social status was categorized as alpha (dominant, breeding individual), beta (subordinate to alphas, dominant over young), or young (off-spring that were subordinate to both alpha and beta coyotes) based upon separate hierarchies of dominance for males and females that were observed within each resident pack (Mech, 1970; Rabb et al., 1967; Schenkel, 1947, 1967).

We classified outcomes of interactions between coyotes and red foxes as deterrence, displacement, or tolerance. Deterrence was recorded when the presence of coyotes caused the fox to avoid the immediate area (i.e., the fox changed direction of travel and moved away from the coyote), or when the fox would not approach and feed on a carcass. Deterrence started when one species noticed the presence of the other, whereas it ended when either one canid moved >500 m from the other, one canid was no longer visible to the other, the coyote displaced the fox, or darkness precluded further observation. Displacement occurred when one or more coyotes approached or chased a fox causing the fox to move away from the immediate area or carcass. A displacement ended when the coyote stopped its approach or chase of the fox. Tolerance was recorded when coyotes appeared to ignore a fox and started when one species noticed the presence of the other, whereas it ended when either one canid moved >500 m from the other, one canid was no longer visible to the other, the coyote displaced the fox, or darkness precluded further observation. Our focus was to understand how coyotes responded to foxes; therefore, only coyotes could deter, displace, or tolerate foxes, not vice versa. However, we observed no interactions that would suggest that foxes displaced or deterred coyotes. Sargeant and Allen (1989) reported only one encounter that described defensive behavior by a fox toward a coyote.

We used a G-test to analyze the frequency of outcomes in the presence and absence of a carcass, and frequency of outcomes among social classes of coyotes (Zar, 1984). We then partitioned the G-value to detect where the differences were that contributed to the overall significant test statistic. We tested for differences in number of foxes and coyotes, distance, and duration with one-way analysis of variance followed by a Tukey's test using the software program SYSTAT (Wilkinson et al., 1992).

RESULTS

We observed 66 interactions between coyotes and red foxes from February 1991 to April 1993; two interactions occurred in winter 1990-1991, three in winter 1991-1992, and 61 in winter 1992-1993. Most observations occurred in the last winter due to an increase in the number of foxes in the valley and to an increase in the monitoring of carcasses. Of the 66 occurrences, 36 were associated with activities of coyotes and foxes at a carcass and 30 were recorded in the absence of an ungulate carcass (Table 1). Deterrence, displacement, and tolerance were observed in 22, 44, and 33% of the interactions near a carcass, respectively. Deterrence, displacement, and tolerance were the outcome in 10, 13, and 77% of the observations, respectively, in the absence of a carcass. The outcome of interactions between coyotes and foxes differed in the presence and absence of an ungulate carcass (G=13.1, d.f.=2, P< 0.005). Coyotes were more tolerant of foxes in the absence of a carcass than in the presence of a carcass (G=12.9, d.f.=1, P< 0.001), whereas no difference was found for deterrence and displacement of foxes by coyotes when a carcass was present or absent (G=0.2, d.f.=1, P> 0.50). We observed that resting and traveling coyotes typically were tolerant of active foxes when no carcass was present. When a carcass was present, we observed that coyotes traveling toward a carcass usually would displace foxes that were feeding on the carcass. Coyotes resting near a carcass often tolerated a fox feeding on the carcass. We found that alpha, beta, and young coyotes similarly deterred, displaced, and tolerated foxes in the presence or absence of an ungulate carcass (presence: G=0.8, d.f. =4, P> 0.90; absence: G=6.0, d.f.=4, P> 0.10).

When a carcass was present, we found that the number of foxes involved in the interaction did not differ among the three outcomes (Table 2; F=0.30, d.f.=2,33, P> 0.70). In contrast, the number of coyotes involved in the interaction did differ among the three outcomes when a carcass was present (F=16.69, d.f.=2,33, P= 0.0001). Coyotes were in larger groups when they deterred foxes (P< 0.001), but groups were similar and smaller when coyotes displaced or tolerated foxes (P> 0.20). We found that in the absence of a carcass, neither the number of foxes, nor the number of coyotes involved in an interaction differed among the three types of outcomes (foxes: F= 0.14, d.f. =2,27, P> 0.80; coyotes: F = 1.38, d.f. = 2,27, P > 0.25). When a carcass was present, mean distance between the two canids differed among the three outcomes (F =3.03, d.f.=2,33, P = 0.06). Coyotes displaced foxes at a shorter distance than when they deterred foxes (P =

TABLE 1.--*Types of interactions and behavior immediately preceding 66 encounters between coyotes and red foxes in Yellowstone National Park, Wyoming, during 1991 to 1993, when an ungulate carcass was present or absent.*

| | Carcass present ||| Carcass absent |||
Behavior	Deterrence	Displacement	Tolerance	Deterrence	Displacement	Tolerance
Red fox						
Travel	3	2	1	3	3	14
Rest	4	2	2	0	1	3
Hunt	1	0	0	0	0	6
Feed	0	12	9			
Coyote						
Travel	0	15	1	3	2	8
Rest	3	0	9	0	2	11
Hunt	0	0	1	0	0	4
Feed	5	1	1			

TABLE 2.--*The mean (+/-SD) number of foxes and coyotes interacting, distance (m), and duration (min) of 66 encounters between coyotes and red foxes in Yellowstone National Park, Wyoming, during 1991 to 1993, in the presence and absence of an ungulate carcass.*

| | Carcass present ||| Carcass absent |||
Observation	Deterrence	Displacement	Tolerance	Deterrence	Displacement	Tolerance
Foxes	1.2+/-0.5	1.2+/-0.4	1.5+/-1.4	1.0	1.0	1.0+/-0.2
Coyotes	5.6+/-2.8	1.1+/-0.3	2.2+/-2.2	2.7+/-1.5	1.2+/-0.5	1.4+/-1.3
Distance	113+/-108	25+/-18	57+/-112	217+/-76	82+/-54	242+/-141
Duration	172.0+/-134.6	1.1+/-0.3	46.8+/-50.6	2.7+/-2.1	3.7+/-2.7	20.6+/-35.1

0.05), but the distance was not different than when coyotes tolerated foxes (P> 0.50). The distance between the two canids was similar when coyotes tolerated and deterred foxes (P> 0.25). Mean distance between the two canids did not differ among the three outcomes when no carcass was present (F =2.56, d.f.=2,27, P=0.09). Mean duration of an interaction between coyotes and foxes was different among outcomes when a carcass was present (F=15.22, d.f.=2,27, P = 0.0001). The duration of an interaction was longest when a coyote deterred a fox (P< 0.003), but similar in length when coyotes displaced or tolerated a fox (P> 0.10). The duration of an interaction was not different when coyotes deterred, displaced, or tolerated foxes in the absence of a carcass (F=0.80, d.f. =2,27, P> 0.40).

DISCUSSION

Observations of encounters between coyotes and red foxes are rare because both canids typically are nocturnal, secretive, and spatially segregated (Harrison et al., 1989; Kleiman and Brady, 1978; Sargeant and Allen, 1989). Most observations of interactions between these canids indicate that coyotes were aggressive toward foxes (Sergeant and Allen, 1989), whereas no reverse aggression by foxes toward coyotes was reported. Foxes appeared to be aggressive only when attacked or defending offspring at a den. In our study, coyotes displaced a fox from the immediate vicinity or from a carcass in 30% of the encounters. In contrast, 53% of encounters of coyotes and foxes resulted in coyotes tolerating foxes in close proximity. In the absence of an ungulate carcass, coyotes were aggressive toward foxes in only 13% of encounters, whereas aggression occurred in 44% of encounters when a carcass was present. Coyotes were more tolerant of foxes in the absence of an ungulate carcass (77%), than when a carcass was present (33%). Intraspecific competition at a carcass occurred among members of a pack of coyotes (Gese, 1995), hence reduced interspecific tolerance of foxes by coyotes near a carcass was not surprising. However, the observations of tolerance of foxes by coyotes, both near a carcass and within the territory of a pack of coyotes, was significant when compared to previous reports about interactions between coyotes and foxes. Wolves (C. lupus) also were tolerant of foxes in their territory and near carcasses (Murie, 1944). Conversely, wolves have been observed to kill red foxes (Mech, 1966).

The number of coyotes present and their behavior before the encounter influenced the outcome of the interaction. When a carcass was present, foxes were deterred more often by a group of coyotes than by a single coyote. A group of coyotes resting or feeding at a carcass was a deterrent to a fox approaching the carcass. A group of coyotes may be more likely to detect and pursue a fox than a single coyote. The presence of a carcass also concentrated a high number of coyotes in a focal area, possibly increasing the risk of predation to a fox. A single coyote approaching a carcass readily displaced foxes, but also was tolerant of foxes at the carcass when the coyote was resting near the carcass.

While we observed interspecific tolerance, we still recognize that only one aggressive encounter with a coyote can result in the death of the fox. Coyotes can kill foxes (Sergeant and Allen, 1989), hence the behavior of the coyote likely dictates whether it tolerates the presence of a fox. We found that in 71% of our observations, coyotes resting near a carcass had fed on the carcass before an interaction with a fox. Coyotes that displaced a fox from a carcass proceeded to feed in 67% of the cases. If a coyote recently has fed on a carcass, the coyote likely would be resting and may be tolerant of a fox at the carcass. In contrast, a hungry coyote would likely displace a fox from a carcass, and deter the fox from approaching until the coyote had finished feeding. Among African carnivores, the amount of food consumed by the dominant species greatly influenced the level of tolerance exhibited toward other carnivores at a carcass (Kruuk, 1972; Schaller, 1972).

Our results are significant because we were able to observe the frequency of different outcomes between coyotes and red foxes, as well as collect detailed information about each encounter. In contrast to previous studies documenting spatial avoidance of coyotes by foxes, our observations indicate that coyotes will tolerate red foxes in their territory and at a carcass. The numerous prey (ungulates and microtines) available within the Lamar Valley during the three winters may have influenced the level of interspecific tolerance observed between coyotes and foxes. Perhaps, in other areas or during years of low abundance of prey, competition for resources would be more intense and interspecific aggression by coyotes toward foxes consequently would be higher, resulting in spatial avoidance of coyotes by red foxes.

ACKNOWLEDGMENTS

Funding and support were provided by the National Park Service, National Geographic Society, Department of Wildlife Ecology and the College of Agricultural and Life Sciences at the University of Wisconsin-Madison, Max McGraw Wildlife Foundation, Biology Department at Montana State University, Earthwatch, United States Fish and Wildlife Service, and the Hornocker Wildlife Research Institute. We thank M. J. Johnson, M. L. Pangraze, and A. M. Whittaker for field assistance, B. Landis for filming interactions of coyotes and foxes and allowing us to view the footage, R. L. Ruff, R. L. Crabtree, and J. D. Varley for logistical support, and A. B. Sargeant and P. A. Terletzky for review of the manuscript.

LITERATURE CITED

Bekoff, M., and M. C. Wells. 1981. Behavioural budgeting by wild coyotes: the influence of food resources and social organization. Animal Behaviour, 29:794-801.

Dekker, D. 1983. Denning and foraging habits of red foxes, *Vulpes vulpes*, and their interaction with coyotes, *Canis latrans*, in central Alberta, 1972-1981. The Canadian Field-Naturalist, 97:303-306.

Despain, D. G. 1990. Yellowstone vegetation: consequences of environment and history in a natural setting. Roberts Rinehart Publishers, Boulder, Colorado, 239 pp.

Gese, E. M. 1995. Foraging ecology of coyotes in Yellowstone National Park. Ph.D. dissert., University of Wisconsin, Madison, 134 pp.

Harrison, D. J., J. A. Bissonette, and J. A. Shurburne. 1989. Spatial relationships between coyotes and red foxes in eastern Maine. The Journal of Wildlife Management, 53:181-185.

Kleiman, D. G., and C. A. Brady. 1978. Coyote behavior in the context of recent canid research: problems and perspectives. Pp. 163-188, in Coyotes: biology, behavior, and management (M. Bekoff, ed.). Academic Press, New York, 384 pp.

Kruuk, H. 1972. The spotted hyena: a study of predation and social behavior. The University of Chicago Press, Chicago, 335 pp.

Major, J. T., and J. A. Sherburne. 1987. Interspecific relationships of coyotes, bobcats, and red foxes in western Maine. The Journal of Wildlife Management, 51:606-616.

Mech. D. 1966. The wolves of Isle Royale. National Parks Fauna Series, United States Government Printing Office, 7:1-210.

---------. 1970. The wolf: the ecology and behavior of an endangered species. Natural History Press, Garden City, New York, 384 pp.

Murie, A. 1944. The wolves of Mount McKinley. National Parks Fauna Series, United States Government Printing Office, 5:1-238.

Nowak, R. M. 1991. Walker's mammals of the world. Fifth ed. The Johns Hopkins University Press, Baltimore, Maryland, 1629 pp.

Rabb, G. B., J. H. Woolpy, and B. E. Ginsburg. 1967. Social relationships in a group of captive wolves. American Zoologist, 7:305-311.

Sargeant, A. B., and S. H. Allen. 1989. Observed interactions between coyotes and red foxes. Journal of Mammalogy, 70:631-633.

Sargeant, A. B., S. H. Allen, and J. O. Hastings. 1987. Spatial relations between sympatric coyotes and red foxes in North Dakota. The Journal of Wildlife Management, 51:285-293.

Schaller, G. B. 1972. The Serengeti lion: a study of predator-prey relations. The University of Chicago Press, Chicago, 480 pp.

Schenkel, R. 1947. Expression studies of wolves. Behaviour, 1:81-129.

---------. 1967. Submission: its features and function in the wolf and dog. American Zoologist, 7:319-329.

Voigt, D. R., and B. D. Earle. 1983. Avoidance of coyotes by red fox families. The Journal of Wildlife Management, 47:852-857.

Wilkinson, L., M. Hill, J. P. Welna, and G. K. Birkenbeuel. 1992. SYSTAT for windows: statistics, version five. SYSTAT, Inc., Evanston, Illinois, 750 pp.

Zar, J. H. 1984. Biostatistical analysis. Second ed. Prentice-Hall, Inc., Englewood Cliffs, New Jersey, 718 pp.

Submitted 7 November 1994. Accepted 16 August 1995.
Associate Editor was Glennis A. Kaufman.

QUESTIONS FOR DISCUSSION

1. What is the research question that this study seeks to answer?

2. What did the research prior to this study suggest about the interaction between these two animals?

3. What do you think motivated these researchers to seek an answer to their research question?

4. Describe the methods used by the researchers. How did they go about finding the answer to their research question?

5. Describe the results achieved by the research. Did this research change previous thinking about interactions between coyotes and foxes?

6. What do you think is the significance of these results? What do the authors say is significant?

7. Take a close look at the statistics presented in the results section of this article. What are the statistics telling us as readers?

8. Are the tables helpful? Why or why not?

9. Have you ever had encounters with wildlife or observed animals in their natural setting? Did anything surprise you about this research or its results?

10. This article is written in the format typical of scientific research reports. Describe the major sections of such a report. Does this format help you as a reader to understand the research and its results?

11. Notice the documentation format for this article. What kind of documentation are these authors using?

Values & Biology Education

James R. Nichols, Abilene Christian University

In an unusual and refreshing article in this journal, Flannery (1989) made a plea for introducing a more "human" side to our biology teaching. She correctly identified how the use of personal examples and even opinion invigorated the class, focused the point, and strengthened the instruction. She noted, however, how personal revelation by a teacher is a "tricky business" and how such exposure made her uncomfortable.

I considered her article a courageous one, not particularly because it introduced new ideas, but because she dared to talk about something every teacher knows to a greater or lesser extent—that how we teach is often as important as what we teach. The article was also one of several that have appeared in recent years with clear calls for honesty, not only in the teaching of science, but in science itself.

In an attempt to expand this concept, I would suggest that not only are honesty and self-exposure (I would say vulnerability) appropriate and necessary for good teaching, but that they lead to a corollary. When a teacher allows his or her own values to be exposed, the teacher becomes, to a certain extent, a value model. Furthermore, if the teacher describes the process of his or her own values clarification, the process itself becomes instructive to students.

Kormandy (1990) has suggested using the "Socratic" method of guiding students through difficult ethical issues. I contend that this approach is appropriate, but that it requires some degree of self-exposure by the teacher. Esbenshade (1993) suggests aiding students in conflict about science and religion by indicating our own positions and how they were reached.

It is even possible to use *another* person's struggle with values as an instructional tool. Hendrick (1991) presents an extensive case study of the life and work of Louis Pasteur. He suggests that a teacher could use historical perspective to show how science and scientists are shaped by forces and factors around them (and decisions based on those) and that scientists are products of value systems they adopt.

About this time your eyes will probably shift to the biographic information for this article and, upon seeing the author's affiliation with a school whose name includes "Christian," say to yourself, "Oh no, here goes some religious nut trying to say we need to coerce students to be conservative Christians." Not so. My plea is for honesty. I contend that it is impossible to teach biology (or anything else) without displaying and imparting values of some kind. We may only subtly indicate racial or sexual favoritism, attitudes toward beauty, or respect (even reverence) or irrespect for life, but the students will not miss the indicators. Overhearing student conversations in the hallways clearly shows how students learn far more about us than the subject matter we teach. One may choose to ignore this part of our impact on students, but it is naive to deny its existence.

WHAT WE WERE TAUGHT

The professional education each of us received as scientists included clear instruction on how science is value-free, at least at the basic level; data are neutral and objective. I can remember a physiology instructor explaining to me that my experimental setup would measure exactly what was occurring . . . for instance, if there were a leak in the system, the data would reflect the leak; I would get an accurate measurement of a leaking system. I see no reason to argue with the objectivity of data, nor should students. We must be honest enough, however, to explain that data are derived from experiments *chosen* by experimenters, humans who may have biases about the phenomena behind the data. Furthermore, the data are *interpreted* by humans. This is not to say the interpreters are dishonest, merely that they *are* interpreting. The data may be value-free; the interpretations may not be.

I believe we scientists have tried too hard to promote the objectivity of science. Certainly there are hard-won, highly significant bodies of information that have changed the course of life in many ways, including such major concepts as our view of the solar system and the germ-theory. But there are also extrapolations that need to be identified as just that. We do the cause of science no favor by confusing nonscientists with what Noll (1986) calls "cosmological musings of self-appointed spokespersons for the scientific establishment." Those of us within the discipline easily accept the tentativeness of data interpretation. We understand how reviewers can see things in our data that we missed, or how our own data book seems to say something different today than it did last month. But somehow when we "go public" with science, even in our classrooms, it comes out being much more definitive than it is.

INSTRUCTOR VALUES; STUDENT VALUES

No matter how uncomfortable it makes us, I believe it is time to admit that a good part of what we do as scientists, particularly science instructors, is value-laden. Our values are exposed and student values are shaped.

Consider with me here a series of topics, some of more importance than others, that have inherent "valuing" to them. Of course, merely saying some are more "important" than others is a valuing process itself. Nevertheless, I find it very difficult to understand how topics such as these could be considered with students in an "objective" and "neutral" way.

1. Attitudes Toward Dissection

Our actions are very clear here: either we use dissection as an instruction method or we do not. If we choose to do so, we face subsequent choices. Should we use freshly killed or preserved material? Should we use dissection for any student no matter what his/her level or should we impose limits? Are the same activities appropriate for 10th and 12th graders? How different should dissection activities be in college compared to high school? Each choice along the way is a reflection of our judgment which has been shaped not only by our professional experience, but by our personal experience.

For more than 20 years both my research and my teaching laboratories have required the sacrificing of many animals, both vertebrate and invertebrate. I have never been totally comfortable with it, but I believe I can justify my actions scientifically, educationally and personally. In a teaching circumstance requiring animal sacrifice, however, I feel compelled to comment to students and explain my reasoning for the use of animals in this way. For several minutes I tell the students that I believe all forms of life are valuable and that the taking of life is a serious consideration. I tell them that I am an avid nonhunter but that I am not a vegetarian. I explain that I can justify killing an animal if I eat it or if I learn from it, but, in either case, I will not "enjoy" the killing. (As an aside, I have found such comments quite provocative to some students and good "dooropeners" to other discussions.) Accuse me of overconcern if you wish, but each student in that lab brings with him or her previous experiences with animals and with death and I would like each student to grow positively from the lab experience, not simply recoil. The students may not agree with my justification (nor must they actually do the killing themselves), but they are going to hear me verbally wrestling with some of their same concerns.

You may not share my emphasis on this topic, but I contend that how each of us deals with dissection communicates some important nonbiology to our students. They can tell what has shaped us and are, subsequently, somewhat molded themselves.

2. Anthropocentricity

Is it appropriate for humans to be the dominant example we use in our discussion of "life?" Our values on this topic, are reflected to students not only in off-hand comments but, often, in the whole organization of courses. Under what circumstances is a biology course to become a "human" biology course? Is this a natural choice to take advantage of an apparently higher student interest in humans? Or is it a cop-out to avoid forcing students to study less appealing organisms like microbes, invertebrates and (worst of all) plants. By the very organism choices we make we communicate subtly to students that some organisms are more valuable than others. I would hasten to say some of you may want to do just that, but let us be clear and meaningful in our intentions. My own view is that an ecologic emphasis noting balance and interdependence of organisms is much more satisfactory. The presence of live material in our classroom helps make this statement. Marine and freshwater aquaria offer not only instruction but beauty. How about some bird cages in the corner? Why do the birds make more noise in the morning classes than in the afternoon? Do you have room for some snakes or a terrarium with carnivorous plants? Indeed, it seems to me that our emphasis on large organisms (mammals and larger angiosperms and gymnosperms) has slanted our perception of life.

3. Evolution

Few would disagree that evolution is the dominant unifying theme in modern biology. Whole textbooks and courses follow this organizational scheme. Molecular techniques allow us to see similarities and differences between organisms at a level of relationships unheard of just a few decades ago.

But problems remain—and, though the problems may be largely solvable, I wonder how honest we are about the problems and what that says about our values.

Students need to understand the necessity of extrapolation in science, that it is reasonable to make specific predictions based upon an accepted generalization or that many specific observations logically lead to a generalized conclusion. But each of us also knows that there are exceptions to these logic tracks. It is important that we keep our students' minds open to the tentativeness of science.

For example, I would mention here the extrapolation from microevolution to macroevolution (Moore 1991). The plausibility of this transition is high, but the mechanism has yet to be explained to the satisfaction of many.

Related to this point are the highly-commented-on fossil "gaps." Students legitimately will ask whether they really exist, how large they are, and what they mean. Our answers to their questions reveal more than just our science knowledge; they speak of our willingness to make inferences based on our knowledge and experiences.

Add to these items a consideration of punctuated evolution and the possibility of organisms directing their own evolution (Gillis 1991), and listening students will learn not only facts from us, but our interpretations.

4. Scientist's Gender

Does it make any difference if a scientist is a male or female? This might appear to be an unusual topic, but may very well be an unasked question by a significant percentage of our students (namely females). Without wading in too deeply, I believe one can ask important questions about how one's life history (and gender) affect one's perspective of science. This is not at all to suggest a gender difference in the quality of science, but to note clearly that the rules of science have been largely determined by males; it seems reasonable to ask if that has slanted science in any way (Galloway et al. 1990; Windle 1992). For example, it is my perception that the increasingly larger number of females attending medical schools has altered the field of medicine in recent decades. I sense now that medicine in general is more aware of individual patient differences and more willing to evaluate patients' physical circumstances in light of their emotional outlook. This change seems reasonable to me as I note the male dominance of medicine for so many years.

Perhaps those four items are sufficient illustrations of my point. If I were to continue the list, I might include such topics as a consideration of the age of the Earth, the Gala hypothesis (Mann 1991), the current state of the "Big Bang" (Is information on this topic really "suppressed?" Arp 1991), and the right of a science publication to remove a potentially embarrassing author (*Scientific American* and the Mims case) (Mims 1991; Caplan 1991). The fact is that it is very difficult to deal with many substantive issues without exposing one's values. My contention is that we should simply recognize that and use it as a strength. Rather than pretending we do not have an opinion, why not use that opinion as a spur? Have the students identify the strengths and weaknesses of your stance. Have one or more students develop (using resource material) alternative stances and have the class critique those. Critical thinking is stimulated alternatives rather than facts to be accepted.

CONCLUSION

Honesty is important in science. It is at or near the top of the list of qualities of a good scientist. For those scientists also involved in education, this honesty will lead to a degree of self-exposure which should not be denied. The corollary of this is that the teacher now also reveals some of his or her values and that those values, themselves, can become instructive.

A discussion of values in science has been denied for too long. We have overemphasized the objectivity of science while failing to recognize degrees of objectivity. Clearly, a composer of a sonnet or a musical piece makes no claim to objectivity. But just because a scientific work is more objective than one of these does not make it truly objective. We have deluded ourselves on this point and, in some cases, it has led to scientific arrogance.

The challenge we have is to recognize values involved in a topic without being coercive. Especially for college students, it is important to introduce them not only to scientific information, but to inform them that decisions based on that information are inevitable. The more science they know, the more competent they will be to decide. But the decisions will not be value-neutral; they will incorporate the history of the student and will influence his or her (or others') future. Science is not just information; it is the expression of that information, and expression is seldom value-neutral.

REFERENCES

Arp, H. (1991). Letter. *Science News, 140*(4), 51.
Caplan, A. L. (1991). Creationist belief precludes credibility on science issues. *The Scientist, 5*(4), 11-13.
Esbenshade, D. H., Jr. (1993). Student perceptions about science and religion. *The American Biology Teacher, 55*(6), 334-338.
Flannery, M. C. (1989). Human biology. *The American Biology Teacher, 51*(4), 250-253.
Galloway, A., Pavelka, M. M., Tarli, S. B., Fedigan, L., Ono, K., Olsen, D. & Reiter, J. (1990). Letter. *Science, 250,* 1319.
Gillis, A. M. (1991). Can organisms direct their own evolution? *Bioscience, 41*(4), 202-205.
Hendrick, R. (1991). Biology, history, and Louis Pasteur. *The American Biology Teacher, 53*(8), 467-478.
Kormandy, E. J. (1990). Ethics and values in the biology classroom. *The American Biology Teacher, 52*(7), 403-407.
Mann, C. (1991). Lynn Margulis: Science's unruly earth mother. *Science, 252,* 378-381.
Mims, F. M. III (1991). Intolerance threatens every scientist—Amateur or not. *The Scientist, 5*(4), 11-13.
Moore, J. (1991). Science as a way of knowing—VII. A conceptual frame work for biology, part III. *American Zoologist, 31*(2), 349-470.
Noll, M. (1986). The war is over. *The Reformed Journal, 36,* 4-5.
Windle, P. (1992). The ecology of grief. *Bioscience, 42*(5), 363-366.

James R. Nichols is a professor of biology at Abilene Christian University in Abilene, Texas.

QUESTIONS FOR DISCUSSION

1. This article begins by discussing other articles about science and values. Does this opening present an appropriate context for the article? Did you find this introduction helpful? Engaging?

2. What was the "exigency" for this author? Why did he write this article? What was he hoping to clarify that hadn't been said previously in other articles on this same subject?

3. Do you agree with the author that there needs to be "self exposure" by the teacher? Do you agree that teachers are "value models"?

4. Oftentimes in science education, teachers try to maintain an objectivity toward their subject and to assert that science is purely objective and unemotional. Do you agree with this assertion? Would this author agree that science is purely objective or value-free?

5. Why the apologia about the author's affiliation with a "Christian" school? How does this affect his "ethos" as a writer? Do you find him a credible, believable author?

6. Outline the topics that the author includes in this article as "value-laden." Are there others you can think of that are not included here? Do you agree with the author that these topics are inherently value-laden?

7. Do you agree with the author that the topics he lists can not be considered with students in an "objective" and "neutral" way?

8. The author asserts in the conclusion that scientists may sometimes have deluded themselves into thinking they are objective and that this may have led to a certain "scientific arrogance"? Do you agree?

9. Notice the documentation format for this article. What kind of documentation is this author using?

Emissaries to the Stars: The Astronomers of Ancient Maya

Anthony F. Aveni, Colgate University

In a sophisticated culture, people turned to astronomers because heavenly events perplexed them. But as times got hard, arcane science seemed hard to justify. It is the story of ancient Maya astronomy, and of modern astronomy.

Of all the astronomers in the history of the world, none are closer to us—yet, in another sense, also more distant from us—than the ancient Mayas of Yucatan. The few documents that survive the passing of their glorious classical age (in the second to ninth centuries) indicate that, like modern astronomy, their science of starwatching was highly specialized. But the knowledge they gleaned from the stars seems to have been directed toward very different ends from our own.

Since I first became involved 25 years ago in studying Mesoamerican cultures through an examination of building orientations, I have tried to sort out the empirical basis of Maya positional astronomy. A lot of my efforts have been directed toward the astronomical cycles and predictions recorded by the Maya in the Dresden Codex, a hieroglyphic book dating from the 12th century. This screen-fold, bark paper text was spirited out of the New World during the great 16th century conflagration of indigenous documents by the invading Spaniards, who believed these books were dedicated to idolatrous nature worship. The Dresden Codex mysteriously turned up in the library of that east German city two centuries later, thus its name.

The Dresden contains a host of almanacs that only can be described as stupendous feats of number juggling and commensuration, among them a Venus Table that generates predictions of the dates of first and last evening and morning appearances of that planet. Next to the Venus Table is the Eclipse Table, which the Maya used to predict eclipses using combinations of sets of numbers composed of lunar semesters (see box on p. 43). Though lacking details of precisely how they work, I have always felt that these mechanically elegant tabulations transport us to the pinnacle of achievement of the ancient Maya skywatchers. Here were astronomers

Copyright 1995, *Astronomical Society of the Pacific*. Reprinted by permission.
[*Mercury*, Vol. 24.1, pp. 15-18.]

ANTHONY F. AVENI

who surely were as fascinated as we are with the mysteries of the unknown, and as driven to discover new insights into expressing those mysteries. I believe that in the codices we may be witnessing the prodigious output of an elite, esoteric "Institute of Advanced Astronomical Studies."

Why elite? There is no doubt that the astronomers who observed sky events and interpreted their portents, as well as the scribes who recorded, recopied, and updated the documents, were members of the ruling class. Recently at the ruins of Copan, Honduras, the tomb of a scribe (brushes, paint pots, and all) was excavated in a prominent position within a major pyramid that also contained the body of a king. Was the scribe an associate, perhaps destined by his innate talents and skills to rise up the ladder of success to his exalted position, or perhaps a member of the royal bloodline simply groomed for the job?

A CODEX THAT THEY LIVED BY

Maya astronomy must have been pretty heady stuff. There is no evidence to indicate that commoners ever directly understood the complicated numbers and their accompanying syllabary of more than 1,000 hieroglyphs. Indeed, we know that the books were strictly a part of the private science sector of Maya culture. The 16th-century Spanish chronicler and bishop, Diego de Landa, said that the priests in charge of religious ritual carried local versions of the codices from town to town. These codices contained predictions and procedures pertaining to the worship of the celestial gods who managed the natural world.

Imagine one such priest-emissary consulting his client, perhaps the chief of an allied city. We can almost see him confidently whipping out his local version of the Venus Table in order to calculate the next impending heliacal rise of Kukulcan, the feathered serpent deity, as the Maya called their male Venus. Might the dawning light anticipate inauspicious occasions relating to the conduct of battles and captures—Maya star wars? Or maybe our astronomer-priest would signal the warning of a forthcoming eclipse at the next full Moon, along with an omen of impending disaster to the maize crop.

There is no getting away from it: Maya astronomy, like all astronomy for much of human history, was driven by astrological concerns [see "The Roots of Astrology," September/October 1994, p. 21]. This is a fact of life that unfortunately turns off most of my serious-minded astronomer colleagues. Just take a peek at that grotesque Kukulcan flinging his daggers of Venusian light across the pages of the Dresden. Would any self-respecting modern astronomer perpetrate a calendar like that on our culture? It's too remote, too unscientific. But the pathway to the secrets of

Maya astronomy lies in understanding the religious belief system that underlies it. Whether contemporary people believe in astrology is not at issue. In archaeoastronomy we are concerned with understanding how and why people looked to the stars for knowledge.

The Venus god that figures into every page of the Venus Table was a contact point between the science of astronomy and the common person, for the Maya believed their future was ordained in the stars. They would periodically renew their perceived cosmic connection by participating in carefully timed, astronomically based rituals. When Venus made its heliacal rising along the axis of a specially oriented temple, the people would go there to witness their living ruling lord show that he was the very incarnation of his heavenly ancestors. Appearing before the altar bathed in the light of his patron star, the exalted ruler would pierce his genitals with a sting ray spine and collect the droplets of blood on a piece of parchment. This was then burned in an incense-scented brazier. Thus the ruler would perform a rite symbolizing the shared belief that he was the blood descendant of the sky gods who created the world and had the power to destroy it. The Maya sky was less a source of objective knowledge, more a device for bonding people together.

FAITH IN ASTRONOMY

In the absence of any knowledge of what was really going on in ancient people's heads, we might be tempted to lament the woeful state of these Maya peasants. Were they superstitious slaves of that elite handful who possessed precise scientific knowledge? Did the ruling class deliberately withhold their know-how of the universe's inner workings from the masses in order to control their behavior?

Today, we would not characterize ourselves as the unwitting dupes of the czars of scientific orthodoxy. Yet who among us is really aware of the intricacies of modern quantum relativity, much less the imaging techniques of the Hubble Space Telescope—products of our modern quest for scientific knowledge? Though few of us really know how it works, most of us share in a collective faith that the scientific process is capable of yielding some objective set of truths that test out in the practical world most of the time. In this sense I think we and the Maya differ little. They shared in a collective faith that they dwelled in a universe that was itself alive. They believed they had a participatory role in a continuing dialog between people and planets. Astronomers acquired the enormous responsibility to set the tone and pace of that dialog.

By the eighth century, the idea that rulership was linked directly to divine descent from celestial deities had propelled astronomy to the fore as a central concern of the Maya state. In a striking parallel to Old World astronomy developed in Alexandria in the first few centuries A.D., knowing the past and future whereabouts of the ancestor gods— "saving the phenomena" as the Greeks termed it in order to learn what their omens foretold for the state of mankind—required ever more accurate sky data. Inscriptions became lengthier and more complex. Long count dates of events, reckoned from that putative creation point 4,000 years in the past, included statements regarding the phase of the Moon, the number of the Moon in a cycle of six, even detailed information regarding its whereabouts in the zodiac. In eighth century Copan, astronomical determinism seems to have reached its zenith. The ruling lords of one particularly long-lived dynasty developed a specialized Venus cult, with astronomical leanings that paralleled those of the Mithraic cult of early Christian Rome. Recently, Maya epigraphers determined that a number of dates on Copan's carved stelae linked significant events in the lives of the rulers—accession to office, marriage, victory in battle, and the capture of neighboring rulers—to key points in the Venus cycle.

One ruler's temple (we call him 18 Rabbit, after the appearance of his name glyph) has a narrow slot on its western facade. The alignment of the aperture correlates with the position of Venus on the horizon at the coming of the rains. Carved in high relief, Venus god symbols, the same ones that we find in the Dresden Venus Table, adorn the body of a two-headed sky serpent perched over the temple doorway. At the site of Palenque, on the western edge of the Maya periphery, inscriptions detailing the life of the ruler Chan Bahlum are built around a chronology keyed to the stationary points in the retrograde loops of Jupiter, evidently his patron planet. The latter discovery is especially significant since we have yet to discover any sort of Jupiter Table in the codices.

LOSING THE COMMON TOUCH

Shortly after the Copan inscriptions were carved, the Maya mysteriously stopped building pyramids, calculating complex dates, and even writing hieroglyphic books. They resorted to a less centralized, more pastoral existence. Did astronomy play a role in the sudden collapse of the Maya?

The Maya cultural downslide is as hotly debated a subject in archaeology as is the existence of cold dark matter in modern cosmology. Crop failure stemming from environmental mismanagement seems to be the most widely accepted explanation. But the social unrest that percolated through pre-Columbian Yucatan at the turn of the ninth century may have been exacerbated by a ruling elite that had grew ever more out-of-touch with the folks in the fields. This leads me back to the fictitious Maya Institute of Advanced Astronomical Studies I conjured up earlier. How, I wonder, could esoteric matters—such as the development of mathematical formulas for computing the arrival of Venus to an accuracy of one day in 500 years—have impacted directly upon the urgent needs of the people, such as putting food on the table, stemming a prolonged drought, or giving proper care to the young and the aged? As people lost faith, I can imagine the astronomers struggling to justify their pet projects, like building that updated temple of Venus or holding a conference to update the Eclipse Table; in the face of more down-to-earth demands unleashed by an increasingly dissatisfied public.

There are historical lessons for all of us in the study of bygone peoples. How shall we make the public aware of the cost-benefits of the long-accepted scientific practice of pursuing knowledge for its own sake? Can we justify living in an ivory tower, ignorant of any obligation to educate the society that supports us? Whether the out-on-a-limb Maya astronomers suffered these experiences or thought these thoughts, I cannot say. But I am convinced that the value of studying ancient astronomies is that such efforts can lift our heads out of the contemporary sands of isolation, which accumulate about us as a natural consequence of the increased specialization of our discipline.

The history of astronomy is too important to be left to the historians. A healthy dose of how and why our forebears viewed the sky belongs in all levels of our curricula. It would go a long way toward bridging the ever-widening gap between our scientific studies and the acquisition of other kinds of knowledge our culture has conveniently compartmentalized into the humanities and social sciences.

Having taught astronomy for 32 years, and archaeoastronomy for the past 25, my most difficult task has been to get across the idea that we should be more concerned with celebrating human rather than only Western, intellectual achievements. You should not be embarrassed, I tell my students, to study and respect a culture whose universe marches to the tune of a different cosmology. In variety there is contrast, and if we gaze intently into the mirror of competing cosmologies, perhaps we can see reflection of ourselves in clearer light.

Anthony F. Aveni is a professor astronomy and anthropology at Colgate University in Hamilton, N.Y. He is a pioneer in archaeoastronomy, one of the top 10 college professors in the country, according to *Rolling Stone*, national Professor of the Year of 1982, and author of *Conversing With the Planets*, *Empires of Time*, and *Ancient Astronomers*.

THE RHYTHM OF A LUNAR BEAT

The 12th-century Dresden Codex was the Maya version of our ephemeris tables for calculating the positions of the planets. In the Venus Table (VT), vertical columns divide the observable synodic period of 584 days into those aspects of Venus that fall between four temporal mileposts: the first and last evening and morning appearances of the planet (see figure on p.15). The Maya appear to have been fascinated with the number 584 because of their penchant for discovering cycles that meshed perfectly together; 584 fits with the tropical year in the almost perfect ratio of 5 to 8.

But Maya astronomers, who always seem to surprise us, cleverly arranged their table so that Venus events also jived with the rhythm of a lunar beat. Thus the four intervals that subdivide the Venusian synodic period are reckoned in integral and half integral multiples of the Moon's phase cycle. This format probably reflects the existence of an archaic lunar time base, such as the one that existed in our own pre-Roman calendar, buried beneath a later solar-based Venus calendar. Astonishing for a low-tech society, the VT features a correction page complete with instructions that tell how to make up for the shortfall of 0.08 days per observed Venus period (583.92 days) with respect to the one canonized in the VT (584 days). The Maya numeration system used neither fractions nor decimals.

The Eclipse Table (ET) has the same format, except that the numbers are replaced by chains of eclipse numbers: (see figure on p. 18) 177+ or -1 and 148 + or -1, written in the standard dot-and-bar, base 20 notation (the dot stands for one and the bar for five, each being an abstraction of handcounting gestures from pre-literate times). These intervals are better known to us as six and five lunar synodic months, respectively. If you know the correct combination of sets of numbers composed of these lunar semesters, like the Maya, you too, can devise eclipse warning periods. For example, the great solar eclipse of July 11, 1991 is separated from the more recent event of Nov. 3, 1994 by six of the former and one of the latter periods. The forthcoming Oct. 24, 1995 eclipse will follow two six-month periods later.

The ET also sports a user's page with a handy multiplication table (of 177s and 148s). And, like the VT, it incorporates dates in a Long count system that marches back several centuries before the effective date of the ephemeris. This implies that the Maya must have been at the business of eclipse prediction for a long time. What is so impressive about the ET is that it needs no orbits, nodes, or other Greek-derived Western geometric concepts to figure out when eclipses might happen. The Mayas appear to have been satisfied with an eclipse astronomy based on time cycles alone, which makes for a very different kind of astronomy from our own.

Elsewhere in the Maya written record, there resides a table that may have clocked the retrograde motion of Mars. But epigraphic astro-skeptics argue over why the Maya would have chosen to divide the 780-day martian synodic period into 10 equal period of 78 days. Were they following Mars across a zodiac? There is a table of 13 (not 10) zodiacal constellations, consisting of peccary, vulture, deer, and maybe even our very own scorpion—animals we might expect to grace a tropical celestial freeway, since each critter is native to that part of the New World. But this time the Maya twist is that their parade of beasties may have been laid out appositionally. That is, they paired a given constellation that makes its first appearance in the east after sunset with one just about to disappear in the west, rather than listing the constellations in a linear sequence.

QUESTIONS FOR DISCUSSION

1. According to the author, what is the purpose of archeoastronomy? Why should we care what the Mayas knew about the stars?

2. Why does the author say it is important to learn about non-western cultures? Do you agree with his argument?

3. Describe how the Maya's social structure may have influenced their astronomy. What does the author say about the "elite" in this culture?

4. What are the theories about the decline of the Maya culture in the ninth century? What does the author suggest may have contributed to this decline?

5. Summarize briefly the information provided in the boxed section "Rhythm of a Lunar Beat." Why do you think the author included this information separately rather than incorporating it into the text itself? Is it a helpful addition to the article?

6. There is no references or works cited page for this article. Why do you think it was not included? Does this make the article less scholarly, less credible?

7. Describe the author's tone in this article. Would you say it is less formal than the other articles in this part of the book?

8. Who do you think the audience for this article might be?

Is Physics Multicultural?

Don S. Lemon, Bethel College

Recently as I was turning through the "Five College Calendar of Events," a brochure listing films, lectures, theater, socials, and concerts in the academic consortium of which Amherst is part, I noticed a new section entitled "E-Pluribus Unum: Multiculturalism in the Five Colleges." Its stated purpose is to ". . . facilitate recognition of the diverse cultures in the Five Colleges and [the] development of an open community." Events listed in this section included a short course on "Latino Cultural Awareness," films on the Yupik Indians, the Israeli-Palestinian conflict, and "Hell Diving Women;" lectures on "Psychoanalysis and Prejudice," and "American Identity;" and a performance by a women's chorus from South Africa. There were also theater, art exhibits, and religious and social gatherings --all deemed "multicultural." There was not, however, a single physics presentation.

One feels a bit discomfited that physics seems irrelevant to a movement which is the focus of so much attention and energy. Physics is clearly an integral part of humanity's attempt to understand the universe. How then can a movement which encompasses so much (politics, history, sociology, literature, art, languages, psychology, and even medicine) and looms so large in university life, and increasingly in our national life, leave out physics?

Perhaps physics doesn't ". . . facilitate recognition of . . . diverse cultures . . . ." Perhaps it isn't multicultural. Or is it? That's my question. No doubt, some physicists will judge the question destructive of the very enterprise it seeks to query. To others it will have an obvious answer.

Even so, in one form or another, the question is pressed upon us. Those of us who work in colleges and universities are asked: "Isn't there an Eastern way of looking at the natural world parallel to or in competition with the physics of the Western Tradition?" Or "Shouldn't there be a science reflecting the concerns and interests of oppressed peoples?" "What about a physics reflecting gender?" Or "Don't persons of diverse cultures make valuable and distinctive contributions to physics? Shouldn't these diverse voices be recognized and encouraged?" Universities have an unwritten law: "All questions are worth asking."

Let's respond by weighing three aspects of modern physics--its origin, its current practice, and its content -- on the scale of multiculturalism.

From the *American Journal of Physics* (1993, Vol. 61.9, p. 777). Reprinted by permission of the author and publisher.

Origin. By origin, physics is, indeed, a Western science. Galileo spoke Italian, Descartes French, and Newton English. One has to look hard to find a non-European scientist active during the 17th and 18th centuries when modern physics began to prosper. Similarly, anthropology is English, sociology French, geometry Euclidean, and dynamics Newtonian.

We could change the terms for this kind of "characterization by origin" by extending the history of physics back to Aristotle, or, alternatively, by searching ethnology journals for precursors to modern science from other cultures. But in doing so we won't change the fact that some cultures have contributed to the origins of physics and some have not. For me, this fact seems no more or less interesting than the fact that some individuals have made outstanding and long lasting contributions to physics while others have not.

Current Practice. Today, physics is practiced worldwide. The American Physical Society has members in 115 countires and the AAPT in 71. A recent UNESCO publication(1) lists significant research and experimental development activities in 76 countries. The Indian and Chinese physics communities are especially active.

The operations of the *American Journal of Physics* illustrates this point. Contributions come from around the world. I feel particularly proud of the Journal when we receive a manuscript from an unfmiliar country, not to mention humbled to find it written in idiomatic English. The "American" in the *American Journal of Physics* describes the circumstances of the Journal's origins sixty years ago, not its current contributors or readers, who as a group are multicultural.

Physics is not a folk science nor can it be; participation requires too much ability and preparation. Yet, it seems fitting and proper that physicists as a group are heterogeneous and widely distributed over the face of the earth. "Physicists are everywhere," as the Chinese physicist and dissident, Fang Lizhi, has emphasized(2).

Content. Physics attempts to describe what is fundamental and universal. In this sense there is no "American physics." All laws of physics are universal. The content of physics is not political; neither is it biographical. Physics is, in Einstein's words, "beyond the merely personal"(3).

Physics progesses from its European origins to universality by a process of testing and criticism which includes experiments, observations, and checks for consistency and coherency. Consider, for example, failed theories and viewpoints. Some of these have been highly beautiful and desirable. Hoyle, Bondi, and Gold's "Continous creation" is, for me, one example. The very existence of failed theories seems powerful evidence that the content of physics is not, ultimately, constrained by social factors but by something else, something fundamental and universal. We often call it Nature.

Is physics multicultural? Physics itself is not multicultural because it doesn't particularly ". . . facilitate recognition of. . . diverse cultures. . . ." Rather, its purpose is to facilitate recognition of what is foundational for all cultures. There is an important social consequence of this fact: because physics is not the property of a particular culture or cultures, persons from all cultures and conditions of life can and do freely contribute to the common enterprise of physics. In a shrinking world this is exactly as it should be.

REFERENCES

1. "UNESCO 1991 Statistical Yearbook" (UNESCO, 1991, Paris), pp. 5-26.
2. "Guest Comment: Physics, physics students, and Tiananmen Square," Fang Lizhi, Am. J. Phys. **58**, 809 (1990).
3. For a discussion of this phrase, see the essay "The Merely Personal," Jeremy Bernstein in Cranks, Quarks, and the Cosmos (Basic, New York, 1993), pp. 122-132.

Don S. Lemon is a professor in the Department of Physics and Chemistry at Bethel College in North Newton, Kansas. He also serves as the Assistant Editor of the *American Journal of Physics*.

QUESTIONS FOR DISCUSSION

1. What do you think motivated the author to write this article, which was included in the *American Journal of Physics* as an editorial?

2. What question about physics is this author addressing?

3. The author divides the question of multiculturalism into three aspects of physics: its origin, its current practice, and its content. Given this discussion, how would you answer the question "Is Physics Multicultural?" Justify your answer.

4. Do you agree with the author's argument in the last paragraph? Why or why not?

2

Readings from the Social Sciences

The social sciences, comparatively young disciplines, have adopted many of the research methods and procedures of the enormously successful sciences, often employing the scientific method to study various aspects of society, such as human behavior and relationships or social conditions and customs. As in the sciences, social science writing tends to fall into two main categories: 1) reports of original research and 2) everything else (including, for example, literature reviews, summaries or precis, case studies, proposals, position papers, critiques, and so on). The readings for Part II include a variety of research reports from several disciplines to illustrate the range of social science research.

The first two articles in this part of the reader exemplify research reports from psychology and health. You will notice that, although these are both examples of primary research, the research questions and the research methods are quite different. The Ballard & Coates article on music and moods uses an empirical method involving numerous experiments and statistical data. The Hastie & Pickwell article on the social system in a dance class uses an observational and interview method of research. Both articles, however, employ the typical research report format also commonly used in the sciences. In contrast, although Jacobs' article on Tewa grandmothers also employs an observational method, she chooses to report her data in a more narrative form. The Brown & Vincent article on political communication uses yet another method—text analysis—and they report their results in a more conventional research report format. Calderon & Farrell in their article on a multiethnic school district use a sociological participant-observer approach, much as Jacobs did with the Tewa grandmothers, but report their results a bit more formally than Jacobs did.

Taken together, these articles show the considerable range of research methods, and subsequently the range in styles of research writing, to be found in the social sciences. All of the articles included in Part Two are reproduced in their entirety from the journals in which they were originally published, by permission of the publisher and/or author(s).

The Immediate Effects of Homicidal, Suicidal and Nonviolent Heavy Metal and Rap Songs on the Moods of College Students

Mary E. Ballard and Steven Coates, Appalachian State University

The authors examined the impact of homicidal, suicidal, and nonviolent heavy metal and rap songs on the moods of male undergraduates under the guise of administering a memory for lyrics test. Subjects heard one of six songs and completed a memory task. Subjects completed several mood inventories as part of a "second study." There were no effects of song content or music type on suicidal ideation, anxiety, or self-esteem. The nonviolent rap song elicited higher Beck Depression Inventory (BDI) scores than the violent rap songs. And, rap songs elicited significantly more angry responses than heavy metal songs.

Rock music has been decried as a scourge of society since it was first introduced to the American public by Bill Haley and His Comets in 1955. This may be because the keystones of rock and roll have been defiance, rebellion, and the expression of youthful angst (Bleich, Zillman & Weaver, 1991; Pareles & Romanowski, 1983; Trzcinski, 1992). Two subgenres of rock, heavy metal and rap, may best exemplify both the insurgency and the disenfranchisement experienced by many adolescents. At the same time, heavy metal and rap music often embody the worst fears of the parents of this generation's youth, that is, sex, drugs, and violence. Thus these two types of rock music have become the center of a controversy that has reached from the sermons of small town churches to hearings on Capital Hill.

HISTORY OF HEAVY METAL AND RAP MUSIC

Heavy metal exploded onto the rock scene in the late 1960s. The term "heavy metal" was coined by William Burroughs in *Naked Lunch*, used

From *Youth & Society* (1995, 27.2: 148-168). Reprinted by permission of Sage Publications.

in the lyrics of Steppenwolf's hit "Born to be Wild," and then adopted by rock critic Lester Bangs to describe this style of loud, guitar-driven rock music (Pareles & Romanowski, 1983). The popularity, and provocative nature, of heavy metal music burgeoned in the mid-1980s (Arnett, 1991a, 1991b).

Rap music appeared on the streets and in the clubs of New York City in the mid-1970s, but rap music as a recorded art form did not appear until the late 1970s (Pareles & Romanowski, 1993). By the early 1980s, rap music was popular among African American youth and it was being integrated into the music of diverse artists (Pareles & Romanowski, 1983). Rap continued to evolve as artists produced songs with more complex music and more subtle lyrics (Simpson, 1990). By the mid-1980s rap had entered the musical mainstream.

LYRICAL CONTENT AND RECORD WARNING LABELS

As the popularity of heavy metal and rap music has grown, so have concerns about the possible detrimental effects of this music. In particular, parents, educators, and religious leaders have voiced concern about songs with themes of drug use, violence (homicide, suicide, and sexual aggression), and Satanism (Prinsky & Rosenbaum, 1987; Record Labeling, 1985). Although many heavy metal and rap songs have positive content (e.g., love, spirituality) or deal with pressing social issues (e.g., abuse, racism, homelessness), a substantive number of songs have violent, degrading, or provocative lyrical content (Thigpen, 1993). Even the names of some groups, such as Suicidal Tendencies, Dead Kennedys, House of Pain, and Public Enemy may elicit concern from some adults. Antisocial themes are not common only to rock music; country music is rife with negative themes (Stack & Gundlack, 1992). Nevertheless, the recent proliferation of heavy metal and rap music into popular culture has focused a spotlight on the negative aspects of these forms of music. These concerns have led groups such as the Parent's Music Resource Center (PMRC) to question music's affects on adolescents (Record Labeling, 1985). The members of the PMRC believe that heavy metal music has a detrimental impact on the moods and behavior of young people and in 1985 requested the U.S. Congress to require consumer warning labels on albums with potentially offensive lyrics (Prinsky & Rosenbaum, 1987; Record Labeling, 1985). The music industry instituted a controversial, voluntary labeling system, placing the warning "Parental Advisory/Explicit Lyrics" on albums that are deemed offensive (Thigpen, 1993). Some music chains also use "18 to Buy/Show" labels (Thigpen, 1993). However, some charge that this practice has led to racially biased labeling, as controversial and explicit recordings by White artists are less likely to be tagged than are similar recordings by African American artists (Thigpen, 1993). And, whereas some stores restrict the sale of potentially offensive material, other stores sell labeled recordings to any consumer, regardless of age (Thigpen, 1993). Thus there is substantial inconsistency in labeling and selling practices.

Recordings also vary in the way "Parental Advisory/Explicit Lyrics" labels are used. Warning labels may be affixed to the outside of the CD or tape case, printed starkly on the cover, or woven into the cover design in an aesthetically pleasing way. Some artists seem to flaunt the fact that their material might be viewed as explicit or offensive. Thus warning labels may have the opposite effect of that desired by the PMRC—more, not fewer, adolescents may be drawn to explicitly violent or sexual lyrics.

The PMRC's main criticism of heavy metal and rap music centers around the belief that the lyrics cause adolescents to display negative moods (e.g., depression, hostility) and to engage in negative behaviors (e.g., aggression, suicide, sexual activity, drug use) that they would not participate in otherwise (Desmond, 1987; Hansen & Hansen, 1991; Record Labeling, 1985). Some religious leaders claim that satanic messages are embedded in rock songs and that this subliminal "backward masking" can lead the listener to commit crimes, use drugs, and worship Satan (Vokey & Read, 1985). Thus two questions arise:

(a) How well does the listener understand and comprehend the lyrics of heavy metal and rock songs (There is no research on rap lyrics.)

(b) Do these lyrics influence the listener's moods or behavior?

LYRICAL COMPREHENSION AND INFLUENCE

The findings of studies examining cognition of heavy metal lyrics are inconsistent and fail to provide a clear picture of either lyrical importance or comprehension. Wass and colleagues (Wass, Miller, & Stevenson, 1989; Wass et al., 1988-1989) found that heavy metal fans were more likely to claim to know the lyrics of their favorite songs than were nonheavy metal fans; there was no measure of comprehension. Heavy metal fans reported that song lyrics made a difference in how the music was experienced. Similarly, Bleich et al. (1991) found that rebellious adolescents reported enjoying song lyrics more than nonrebellious adolescents. Alternatively, both Arnett (1991b) and Rosenbaum and Prinsky (1987) found that most adolescents, including heavy metal fans, focused on music, while a minority paid more attention to the lyrics.

When young adolescents do attend to song lyrics their interpretation of the lyrics tends to be literal, not taking into consideration the complex metaphors often employed by songwriters (Greenfield et al., 1987;

Rosenbaum & Prinsky, 1987). Even when adolescents were provided with song lyrics they were no better than casual listeners in determining the songs' themes (Greenfield et al., 1987; Hansen & Hansen, 1991). By late adolescence or early adulthood, people are more capable of interpreting the abstract subcontext of heavy metal songs (Greenfield et al., 1987; Rosenbaum & Prinsky, 1987). Adults perceive more satanic and sexual content in songs than adolescents (Rosenbaum & Prinsky, 1987), perhaps because they have greater experience with and knowledge of such concepts (Greenfield et al., 1987).

There is no evidence to support claims that "backward masking" influences behavior. Thorne and Himelstein (1984) and Vokey and Read (1985) found that suggestion played a large role in whether or not backward masked messages were heard at all when materials were played backwards. Thus backward masked messages may be the result of construction on the part of the listener, rather than purposely planted messages. In addition, Pokey and Read (1985) found no evidence that even intentionally planted backward masked messages influenced the listener's behavior.

HEAVY METAL AND SUICIDE: IS THERE A LINK?

One of the most frightening claims made by the detractors of heavy metal music is that the music causes adolescents to attempt or to commit suicide. This was illustrated by highly publicized cases where parents charged that songs by Judas Priest and Ozzy Osbourne were linked to the suicides of their adolescent children. Recently, "Jeremy," by Pearl Jam, spawned controversy, as the song relates the tale of a neglected and alienated boy's public suicide. Eddie Vedder (1993), Pearl Jam's lead singer and lyricist, defends the song, saying that rather than promoting suicide it should have the opposite effect.

There is no empirical data to link depression or suicide attempts or completions to heavy metal or rap music. Few studies have addressed these questions even indirectly. Wass and colleagues (1988-1989) found that adolescents who disliked heavy metal music were significantly more likely than heavy metal fans to believe that listening to heavy metal music with violent or satanic themes could increase the risk that someone would commit suicide or homicide. Stack and Gundlack (1992) did not study rock music, but found significant positive correlations between the suicide rates of Whites and the amount of airplay dedicated to country music.

HEAVY METAL AND ANTISOCIAL AND RECKLESS BEHAVIOR

Although there is little research on links between music and mood, there are links between reckless and antisocial behavior and preference for heavy metal music. Correlational studies by King (1988) and Wass, Miller, and Redditt (1991) indicate that heavy metal music is more popular among antisocial youth than among the general population. King (1988) found that among adolescents hospitalized for psychiatric or behavioral disorders, heavy metal music was more popular with adolescents who abused drugs than among those who did not. In a study of adolescent offenders, Wass et al. (1991) found that a majority of the White youths were fans of heavy metal music. (None of the African American subjects preferred heavy metal music.) Neither King (1988) nor Wass et al. (1991) studied control groups in relation to these clinical populations.

Arnett (1991a) examined the relation between heavy metal music and antisocial behavior among a community sample of adolescents. Although the sample may not be representative due to recruitment procedures, the results are striking. Male fans of heavy metal music scored higher on sensation seeking and engaged in behaviors such as reckless driving, casual sex, and drug use significantly more often than male nonfans of heavy metal music. However, reckless and destructive behaviors were pervasive, regardless of the boys' musical preferences (Arnett, 1991a, 1991b).

Female heavy metal fans were more likely to engage in sex without contraception, marijuana use, shoplifting, and vandalism than female nonheavy metal fans (Arnett,1991a). Overall, females were less likely to engage in reckless behaviors than males, regardless of musical taste. Female heavy metal fans also had higher sensation seeking scores than nonfans. Arnett (1991a) suggests that sensation seeking may be the strongest link between a preference for heavy metal music and reckless behavior.

All of the studies cited above (Arnett, 1991a; King, 1988; Wass et al., 1991) singled out heavy metal music and fans. Therefore, the rate of preference for other music types, such as rap or country, among antisocial or reckless youths has not been examined. So, it is impossible to compare the behavior of heavy metal fans to the behavior of fans of other types of music.

Although there is evidence that a preference for heavy metal music is related to increased risk for reckless or antisocial behavior, this link is tenuous at best. And, there is no empirical evidence that a preference for heavy metal music places adolescents at risk for suicide. However, even psychologists seem beguiled by the deluge of media attention on the subject. Rosenbaum and Prinsky (1991) report that 83% of psychiatric facilities contacted recommended inpatient admission for a hypothetical youth who presented no behavioral or emotional problems, but who preferred heavy metal music, "punk" fashion, and had a messy room decorated with "awful looking" posters.

STATEMENT OF PROBLEM AND HYPOTHESES

To date research examining the impact of music on adolescents' moods and behavior has been correlational and has not examined the impact of lyrical content on mood. In addition, much of the extant research is limited by either (a) biased populations, (b) a singular focus on heavy metal music, (c) a negative bias against heavy metal music, or (d) a lack of understanding of the subgenres of rock music.

This study is an effort to investigate the links between lyrical content and mood in an experimental fashion. We examined the immediate impact of exposure to heavy metal and rap songs with nonviolent, homicidal, and suicidal themes on the moods of college students, under the guise of administering a memory for lyrics test.

Because music videos with violent content were found to be more unpleasant and arousing than those with less violent content (Hansen & Hansen, 1990), we expected that the undergraduates' state moods, such as anxiety and anger, would vary as a function of lyrical content (i.e., subjects would have higher levels of anxiety and anger after exposure to violent lyrics than after exposure to the nonviolent control). We did not expect that nonstate measures, such as depression, self-esteem, and suicidal ideation, would vary as a function of lyrical content, as these characteristics are not as vulnerable to the immediate context of the situation unless it has a strong personal valence.

As there is no precedent for examining rap versus heavy metal music, we had no explicit hypotheses regarding the impact of music type on mood. However, as rap and heavy metal music are both viewed as highly arousing by students in another study in progress, it might be expected that they would affect mood similarly.

PILOT STUDY

METHOD

Participants

Sixteen volunteer subjects from upper-level psychology courses participated in the pilot study.

Materials

Eighteen songs were selected for use in the pilot study, fans of heavy metal and rap music were polled for suggestions and these were narrowed down by the investigators, based on length, content, and year of release. (We failed to find unfamiliar country and Top 40 songs with homicidal and suicidal themes.) These 18 songs included three songs from each of three lyrical content categories (nonviolent, homicidal, and suicidal) for both types of music under investigation (heavy metal and rap). One-minute segments of each song were prerecorded for use in the pilot study. The song segments included a portion of the verse and the chorus of the song.

Procedure

Pilot testing was used to identify three heavy metal and three rap songs that (a) fit into the content categories of interest, (b) were low in familiarity, and (c) were relatively high in coherence. (Rap music is by definition more coherent than other types of popular music.) The 18 song segments described above were played for participants one at a time. After each song segment was played, subjects were asked to rank the familiarity and coherence of the song on Likert-type scales. They were also asked to choose which theme (i.e., love/relationships, suicide, violent or degrading sex, homicide, other) best fit each song and to categorize the songs as either rock, country, rap, alternative, or heavy metal.

RESULTS

The six songs that best met the criteria cited above were selected for use in the study. The three heavy metal songs that were selected were "Of Wolf and Man" (nonviolent/control), "Assassin" (homicidal), and "Falling Asleep" (suicidal). The rap songs that were selected were "Sunny Meadowz" (nonviolent/control), "Peel Their Caps Back" (homicidal), and "Ever So Clear" (suicidal). See Table 1 for familiarity and coherence rankings.

TABLE 1
Pilot Study Means for Familiarity and Coherence

	Familiarity Scores	Coherence Scores
Rap		
Nonviolent	1.14	3.94
Homicidal	1.33	3.36
Suicidal	1.37	4.37
Heavy metal		
Nonviolent	1.10	2.43
Homicidal	1.31	2.62
Suicidal	1.10	2.74

NOTE: Familiarity scores range from 1 (not familiar) to 5 (very familiar), coherence scores range from 1 (not at all coherent) to 5 (very coherent).

EXPERIMENTAL STUDY

METHOD

Participants

The participants consisted of 175 (82 males and 93 females) volunteer psychology undergraduates from Appalachian State University. They were primarily non-Hispanic Caucasian (N = 165). Six subjects were African American, 4 were Asian American, and 2 were Native American. The mean age of the subjects was 19.71 years. Mean socioeconomic status of the participants was upper-middle class.

Eleven subjects (all non-Hispanic Caucasian) opted not to complete the personality questionnaires. Of the remaining 164 subjects 77 were male and 87 were female. Males and females were fairly evenly represented across conditions. Subjects were randomly assigned to one of the six conditions in the 3 (song content) x 2 (music type) design.

Materials

Songs. The six songs listed above were used in the experiment. Two styles of popular music (heavy metal and rap) were crossed with three lyrical content themes (nonviolent/control, homicidal, or suicidal lyrics). The songs were approximately the same length (song length varied no more than 30 seconds) and came from 1986-1991.

Memory-for-lyrics test. A memory test was developed for use in the study for two reasons: (a) to assure that the participants would focus on the lyrical content of the songs (to maximize the affect of the lyrics on mood) and (b) to divert the participants' attention from the true purpose of the study and to decrease demand characteristics. The memory test included (a) a free recall task where subjects were asked to recall from memory as many salient words as possible from the songs (excluding words such as "and" and "the"), (b) specific questions about lyrical content (e.g., Were any names mentioned in the song? Was any profanity used in the song?), and (c) categorization items (music type and thematic content).

State-Trait Anger Expression Inventory (STAXI). Subjects completed the STAXI, a 44-item measure that taps how people usually experience and express anger (Spielberger, 1988a; Spielberger et al., 1985). The STAXI yields scores for anger-in, anger-out, anger expression, state-anger, trait-anger, and anger-control and has convergent and divergent validity and good reliability (alphas range from .84 to .93; Spielberger, 1988b, 198&; Spielberger et al., 1985).

Beck Depression Inventory (BDI). The BDI (Beck, Wad, Mendelson, Mock, & Erbaugh, 1961) was used to measure subject's levels of depression after exposure to the song. The reliability and validity of the BDI is well accepted.

Self-Esteem Scale (SES). On this 10-item measure of self-esteem (Rosenberg, 1965) subjects respond to a variety of self-statements on a point Likert-type scale. The SES has good internal consistency ($r = .77$ to .88) and is positively correlated with general self-regard ($r = .78$) and negatively correlated with anxiety ($r = -.64$) and depression ($r = -.54$) (Blascovich & Tomaka, 1991).

State-Trait Anxiety Inventory (STAI). The STAI is a Subitem questionnaire that measures state- and trait-anxiety. Metzger (1976) reports that the STAI has good validity ($r = .81$ to .92) and excellent internal consistency (alphas range from .86 to .95). Test-retest reliability scores for the state anxiety subscale are low, which is appropriate for a state measure (Metzger, 1976).

Adult Suicidal Ideation Questionnaire (ASIQ). The ASIQ (Reynolds, 1991) assesses current suicidal ideation. The ASIQ is comprised of 25 items that subjects rate on a 7-point Likert-type scale as to how often they have had suicidal ideas in the past month. The ASIQ was standardized with nonclinic populations of adults. The ASIQ has excellent internal consistency for both college males (.97) and college females (.96). The median content validity correlation was $r = .70$. Criterion validity, with scores on the Hamilton Depression Rating Scale, was .77 (Reynolds, 1991).

Procedure

Participants were randomly assigned and were run in groups of 5 to 10 by assistants who were blind to the purposes and the hypotheses of the study. Participants volunteered for a study that ostensibly examined the relation between music type and memory for lyrics. The research assistant informed subjects that they would hear one song, played twice, and that they should pay particular attention to the lyrics of the song, as they would be tested on their memory for the lyrics. They were also told that the memory experiment would only take up half of the allotted time and that another experimenter had agreed to let them participate in a second study, on personality, after the music study, so they could receive one full hour of extra credit for their participation. After subjects signed the informed consent for the memory experiment they were exposed to one of the six songs, which was played twice. Participants were then given the memory task. On completion of the memory task subjects were told that they could either leave or that they could stay to participate in the second study for additional extra credit. If the subjects agreed to stay they signed another consent form and completed the personality inventories. The purpose of this subterfuge (the memory task, the "second" experiment, and the second consent form) was to decrease the possibility that the subjects would directly link exposure to the music to completing the personality measures. Subjects were allowed to leave after completing the questionnaires. They were debriefed regarding the true purpose of the study as soon as possible after the completion of the experiment. Great care was taken to assure the subjects that the experimenters had taken elaborate precautions against demand characteristics in this study.

Table 2
Means and SDs for Familiarity and Coherence

	Familiarity Scores	Coherence Scores
Rap		
Nonviolent 1.06 (.25)	2.87 (.88)	
Homicidal	1.07 (.25)	3.47 (.89)
Suicidal	1.25 (.51)	4.39 (.57)
Heavy Metal		
Nonviolent	1.53 (.59)	2.62 (1.10)
Homicidal	1.04 (.19)	3.00 (.82)
Suicidal	1.04 (.19)	2.43 (.88)

NOTE: Familiarity scores range from 1 (not familiar) to 5 (very familiar); coherence scores range from 1 (not at all coherent) to 5 (very coherent). SDs are in parentheses.

RESULTS

Song Classification

Overall, subjects correctly categorized the songs as either rap (96%) or heavy metal (95.4%). Some subjects categorized the rap songs as rock (3%) or alternative (1%) music. A few subjects classified the heavy metal songs as rock (2.3%), rap (1.1%), or alterative (1.1%) music.

Thematic classification was less consistent. In general, subjects categorized songs in the category that they were meant to represent. The homicidal songs were typically correctly classified (95%). Suicidal songs were classified as violent in content by 91% of the subjects, but as specifically suicidal by only 38% of the subjects. Nonviolent songs were classified as nonviolent by most (63%) of the subjects, but 37% of the subjects classified these songs (which had no violent lyrics) as homicidal in nature.

Although the songs used in the study were equated on coherence and familiarity during pilot testing, ratings of song coherence and familiarity were reexamined for the study population. In general, on a scale of 1 to 5, all of the songs used in the study were unfamiliar to the subjects (see Table 2 for means and standard deviations). On the other hand, there was substantial variation in song coherence. To see if the songs varied significantly in regard to either coherence or familiarity, 2 (music type) x 3 (song content) ANOVAs were executed.

There was a significant interaction between music type and song content for coherence, $F(2, 169) = 14.17$, $p < .001$. Simple effects tests show that the suicidal rap song ($M = 4.39$, $SD = .57$) was rated as more coherent than the homicidal rap song ($M = 3.47$, $SD = .90$) or the nonviolent rap song ($M = 2.87$, $SD = .88$), $F(2, 86) = 26.59$, $p < .001$. The homicidal rap song was rated as more coherent than the nonviolent rap song. There were no significant differences in the coherence ratings of the heavy metal songs, regardless of content. Main effects of music type and song content for coherence indicate that the rap songs ($M = 3.55$, $SD = 1.01$) were significantly more coherent than the heavy metal songs ($M=2.61, SD=2.61$), $F(1,169) =49.86$, $p< .001$. Subjects rated the nonviolent songs ($M = 2.66$, $SD = 1.02$) as less coherent than the homicidal ($M = 3.24$, $SD = .88$) or suicidal ($M = 3.41$, $SD = 1.23$) songs, $F(2, 169) = 12.19$, $p < .001$.

Although all six of the songs ranked very low in terms of familiarity to the subjects, there was a significant interaction between music type and content for familiarity, $F(2, 169) = 8.58$, $p < .001$. Simple effects tests show that the rap songs did not differ in familiarity. Subjects rated the nonviolent heavy metal song ($M = 1.53$, $SD = .90$) as more familiar than the homicidal ($M = 1.04$, $SD = 1.89$) or the suicidal ($M = 1.04$, $SD = 1.89$) heavy metal songs, $F(2, 83) = 7.91$, $p < .001$. There was a main effect for content, $F(2, 169) = 4.17$,

$p < .05$. The nonviolent songs (M= 1.30, SD = .69) were rated as more familiar then the homicidal songs (M = 1.05, SD = .22), but this finding is qualified by the interaction.

Due to the significant interaction effects for song coherence and familiarity, analyses for the personality variables were first run using coherence and familiarity as covariates. But as neither coherence nor familiarity were significant covariates, noncovariate analyses are reported.

TABLE 3
Means and SDs for Adult Suicide Ideation Questionnaire (ASIQ), Beck Depression Inventory, (BDI), State-Trait Anxiety Inventory (STAI), and Self-Esteem Scale (SES)

	ASIQ	BDI	SW	SES
Rap				
Nonviolent	52.58 (13.39)	9.83 (8.01)	38.00 (11.53)	19.39 (5.85)
Homicidal	53.12 (17.58)	5.55 (4.33)	37.79 (11.92)	19.21 (5.45)
Suicidal	49.43 (10.96)	5.25 (3.45)	36.15 (9.11)	17.93 (4.62)
Heavy metal				
Nonviolent	79.87 (13.68)	6.08 (5.80)	35.21 (8.85)	18.00 (4.61)
Homicidal	49.82 (13.63)	7.26 (8.51)	41.36 (15.34)	19.11 (5.14)
Suicidal	46.04 (4.68)	7.07 (3.41)	37.48 (7.69)	17.24 (4.53)

NOTE: Standard deviations are in parentheses.

Interactions with Gender

To determine if gender interacted with music type or song content, 2 (gender) x 2 (music type) x 3 (song content) ANOVAs were conducted for each of the dependent measures. There were no significant interactions, so gender was not included in the analyses.

Mood Inventories

Two (music type) x 3 (song content) ANOVAs (or MANOVA, where appropriate) were used to examine the impact of the experimental variables on responding to the mood inventories. Because preliminary analyses indicated that (a) neither familiarity nor coherence of the songs significantly covaried with responding to the personality measures and (b) gender did not interact with music type or song content to predict responding to the personality measures, simple 2 x 3 ANOVAs were used for the ASIQ, BDI, STAI, and SES. A 2 x 3 MANOVA was used to examine the subscales of the STAXI. The MANOVA indicated a main effect of music type, $F(8, 146) = 2.5$, $p = .014$), but there was no significant main effects for song content, nor was there a significant music type by song content interaction. Thus univariate analyses are reported for the main effect of music type on the STAXI subscales. Univariate analyses are not reported for song content or interactions for the STAXI, as the overall MANOVA was not significant for these effects. Means and standard deviations for the personality measures by music type and song content are in Table 3.

BDI. There was a significant music type by song content interaction for responses to the BDI, $F(2, 124) = 3.03$, $p < .05$. Simple effects tests were performed holding music type constant. There were no significant differences due to song content among the heavy metal songs. But, subjects who heard the nonviolent rap song ($M = 9.83$, $SD = 8.01$) had higher BDI scores than subjects who heard either the homicidal ($M = 5.55$, $SD = 4.33$) or the suicidal ($M = 5.25$, $SD = 3.45$) rap song. A second set of simple effects tests were performed holding song content constant; there were no significant effects of music type. There were no main effects for song content or music type.

STAXI-Trait Anger. There was a main effect for music type on the Trait Anger subscale, $F(1, 155) = 3.96$, $p < .05$. The rap songs ($M = 51.13$, $SD = 10.69$) were related to higher scores on Trait Anger than the heavy metal songs ($M = 47.95$, $SD = 9.50$). (The MANOVA performed across STAM subscales was not significant for song content or for music type by song content interaction, thus only univariate analyses for the main effects are reported for the STAXI subscales.)

STAXI-Trait Anger Reserve. There was a also a main effect for music type on the Trait Anger Reserve subscale, $F(1, 155) = 12.81$, $p < .001$. Again, subjects who were exposed to the rap songs ($M = 52.41$, $SD = 10.57$) displayed higher levels of Trait Anger Reserve than the subjects who were exposed to the heavy metal songs ($M = 46.81$, $SD=8.74$).

STAXI-Anger In. There was main effect for music type for the Anger In subscale, $F(1, 156) = 5.96$, $p < .05$. Again, subjects who were exposed to rap songs ($M = 54.55$, $SD = 11.15$) displayed higher scores than subjects exposed to the heavy metal music ($M = 50.60$, $SD = 8.48$).

STAXI-Anger Expression, Anger Control, Anger Out, Trait Anger Total, State Anger. There were no main effects of music type for these variables, largest $F(1, 153) = 1.53$, $p =.22$.

ASIQ, STAI, Self-Esteem Scale. There were no main effects of music, song content, or interactions, for these variables, largest F(1, 155) = 2.... = .13.

DISCUSSION

The hypotheses were partially supported. As expected, lyrical content did affect students' immediate response to state mood questionnaires, but only in regard to one measure. Contrary to expectation, music type was related to differing responses on several measures, particularly anger. However, neither music type nor lyrical content affected subjects' responding on the ASIQ or the STAI. Thus the results of the study do not provide any evidence that lyrical content or music type (i.e., heavy metal vs. rap) has an immediate effect on either suicidal ideation or state anxiety.

In regard to rap song content, students who heard the nonviolent song had higher scores on the BDI than those who heard the violent songs. It may be that they felt relatively good about their own lives after listening to the violent and depressing rap songs, and thus reported fewer depressive symptoms than the subjects who heard the nonviolent, control song.

Surprisingly, rap music elicited more anger than heavy metal music on three of the STAXI subscales. Participants who were exposed to the rap song scored higher on the trait anger, trait anger reserve (a tendency to react with anger when criticized or treated unfairly) and anger-in (anger suppression) subscales. Several factors might be related to this finding. First, it has been suggested that listening to heavy metal music has a cathartic emotional effect. Arnett (1991b) found that male adolescents reported feeling a release of negative emotions, in a positive, nondestructive way, when listening to heavy metal music. Thus the heavy metal songs may have provided a release of anger for the listeners resulting in lower STAXI scores. But, musical preference may have affected subjects' responses. More subjects reported a preference for rock (N= 90), heavy metal/alternative (N= 39), and country (N= 22) than for rap (N = 22). Thus the subjects may have responded to the rap music more negatively simply because they did not like it. In addition, the lyrics of the rap songs contained more profanity than the lyrics of the heavy metal songs and this may have elicited more anger.

Other explanations for the effect hinge on the nature of rap music, which has become a mouthpiece for the oppressed and those seeking sociopolitical change. Thus, rap music may arouse righteous anger related to dismay over sociopolitical issues, due to the music's political salience. Or, the angry reactions to rap music may reflect an underlying, covert racism. If the mostly White subjects have internalized racism, then they might react to rap (typically considered an African American music style) with higher trait anger reserve scores because of internalized fears, prejudices, or both. Likewise, because overt racism is socially unacceptable, the subject would be likely to suppress such feelings of anger, leading to higher anger-in scores. Thus, it is may not be rap music per se that elicited greater anger, but the cognitive stereotypes associated with rap. It would be interesting to use a more ethnically diverse population in extensions of this study.

A few limitations of the present study should be noted. First, the procedure was carried out in the relatively sterile environment of a college classroom; this setting may have restricted the impact of the music on the subjects' moods. In addition, the subjects heard the song to which they were exposed just twice, at a moderate volume. Because we examined subjects' responses to brief exposure to the music in controlled context, the results of this study might underestimate the impact of music on those who often listen to heavy metal or rap music. Additionally, the results might not reflect how people would respond to similar music in a natural environment, such as their room or a party. And, because the memory test was administered after the songs as a distracter, this may have moderated the impact of the songs on the subjects' emotional responses. Clearly there are limits as to how one can examine responses to music in a laboratory setting, but future studies could focus on increasing the length of exposure to musical stimuli, varying volume, conducting studies in more comfortable settings, and gathering emotional responses immediately.

A few other findings warrant discussion. First, gender did not interact with music type or lyrical to affect responding on the dependent variables. Although no effects were hypothesized, the lack of gender effects is interesting given that more males than females prefer heavy metal music (Arnett, 1991a; Wass et al., 1988-1989). Second, the substantial lack of consistency in thematic classification of songs is related to findings that people often do not accurately analyze song content (Greenfield et al., 1987; Hansen & Hansen, 1991; Rosenbaum & Prinsky, 1987). The failure of some subjects to correctly classify the songs' themes may have influenced the results. A substantial minority of subjects incorrectly classified the nonviolent control songs as violent in nature. Some students may hold the belief that heavy metal and rap music are inherently violent, particularly because this belief is reinforced by the media, and thus failed to categorize the songs in light of lyrical content. If so, the differences between the songs were truncated and decreased variability.

Future studies should also include a broader range of music conditions, such as country and pop music. We did not include other types of music in this study because we could not find unfamiliar country or pop songs with violent themes. Rap and heavy metal music are both highly arousing and may elicit similar reactions in regard to moods other than anger. Other types of music may elicit different sorts of mood changes (e.g., such as depression) than those elicited by heavy metal or rap. And, if musical preference is related to emotional responding to music, there may be interactions between musical preference and responses to varying types of music. There is anecdotal evidence that people become irritable when exposed to music they do not like. Thus, although heavy metal fans may respond positively to listening to heavy metal music, they may respond negatively if forced to listen to country music and vice versa. Future research must also broaden the age range studied. These findings, from a sample of college students, may not be indicative of how individuals in early and midadolescence would respond to heavy metal and rap music.

Despite these limitations, the results of this study yield an experimental look at the impact of types of rock music on college students. As the media continues to permeate our lives to a greater degree, such research will become more important.

REFERENCES

Arnett, J. (1991a). Heavy metal music and reckless behavior among adolescents. *Journal of Youth and Adolescence, 20*, 573-592.

Arnett, J. (1991b). Adolescents and heavy metal music: From the mouths of metalheads. *Youth & Society, 23*, 76-98.

Beck, A. T., Ward, C.H., Mendelson, M., Mock, J., & Erbaugh, J. (1961). An inventory measuring depression. *Archives of General Psychology,4*, 561-571.

Blascovich, J., & Tomaka, J. (1991). Measures of self-esteem. In J. P. Robinson, P.R. Shaver, & L. S. Wrightman (Eds.), *Measures of personality and social psychological attitudes: Volume I* (pp.115-160). San Diego: Academic Press.

Bleich, S., Zillman, D., & Weaver, J. (1991). Enjoyment and consumption of defiant rock music as a function of adolescent rebelliousness. *Journal of Broadcasting & Electronic Media, 35*, 351-366.

Desmond, R.J. (1987). Adolescents and music lyrics: Implications of a cognitive perspective. *Communication Quarterly, 35*, 276-684.

Greenfield, P. M., Buzzone, L., Koyamatsu, K., Satuloff, W., Nixon, K., Brodie, M., & Kinsdale, D. (1987). What is rock music doing to the minds of our youth? A first experimental look at the effects of rock music lyrics and music videos. *Journal of Early Adolescence, 7*, 315-329.

Hansen, C. H., & Hansen, R. D. (1990). The influence of sex and violence on the appeal of rock music videos. *Communication Research, 17,* 212-234.

Hansen, C. H., & Hansen, R. D. (1991). Schematic information processing of heavy meal lyrics. *Communication Research, 18,* 373-411.

King, P. (1988). Heavy metal music and drug abuse in adolescents. *Postgraduate Medicine, 83,* 295-304.

Metzger, R. L. (1976). A reliability and validity study of the state-trait anxiety inventory. *Journal of Clinical Psychology, 32,* 276-278.

Pareles, J.,& Romanowski, P. (Eds.). (1983). *The Rolling Stone Encyclopedia of Rock and Roll.* New York: Rolling Stone Press.

Prinsky, L.E., & Roserbaum, J. L. (1987). Leer-ics or lyrics? *Youth & Society, 18,* 384-394.

Record labeling: Contents of music and lyrics of records. (1985, September). Hearing before the Committee on Commerce, Science, and Transportation, United States Senate, 99th. Congress (S. Hrg. 99-529). Washington, DC: U.S. Government Printing Office.

Reynolds, W. M. (1991) . *Adult Suicidal Ideation Questionnaire: Professional manual.* Odessa, FL: Psychological Assessment Resources.

Rosenbaum, J., & Prinsky, L. (1987). Sex, violence and rock and roll: Youth's perceptions of popular music. *Popular Music and Society, 11,* 79-90.

Rosenberg, M. (1965). *Society and the adolescent self-image.* Princeton, NJ: Princeton University Press.

Simpson, J. C. (1990, February 5). Yo! Rap gets on the map: Led by groups like Public Enemy, it socks a black message to the mainstream. *Time,* pp. 60-62.

Singetary, M. W. (1983). Some perceptions of the lyrics of three types of recorded music: Rock, country, and soul. *Popular Music and Society, 9,* 51-63.

Spielberger, C.D. (1988a). *Manual for the Stait-Trait Anger Expression Scale (STAXI).* Odessa, FL: Psychological Assessment Resources.

Spielberger, C. D. (1988b). Anger Expression Scale. In M. Hersen & A. S. Bellack (Eds.), *Dictionary of behavioral assessment techniques* (pp. 27-29). New York: Pergamon.

Spielberger, C. D. (1988c). Stait-Trait Anger Scale. In M. Herson & A. S. Bellack (Eds.), *Dictionary of behavioral assessment techniques* (pp. 446-448). New York: Pergamon.

Spielberger, C. D., Johnson, E. H., Russell, S. F., Crane, R. J., Jacobs, G. A., & Worden, T. J. (1985). The experience and expression of anger: Construction and validation of an anger expression scale. In M. A. Chesney & R. H. Rosenman (Eds.), *Anger and hostility in cardiovascular and behaviors disorders* (pp. 5-30). Washington, DC: Hemisphere.

Stack, S. & Gundlack, J. (1992). The effect of country music on suicide. *Social Forces, 71,* 211-218.

Thigpen, D. (1993, September 16). Restricted access. *Rolling Stone,* p. 13.

Thorne, S. B., & Himelstein, P. (1984). The role of suggestion in the perception of satanic messages in rock and roll recordings. *Journal of Psychology, 116,* 245-248.

Trzcinski, J. (1992). Heavy metal kids: Are they dancing with the devil? *Child & Youth Care Forum, 21,* 7-22

Vedder, E. (1993, September 2). *MTV Tenth Anniversary Music Video Awards.* New York: MTV.

Vokey, J. R., & Read, J. D. (1985). Subliminal messages: Between the devil and the media. *American Psychologist, 40,* 1231-1239.

Wass, H., Miller, M. D., & Redditt, C. A. (1991). Adolescents and destructive themes in rock music: A follow up. *Omega, 23,* 199-206.

Wass, H., Miller, M.D., & Stevenson, R. G. (1989). Factors affecting adolescents' behavior and attitudes toward destructive rock lyrics. *Death Studies, 13,* 287-303.

Wass, H., Raup, J. L, Cerullo, K., Martel, L. G., Mingione, L. A., & Sperring, A. (1988-1989). Adolescent's interest in and views of destructive themes in rock music. *Omega, 19,* 177-186.

Mary E. Ballard is an assistant professor of psychology at Appalachian State University. She received her B.S. and M.S. from Eastern Kentucky University and her Ph.D. from West Virginia University. Her research interests include the impact of media (particularly music and video games) on adolescents and children, attachment, and stress and coping. Recent publications include articles in *Journal of Youth and Adolescence* (in press; with Bush and Fremouw), *Journal of Abnormal Child Psychology* (1994; with El-Sheilkh and Cummings), and *Child Development* (1993; with Cummings and Larkin).

Steven Coates is a staff psychologist at the Roanoke Rapids Mental Health Center in Roanoke Rapids, NC. He received his M.A. from Appalachian State University in 1994. His primary research interest is in antisocial adolescent behavior.

QUESTIONS FOR DISCUSSION

1. The authors begin their article by providing a history of heavy metal and rock music and by reviewing previous literature on related topics. Summarize briefly this background information. What questions are left unanswered in previous literature?

2. What is the starting question for this research? How did the authors arrive at a hypothesis to test their starting question?

3. From their hypothesis, the authors design a research method. Describe the method they used to test their hypothesis. Was this an appropriate method, in your opinion? Will it answer the starting question?

4. Why did the authors conduct both a pilot study and an experimental study? What is the purpose of a pilot study? What did the authors learn in the pilot study?

5. The authors use a typical research report format for presenting their study; what are the parts of the typical research report used in this article?

6. The results section of the report is heavily laden with statistics. What did you learn from these statistical reports?

7. Many of the statistics are reported in the form of tables. Did this help you understand the results? Why or why not?

8. Read the discussion section of the report very carefully. Do you agree with their explanations? Are there other interpretations of their data that are possible besides the ones they provide?

9. Did anything surprise you about the results of this research? Discuss your own opinion about the connection between music and mood.

10. Notice the documentation style used for this research report. What style is it and why do you think it was chosen?

Take Your Partners: A Description of a Student Social System in a Secondary School Dance Class

Peter A. Hastie, Auburn University and Andrew Pickwell, Ipswich Grammar School, Australia

This study examined the operations of a student social system within an elective physical education dance class. Its methodology is based on the findings of Allen (1986), who determined that students have two main agendas in classes, namely, to give teachers what they want while having fun and socializing with classmates. Consistent with previous findings, many students in this study were particularly adept at finding ways to minimize work and have fun while still doing enough to pass the course. These findings are explained in conjunction with the task structure and accountability systems put in place by the teacher. That is, the teacher seemed to be content to trade off lower levels of participation in the instructional task system for at least nondisruptive behavior, thereby allowing a relatively unimpeded achievement of the students' social objectives.

As the field of research on physical education develops, a number of devices are becoming available for studying students and teachers in classes. One particular concept that has been lauded as providing a particularly incisive explanation of classroom processes is the ecological model and the study of academic tasks. The focus of such a research agenda is to explain how work gets done, acknowledging the dual directionality of teacher-student behaviors.

The stimulus for the development of an ecological model of classrooms was provided by Walter Doyle in a series of studies in the 1970s (Doyle, 1977a, 1977b, 1979a). Doyle had two primary concerns. First, he contended that too much attention was placed on the teacher as a causal effect in classrooms. Doyle explained that research focusing on teachers had failed to explain how teacher effects actually took place, and he

Reprinted by permission from P.A. Hastie & A. Pickwell, 1996, "Take Your Partners: A Description of a Student Social System in a Secondary School Dance Class," *Journal of Teaching Physical Education*, 15 (2): 171-87.

commented that "in the absence of formal explanatory propositions, it is difficult to interpret contradictory findings or select potentially fruitful avenues for investigation" (Doyle, 1977a, p. 167). Second, and perhaps more important, Doyle believed that focusing only on teacher variables oversimplified the picture of causality in classrooms. In Doyle's view, students could affect classroom actions almost as much as the teacher. He commented that several investigators had reported evidence to support the proposition that student behaviors were a cause of observed teacher behaviors (Doyle, 1977a).

Doyle conceptualized teaching-learning as a set of interrelated task systems, all under the influence of the accountability strategies utilized by the teacher. This model was called the "ecological paradigm," and the key to the model was that changes in one system are likely to influence behavior in another. The original systems identified in classroom studies (Doyle, 1979a, 1980) were the managerial and instructional task systems. The managerial task system consists of those nonacademic tasks that relate to appropriate standards of behavior and the maintenance of the learning environment. The instructional task system consists of the academic work of the class (Doyle, 1983), that is, the tasks relating to the subject matter and subsequent intended learning.

A brief summary of the research on the ecology of physical education (e.g., Lund, 1992; Son, 1988/1989; Tousignant & Siedentop, 1983) provides a number of key issues. Most importantly, accountability drives a task system, be it managerial or instructional. Without accountability there is no task, and students will only do as much as they are motivated to do by their own interests. In addition, the answers a teacher actually accepts and rewards define the real tasks in classrooms, and the strictness of the criteria a teacher uses to judge answers has consequences for task accomplishment. Thus, students tend to treat seriously only those tasks for which they are held accountable (Doyle, 1983).

The level of accountability will determine the difference between the "stated task," (that is, the instructions given to the student by the teacher) and the "real task" (that is, what the students are allowed to produce that is accepted by the teacher). This acceptance or reinforcement can be overt, such as a comment, or can be covert, such as ignoring.

As described, it is important to note that these task systems are interdependent. Changes in student behavior in one system will have consequences for what is achieved in another. For example, if a group of students should become bored with the instructional tasks and decide to act out, thereby exceeding the boundaries of the managerial system, the teacher must decide whether to ignore the misbehavior (and thereby informally accept it) or react to bring the students to order. The extent to which the teacher moves away from an instructional role to a managerial role will have implications for the instructional task system. If full attention is placed onto the miscreant students, and the attention of the whole class is brought to bear upon them, it is possible that the instructional task system will temporarily be suspended. If the teacher is able to deal with the issue while still attending to the instructional goals of the lesson, the instructional task system may not be affected at all, at least for the rest of the class.

The study of Tousignant and Siedentop (1983) provided clear examples of these notions in physical education. In a detailed examination of secondary school physical education teachers, these authors investigated behaviors for which physical education students were held responsible. Tousignant and Siedentop determined that teacher follow-up determined the nature of tasks more than teacher instruction, and that students often learned more about the requirements for the task from a teacher's reactions to performance than they did from the teacher's original instructions.

Studies in physical education have focused primarily on the instructional and managerial task systems. Tousignant and Siedentop's (1983) first observations included secondary school track, gymnastics, tennis, and volleyball. Since then, there have been examinations of a secondary golf unit (Alexander, 1982/1983), of middle school volleyball (Graham, 1987), and of the varieties of techniques used by teachers to hold students accountable for accomplishment in instructional tasks (Hastie, 1994; Lund, 1992).

Throughout this program of research, one additional dimension of class life has been identified. In addition to the instructional and managerial task systems put in place by teachers, a student social system has also been shown to affect the extent of task development and the amount of work that gets done in lessons. The social world of the student has been described in most enlightening form by Emmers (1981). She describes schools from the perspective of students and makes two particularly poignant comments. The first describes the social world of the student:

> Learning American history pales in comparison to hearing about a previous night's party; solving algebraic equations intrigues less than figuring out how to be acceptable before one's peers. Rarely will academic achievement be more vital to a student than his social development; rarely will studying consume more of his energy than socializing.
> (Emmers, 1981, p. 2)

Emmers's (1981) second key point relates to student behavior in the classroom, and how it is designed to achieve social objectives or minimize work:

> Students not only like to get off the subject, they also like to get "out of" the subject, and they are ingenious inventors of reasons to do so. One student must consult with the guidance counselor briefly; another has to make an urgent phone call; another picked up by mistake the wrong book from his locker. (p. 90)

In a participant observation study, Allen (1986) identified that students have two major goals in classes: to socialize and to pass the course, and he presented a model that described the key features of students' classroom agenda.

Allen (1986) noted that students use two major strategies to achieve their goals of socializing and passing, namely having fun and giving the teachers what they want. To successfully achieve both agendas, students will use tactics to minimize work and reduce boredom, while attempting to stay out of trouble. The more subversive or submissive tactics are occasionally used, depending upon the managerial focus of the teacher.

To date, there has been little attention placed upon the student social system in physical education, and comment has been made on the need for research in this area (Siedentop, 1988). Although Tinning and Siedentop (1985) identified a social tasks system operating in student teaching, their study focused on how the student teacher developed and maintained cordial relations between himself and his supervisor and cooperating teacher. The study did not provide detail of a student-social system from the perspective of the pupils in the class.

One further concept relating to the ecological paradigm needs to be addressed. This is the concept of negotiation. Identified by Woods (1978), negotiation occurs as students confront tasks in either the managerial or instructional task system. In facing these tasks, students will get some idea how successful they can be in achieving the demands of these tasks. Negotiation involves interactions between students and teachers whereby students attempt to reduce the demands of a particular task or at least have the teacher give more information about how to achieve its objectives. Although negotiation in classrooms is typically verbal (Doyle, 1981), in physical education it is mostly enacted through the physical modification of tasks, either to make the tasks easier or to make them more challenging (Marks & Hersh, 1990). Students will actively change the set tasks to make them more easy or difficult, depending upon their skill level, and the reactions of the teacher to this modification will affect the success of this negotiation.

Negotiation can also have impact across systems. For example, Son (1988/1989) described how highly skilled students would modify tasks to make them easier, which would allow the students to socialize more with their friends. By performing at a moderate skill level, students could socialize without drawing attention from the teacher.

PURPOSE

The purpose of this study was to examine the student social system in a secondary school physical education class. Dance was chosen as the unit, because it historically is one content area of physical education in which teachers meet resistance (e.g., Cunningham, 1982; Lloyd & West, 1988; Williams, 1986), especially with male students. Dance also provides a number of opportunities for student social engagement, in spite of the rigor of teacher accountability.

Three research questions provided the focus for this study:

1. What is the level of student engagement in these dance classes?
2. At what level does the teacher hold the students accountable for instructional tasks?
3. What strategies do students use to socialize and still pass?

In answering these questions, the efficacy of adopting Allen's (1986) model of students' classroom agenda as a useful tool for further study in physical education could be evaluated.

METHOD

Participants

Students. The class in this study consisted of twenty-two 11th-grade students (ages 16-17) at an Australian metropolitan high school. Full enrollment was 14 boys and 8 girls, although rarely was full attendance achieved. However, on no occasions during this study did girls outnumber boys in attendance. Although the students at the school were from a wide ethnic background, the students in this class were exclusively Caucasians.

Teacher. The teacher was one of five specialists who taught the optional program in physical education at the school. Ms. Samba, who had been teaching for 6 years (the last 4 at this school) had previous experience teaching dance, and had taught the same unit at this school for the past 4 years, and had also taught dance to 12th-grade students for that time.

The School Curriculum

At this school, like all other schools in the state, the students were required to select four optional subjects in addition to English, and these subjects were graded on progressive assessment over the four semesters of Grades 11 and 12. All of the students in this class had therefore chosen health and physical education as one of those four electives. This subject was graded in the same fashion as all others on the curriculum. Grades could be awarded solely on measured performance, such as practical skills tests, or written examinations and assignments. No marks could be awarded for effort during class or for attendance, nor could deductions be made for misbehavior or laziness.

Dance was one of seven content areas that made up the practical component of the health and physical education course. This practical component counted toward 60% of the final grade. Foundations of physical education and health education (commonly known as the theory component) contributed the other 40%. Dance, then, contributed nearly 10% of the final grade for this subject. The students in this class had either little or no previous experience with dance within the physical education program at the school. Those who had taken physical education in the 10th grade had experienced square dance, but those enrolling for the first time in this grade had no previous exposure, at least at school. The dances completed in this unit were the jive, cha-cha, and waltz. The class met three times a week for a 40-minute period, and the unit extended over 6 weeks, allowing 2 weeks per dance.

Data Collection

Data were collected over the 6-week period for at least two periods per week. A total of 14 lessons were observed. Data were collected through passive participant observation (Spradley, 1980). That is, although we attended the dance lessons, we did not actively participate in a teaching role, and we only interacted with the teacher and students for the purposes of informal interviews. As Spradley (1980) comments, "If the passive participant occupies any role in the social situation, it will only be that of 'bystander,' 'spectator' or 'loiterer'" (p. 59).

The Nature of Tasks and Task Accomplishment. A modified version of Marks's (1988/1989) Task Structure Observation Instrument (TSOI) was used to collect data on the stated tasks and on student accomplishment of those tasks in the dance classes. Included on the recording sheet was the stated task given to students, the subsequent students' response, and the accountability strategies used by the teacher during that instructional episode. A sample of one completed segment is shown in Figure 1.

Stated task	Students' response		Teacher's response	Comments
OK. This time we will go through the whole sequence four times. Start as I count you in.	On-task Modified up Modified down Off task Deviant	16 0 2 4 0	None Feedback * to student she Desist is dancing with Prompts Restates task	One pair is not doing the turn. Two other pairs are standing and watching.
Boys, change over.	On-task Modified up Modified down Off task Deviant	20 0 0 0 2	None Feedback Desist Prompts Restates task	Two boys move up to the line, but do not change over. T is changing tape, does not see them.

Figure 1--Modified task structures observation instrument.

Field Notes. Field notes were used to provide an account of how students achieved social objectives. The field notes focused on the primary tasks of students' classroom agenda identified by Allen (1986). In addition, the students' grades for this dance unit and all other units were collected.

Interviews. Interviews were conducted with selected students and the teacher in order to provide support for the hypotheses developed from the field notes. Interviews commenced from the first week with the teacher and from the 3rd week with the students. The purpose of the early interviews with the teacher was to gain a perspective on the teacher's feelings about the importance of student participation in the unit, and the extent to which she was going to accept nonparticipation, as there were more boys in the class than girls.

Interviews were conducted informally and incidentally. They were typically characterized by brief questions, usually on the way to or from class and, in the teacher's case, in the stateroom during recess. The interviews were not audiotaped since most questions were simple and responses easily recorded using a note pad. To confirm responses and improve reliability, a number of students were also asked prepared questions such as the following:

Do you like dance?
Are you taking this unit seriously?
What is your main concern when taking this unit?

Data Analysis

Reducing Data and Developing Categories. A process of progressive reduction was used to develop the categories discussed in this study. Quantitative observation data, together with field notes and interview data, were analyzed to identify any recurring patterns of class participation and student/teacher responses. Original categories were derived from prior studies using the ecological paradigm and included instructional and managerial tasks, as well as accountability. Also included were the factors of Allen's (1986) model. These categories served as useful initial placements of data. From these categories, new categories were derived. Examples include the nature of the different mechanisms used to promote the students' social agenda.

Trustworthiness of the Data. Verification of our findings was achieved be seeking consistency of both student actions and verbal accounts over the entire unit. Where the same patterns of task involvement were demonstrated, this suggested a strong tie to our hypotheses. This consistency was also sought through the analysis of discussions with students and in more lengthy discussions with the teacher. If students gave the same or similar responses to identical questions, that data was considered reliable. If the teacher agreed with a particular hypothesis, that suggestion became more plausible.

Informed Consent

The teacher in this class provided informed consent to the conduct of the research and the presence of the researchers in the lessons. We were both known to the teacher and had previous experience in the school. The first author had visited the school many times during internship visits, and the second author had been Ms. Samba's student teacher during his internship. The students in the class were told that the purpose of the research was to understand how they liked dance and to examine how well they performed the set tasks during lessons.

RESULTS

Accomplishment of Instructional and Managerial Tasks

The Setting. Every lesson in this dance unit took a familiar organizational structure, because the unit plan consisted of a number of modern dances. First, the students would form two lines, boys facing girls. The teacher would walk through the girls' steps with them while the boys were expected to listen and watch. The teacher would then repeat this exercise with the boys. The students would then go together with a partner, walking through the steps to the count of the teacher. On occasions, the teacher would get one of the boys to be her partner—usually one of those who seemed unwilling to participate or who was not putting in much of an effort (confirmed by the teacher in an informal interview)—and would demonstrate the steps in front of the class. The students would complete segments of a dance routine, then progress to the whole dance, finally completing the dance to music. The teacher expected that this progression up to completing the routine for the test to music would be achievable in each lesson (informal interview with teacher).

Student Participation. All students were expected to participate in the class. When individual tasks were set, such as walking through the steps of the dances or watching the teacher demonstrate, all students were active and attentive. The teacher would direct attention to those not listening or watching and direct them to do so.

However, when students were expected to work with a partner, different participation patterns were evident. One critical factor in determining the level of student involvement in partner work was class attendance. Given the ratio of boys to girls in the class, not every boy could work with a girl partner. A number of boys, then, were without partners. The teacher tried to get those students involved, but with little success. The stated task of, "You people stand at the back, in line with the other guys, and walk through the steps by yourself," was effective for the first one or two sequences, but soon, through a lack of reinforcement and therefore a lack of accountability, this stated task resulted in no participation. The real task that resulted was simply to avoid having to "get a partner."

As a result, on days when there was full attendance, as many as 6 boys would be waiting for a partner, because the teacher did not require boys to dance with boys. During this unit then, especially in the later stages of learning each dance, boys were able to sit out. The teacher did not make them practice the steps by themselves, nor did she make them watch or provide feedback to partners who were practicing. The girls had no such opportunity, since at no stage did they outnumber the boys in attendance.

When asked why she did not require the leftover boys to act as partners, the teacher gave two reasons:

> First of all, they wouldn't do it. They would just fool around, and I'd end up spending more time disciplining than teaching. But the main reason is that it would be too confusing. One minute they'd be doing the girls' steps and then the boys'. They have enough trouble just learning their own without having to switch back and forth. I'd prefer they just get in the back of the line and practice one set of steps well. (informal interview)

Task Modification. During practice, there were rare occasions when some girls would modify the set task to make it more challenging or interesting. That is, they would walk or dance through the steps while the teacher was explaining the sequence. The stated task here was simply to watch and listen. The teacher never desisted this upward modification. The boys in the class never did anything extra beyond the actual stated task, although there were considerable (and successful) attempts to reduce participation or modify tasks in a downward direction.

All students were at their best (in terms of task congruence) when performing with a partner, with no music, and following the teacher's count. The quality of dance at this time was even better than when students were practicing by themselves. There were fewer errors, and the sequences seemed more smooth. By having a partner, the boys could at least follow the girls if they did not know what to do, and could learn the steps in this way. This was confirmed by the teacher: "The girls tend to lead them around if they don't know what to do. They've [the boys] got someone else's feet to watch and follow. When they're by themselves, they're on their own" (Ms. Samba, Lesson 5).

The Teacher's Accountability System. Ms. Samba seemed content to hold students informally accountable for participation only, without any regard for the quality of performance. Little individual feedback was given to students during lessons, and the feedback that was given focused on effort rather than on technique. Most often, the provision of feedback was limited to the student dancing with the teacher.

One informal accountability strategy the teacher used was to have male students dance with her. It was on these occasions that we could see that most of the boys could actually perform the tasks, and were more unwilling than unable to participate.

The teacher also used grade-related threats to promote participation. "You are going to get an E if you don't get up and practice," was a common statement directed to those who avoided participation. Although the teacher could not take marks off for lack of participation, she was hinting that if they did not practice their performance on the test would suffer (informal interview).

This grade-related strategy seemed ineffective when it was presented in a public context. A lot of students would laugh at this statement in front of their friends. However, when the teacher discussed the prospects of a poor grade to students in private, the effort and participation of the targeted student did improve, at least in the next lesson (field notes, informal discussion with teacher, Lessons 6 and 7).

The threat of public exposure was also used. During one lesson, the students were forced to work underneath a building due to the school's gymnasium being used for statewide aptitude testing. As the lesson was approaching its scheduled conclusion and some students were beginning to pack up, the teacher stated,

> No one is leaving until everyone has gone through this with the music. If the bell goes, and you haven't finished, we are still going to go through it, and everyone coming down for lunch can come and sit here and watch you dance.

At this point, student effort and participation increased and the class quickly completed the set tasks.

<u>The Student Social System</u>

This section describes how the students achieved a social agenda during the dance unit. It follows the steps of Allen's (1986) model.

Figuring Out the Teacher. This element is essentially equivalent to the discussion relating to Ms. Samba's accountability system. Students in this class knew that very little monitoring took place and that there could be no ongoing grading of their performance until the formal examination. It is important to recall here that in the specialist course in physical education in which these students were enrolled, teachers are unable to grade for effort or participation. They are locked into a central, state-wide mechanism in which only formal, performance-based assessment counts for student grades. The students knew, then, that during the lessons of the unit, the teacher was only able to enact informal, rather than grade-related, accountability strategies. One student stated:

> You know that the test is what counts. As long as you do it on the day, that's all that matters. So why work hard when you don't have to? Besides, it's easy to hide. You just look where she is. (Sam)

Giving the Teacher What She Wanted. In this class, as reinforced through the teacher's inaction in enforcing students to practice by themselves, the students were able to be in good standing provided no girls were left without a partner. As a whole, students were able to attend to their social agendas provided they had at least a couple of turns during the lesson and did not disrupt those who were practicing.

Having Fun. It was clear that many of the boys in this class did not enjoy dance. Indeed, for many, their primary goal was to limit their involvement in the instructional tasks. When asked about his feelings towards the unit, Bill commented, "Yeah, I hate it. You look like a dork, and besides, you won't use it anywhere. The only time we do this stuff is in PE."

Clearly then, the set activity in this class was not conducive to having fun for these boys. However, what became fun was inventing ways to avoid participating. By missing out on a partner, the boys were able to engage in socializing activities, such as discussing the week's football game or planning events for the weekend. Some boys would also spend this time calling out to their mates on the dance floor, engaging in a common practice known as "paying out." "Yeah, good move Joey," and, "That's the way to step on her feet. Just kick him back Sara," are two examples of how boys attempted to embarrass their classmates. However, this paying out was not seen as a serious attempt to belittle the classmate; it was more a case of scoring points on the social popularity scale. Two students explained:

> No one really worries about it. It's just a bit of fun. (Ted)

> Yeah, if we really didn't like him, we'd find something much better to do. (Jim)

How Did Students Avoid Participation? The female students in this class did not have any chance to avoid participation, unless they were sick or injured. Indeed, such tactics were never used by the female students. However, the "Oh Miss, I hurt my knee in soccer" strategy was effectively used by one male student, which sponsored a number of false claims in the next lesson. "Big soccer game yesterday, Miss. Sore knee," was one excuse made by a boy who less than an hour later was seen playing rugby during lunch.

Other boys used more subtle and selective techniques to limit their participation. Every 5 to 10 minutes, the teacher would call out for the boys to change places with those who were waiting. The boys used a number of strategies to avoid getting a partner in this changeover period. The first involved a boy moving up to the line of dancers, and then moving back out of it again, as though he had been in line. He would then sit around the corner and try to remain inconspicuous. Others were more elaborate. When the teacher challenged students about participation, the typical exchange would be similar to the following:

James, you haven't had a go, have you?

Oh, no Miss.

Well, you'd better get in this time.

The boy would then move up to the line and almost link up with a partner. However, he still managed to move towards a girl where another boy has already traded places. He then resumes his seat. A couple of minutes later, the teacher realizes that James still hasn't got a partner:

James, have you got your partner?

Oh! Oh no Miss, I was just about to. . . .

Students would also go and sit down before it was their turn. While this tactic sometimes worked, it was not always supported by their classmates. At times, when too many would leave the floor at once, a number of girls would be left, prompting teacher action. When questioning the boys about whose turn it was, Ms. Samba was supported by calls of, "You haven't gone, you haven't gone," and, "Miss, Bob hasn't been out yet."

The further avoidance strategy was to simply move out to the line too slowly, where by all exchanges would have been made. The boys then, had developed a series of skills and strategies to allow minimal participation in the instructional tasks of the unit. In particular, they had become competent bystanders.

Tousignant and Siedentop (1983) described the *competent bystander* as the student who rarely makes contact with the instructional tasks, but is adept at not placing attention on him- or herself. This is achieved by staying within the boundaries and requirements of the managerial task system and through attachment to better skilled students, thereby looking as though the student is involved.

In this class, although no dancing partners were deliberately off task, the pairs who were not very good spent more time in the back corners furthest from the teacher. Since the teacher did not vary her position much during lessons, the chances of being monitored were slim. Only the good pairs moved closer to the teacher, in order to check whether they were performing the correct sequence. Isolation was also accompanied by downward task modification. For example, during the waltz, the stated task was to perform the correct sequence of steps to complete the full waltz turn. The distant pairs were more likely to simply twirl with their partners backwards and forwards. However, when the steps became more complex, many would simply stop and watch (Lesson 9). This movement to the back of the teacher's view was the only strategy available for the girls who desired less participation. It was consistently the same two girls who were more distant from the teacher.

A Special Case. Although most of the boys in the class were prepared to forego any work to engage in socializing, there was one particular student who achieved success in both systems. Toby was an A-level student in physical education who clearly was not prepared to score poorly in this unit, but at the same time, did not want to be isolated from his mates (informal discussion).

Toby's strategy was carefully constructed. First, he would always do the steps well, but he would never modify upwards. This served a particular purpose. Adequate performance would not draw any praise from the teacher, thereby not drawing attention from his friends that he was achieving well at dance, clearly against the norm for the group.

Second, to remain in good standing with the nonperformers, Toby only completed the minimum task requirements. He only went to the dance line when it was his turn, and he did not misbehave when he was sitting out. In this way, he could maximize the time he spent with his friends, which in turn served to withdraw any attention on him during practice. By not being under the scrutiny of his friends during practice, he could be conscientious in attempting to achieve a high grade for the unit.

Critical Instances in Class. Allen (1986) describes two cases that arise when the student social system is not allowed to fully develop, that is, when the teacher's agenda conflicts with the routine of the students' agenda. The first occurs when students find the class boring. In this case, students invent strategies to reduce that boredom, such as trying to embarrass the teacher and get him or her mad. The second critical incident occurs when the teacher is so strict as to control students' socializing. In this case, Allen (1986) comments that students move into damage control, and initiate strategies for staying out of trouble. These include the termination of talk and play activities or changing of seats to move away from troublemakers.

In this dance class, these critical incidents did not seem to arise. First, because the teacher employed only a limited and irregular accountability system, the boys' social agenda was allowed to operate unimpeded. Second, because the teacher could not deduct points from the final grade, the need to behave perfectly to "pass the course" was removed. Furthermore, many of the boys were not concerned with obtaining a passing grade for this unit, socializing objectives (through minimizing work) could be better achieved. Failing dance, after all, was not seen as critical, since it counted only 10% toward the final grade and with some success in other units, a passing grade could be achieved. Two students explained:

> It doesn't really matter if you don't pass this stuff. I don't even care if I don't get a good mark for dance. It isn't a real sport anyway. (Terry)
>
> It's boring, and I won't ever do it again outside of this unit. So why bother? (Jack)

In terms of reducing boredom, although the dance activities might have been boring for the boys, they were at least able to achieve their social agenda without threat, and therefore, they did so without significant disruptions to the class.

DISCUSSION

The results from this study provide evidence for suggesting that Allen's (1986) model might be a useful framework for describing students' agendas in physical education. The components of the model were evident in this dance class, at least from the observation of the boys. It was more difficult to determine the extent of socializing for the girls, since the girls were almost totally involved in the instructional task system.

However, it is important to recall that the girls did not invoke any strategies to minimize work. The girls did not come to class with injury excuses, as some of the boys did, nor did the girls put any boredom-reducing strategies in place. One could suggest however, that even if one of the girls had been successful in avoiding participation, a girl talking to a group of boys would have drawn the attention of the teacher, who would have taken steps to ensure both parties became active.

It was clear that this class demonstrated clear inequities in the treatment of the boys and girls. The teacher interacted differently with boys and girls and provided different demands for the boys' and girls' participation. Different patterns of acceptable participation were also evident.

Griffin (1983) comments that the resulting interaction and participation patterns are not solely the result of the teacher, because students already have sex-stereotyped beliefs about themselves, each other, and the activities being taught. However, it is perhaps more important to note that teacher inaction can further perpetuate these notions, as was evident in this class. Griffin (1983) comments that

> to the extent that teachers and students accept the resulting interaction and participation patterns as a normal part of the day-to-day experience in sex-integrated classes, the opportunity to team activity skills will be limited to student perceptions of sex-appropriate behavior. (p. 84)

In this class, these perceptions seemed not only limited to the students. For example, Ms. Samba had commented during informal discussion that "this is one unit where the girls can do really well. They like dance and are better than the boys, so the unit gives them a chance to show that they can do things as well as the boys."

It also needs to be reinforced that the key to understanding any ecology is that the task systems are interdependent and that one cannot be fully understood in isolation or without examining the implication for others. While previous research in physical education has examined the interdependency of the managerial and instructional task systems, it can now be demonstrated that the student social system has a strong influence on this interdependency.

In Ms. Samba's class, it was clear that there were some male students who were not prepared to give up the socializing opportunities available to them. To fully conform with the teacher's task demands in the instructional task system, by dancing with a partner and practicing when alone, these students would have had to suspend the social system altogether. Furthermore, there was an "antidance" ethic that served to strengthen the value placed upon nonparticipation. For instance, it seemed that it was more dignified for a boy to fail without effort than it was to try to get a good grade. This statement can be supported through the actions of Toby, who wanted to maintain his A status in physical education, but not at the cost of isolating himself from his classmates.

The effects of peer pressure in developing a social agenda in physical education cannot be overlooked in future studies, particularly given the public context of the subject. It is pertinent to note the boys in this class earned a significantly lower score for this dance unit than their average for all physical education topics ($t = 3.7$, $p < .005$). The irony however, was that while no boy scored an A for dance, none scored lower than a C. There was no significant change in girls' scores, with the average being a B+.

The results of this study might provide an explanation of the classes in Placek's (1983) well known "busy, happy, and good" findings. Placek (1983) reported that teachers are more concerned with students participating in the activities and enjoying themselves in a nondisruptive manner than they are with student learning and achievement. As found by Allen (1986), the best classes from students' perspectives are ones that allow them to socialize while learning something interesting. A busy, happy, and good class might well fit this criteria. By being busy, happy, and good, the students can give the teacher what he or she wants, and through a weak demand on the concern for achievement, the students can achieve their classroom agenda. Importantly for the teacher, there is the absence of critical events that lead to misdemeanors and deviant student behavior, and the need for the teacher to implement a harsh disciplinary climate is avoided. Both these factors make the gym livable, and because a teacher's first task is to "gain and maintain cooperation in classroom activities" (Doyle, 1979b, p. 47), the gym becomes an eminently livable place.

Nevertheless, it is debatable how much work is being done in these classes, a key concern of Placek (1983). Like those classes, it would appear that in the dance class in this study, little work was being done, at least by the boys. In this study, Ms. Samba seemed content to trade off nonparticipation in instructional tasks for at least sensible behavior by those sitting out. By giving the teacher what she wanted (minimal disruptions and a full quota of boys to dance with the girls), the boys were able to achieve their social objectives relatively unimpeded.

Bloome, Puro, and Theodorou (1989) have described this nonacademic but livable environment as an example of "procedural display," which they defined as follows:

> Procedural display occurs when teachers and students are displaying to each other that they are getting the lesson done, constructing a cultural event within a cultural institution—which is not at all the same thing as substantive engagement in some academic content. (p. 272)

It is more likely, however, that the display by the boys in this study is more appropriately refered to as *mock participation* (Broome, 1984), a term used to describe the situation in which students pretend to be participating in the lesson by mocking the appropriate behaviors, but indeed are actually achieving little academic content. Doyle (1979b) refers to this as counterfeit work, work that is done without understanding, thereby circumventing the purposes of the curriculum.

As Allen (1986) noted, a teacher's expression of his or her academic and behavioral expectations to students is a key feature affecting students' views on classroom management. This view on classroom management has serious implications for the student social system that can operate in a class. Students like to have fun in class, and as Emmers (1981) comments,

> Students don't have to be particularly concerned that their school operates effectively and efficiently. They set out each day to have as pleasant a time as possible in a place where they must spend most the days for most of each year. (p. 1)

However, it is also important to note Allen's (1986) finding that students will accept high work demands and routine structures. The proviso is that they can concurrently socialize. It would have been interesting to see the ramifications if there had been stricter demands for the boys to practice while waiting for a partner, or if the teacher had required the boys to dance with each other. From the results of Allen's (1986) study, one could hypothesize that there may have been more defiant or subversive actions taken by students. However, because sitting out was accepted in this class, the boys did not need to employ such tactics because of the ample opportunities for socializing and having fun.

Classes not conducive to the development of a social system are those in which academic demands are high, the instructional pace is fast, and they are managed in a controlled and disciplined manner. Future research into how students react in classes where there is no opportunity to socialize is needed.

In terms of generalizing the results of this study to other physical education classes, two important factors need to be considered, one dealing with grading procedures and the other dealing with subject matter. First, in this class, grades could only be awarded for student performance in the formalized testing sessions. Had the teacher been able to award points toward a final grade from effort, participation, or even behavior, the students may have taken different approaches toward the subject. Nevertheless, the fact that the unit was on dance might be a confounding variable in this hypothesis, especially considering that a number of boys stated they were prepared to fail this unit rather than perform.

Second, as Tannehill and Zakrajsek (1993) have noted, secondary school students like physical education particularly from the fun and enjoyment they derive from it. Furthermore, 72% of boys opposed learning dance skills. Tannehill and Zakrajsek (1993) reported that students of all ethnic backgrounds have a penchant for team sports. Had the unit in the current study been on rugby or basketball, the participation patterns of the boys (and also the girls) may well have changed, and so too the students' social agenda. It is valuable at this point to consider another of Emmers's (1981) comments about student involvement and motivation: "It is not that students object to learning difficult material....Rather students resist anything that seems unimportant to them" (p. 37). This statement provides perhaps the best explanation of the involvement of many of the students in the dance class of this study.

CONCLUSION

This study provided a preliminary explanation of a social agenda operating in physical education. Although limited in terms of examining only one class, this study has provided a number of significant implications for teaching physical education and for future research.

From a teaching perspective, the student social system has proven to be a strong force in determining classroom events, further supporting Doyle's notion that teaching-learning is not a one-way process. In this class, the action of the boys in ignoring requests to follow the partners in individual practice resulted in the teacher giving up attempts to force participation and instead accepting nondisruptive sitting out. One can also see how students react negatively to subject matter that they consider unimportant. For teachers who follow a prescribed curriculum, this study has implications, particularly for the accountability systems and the extent of negotiation they must accommodate in those classes. Should the teacher "give in" to students' task modification and accept lower standards of work, or should the teacher employ a strict accountability system and attempt to override the student social system? The resulting class dynamics in either case are less than desirable.

From a theoretical perspective in particular, this study has verified Allen's (1986) model as a useful heuristic for planning future studies on the social agenda of students in physical education. Three cases in particular deserve attention. The first involves a class in which most students have a positive attitude toward the subject matter, which is most likely to occur in a team sports context. A study of this situation would provide more opportunities to examine students' social interactions in a potentially positive class environment. Such a study could also encapsulate the second situation, an investigation of a teacher who is successful at accommodating the student social system with the instructional task system. Research into the student social system within units of sport education (see Siedentop, 1994) would be particularly valuable.

The third context deserving research is a class having a strong academic focus accompanied by strong and effective accountability. Such a study would be useful in comparing teachers who achieve this through aversive or negative control, or through positive means; the latter teachers possessing what Siedentop (1988) refers to as "a certain kind of technical virtuosity" (p. 121). The question that remains however is, How many of these two types of teachers exist within our schools? Nevertheless, the examination of students' social agendas in varying accountability contexts would further aid our understanding of how work gets done in class, the ultimate task of the ecological paradigm.

REFERENCES

Alexander, K. (1983). Behavior analysis of tasks and accountability in physical education. (Doctoral dissertation, Ohio State University, 1982). *Dissertations Abstracts International, 43*, 3257A.

Allen, J.D. (1986). Classroom management: Students' perspectives, goals and strategies. *American Educational Research Journal, 23*, 437-459.

Bloome, D. (1984). A social-communicative perspective of formal and informal classroom events. In J. Niles & L. Harris (Eds.), *33rd Yearbook of the National Reading Conference* (pp. 117-123). New York: National Reading Conference.

Bloome, D., Puro, P., & Theodorou, E. (1989). Procedural display and classroom lessons. *Curriculum Inquiry, 19*, 265-291.

Cunningham, J. (1982). Sports are masculine, dance is . . . ? Thoughts on boys' dance in physical education. *CAHPER Journal, 48*(4), 19-20.

Doyle, W. (1977a). Paradigms for research on teacher effectiveness. In L.S. Shulman (Ed.), *Review of research in education* (Vol. 5, pp. 163-198). Itasca, IL: Peacock.

Doyle, W. (1977b). The use of non-verbal behavior. *Merrill-Palmer Quarterly, 23*, 179-192.

Doyle, W. (1979a). Classroom tasks and students' abilities. In P.L. Peterson & H.J. Walberg (Eds.), *Research on teaching: Concepts, findings and implications* (pp. 183-209). Berkeley, CA: McCutchan.

Doyle, W. (1979b). Making managerial decisions in classrooms. In D.L. Duke (Ed.), *Classroom management: Seventy-eighth yearbook of the National Society for the Study of Education* (Part 2, pp. 42-74). Chicago: University of Chicago Press.

Doyle, W. (1980). *Student mediating responses in teacher effectiveness*: Final report. Unpublished manuscript, North Texas State University. (ERIC Document Reproduction Services No. ED 187 698)

Doyle, W. (1981). Research on classroom contexts. *Journal of Teacher Education, 32*(6), 3-6.

Doyle, W. (1983). Academic work. *Review of Educational Research, 53*, 159-199.

Emmers, A.P. (1981). *After the lesson plan: Realities of high school teaching.* New York: Teachers College Press.

Graham, K.C. (1987). A description of academic work and student performance during a middle school volleyball unit. *Journal of Teaching in Physical Education, 7*, 22-37.

Griffin, P.S. (1983). "Gymnastics is a girl's thing": Student participation and interaction patterns in a middle school gymnastics unit. In T. Templin & J. Olson (Eds.), *Teaching in physical education* (pp. 71-85). Champaign, IL: Human Kinetics.

Hastie, P.A. (1994). Selected teacher behaviors and student ALT-PE in secondary school physical education classes. *Journal of Teaching in Physical Education, 13*, 247-259.

Lloyd, M.L., & West, B.H. (1988). Where are the boys in dance? *Journal of Physical Education, Recreation and Dance, 59*(5), 47-51.

Lund, I. (1992). Assessment and accountability in secondary physical education. *Quest, 44*, 352-360.

Marks, M. (1989). Development of a system for the observation of task structures in physical education (Doctoral dissertation, Ohio State University, 1988). *Dissertations Abstracts International, 49*, 2579A.

Marks, M.C., & Hersh, S.B. (1990, April). *Student negotiation of tasks in physical education and special education settings.* Paper presented at the American Educational Research Association Annual Meeting, Boston, MA. (ERIC Document Reproduction Services No. ED 321 459)

Placek, J. (1983). Conceptions of success in teaching: Busy, happy and good? In T. Templin & J. Olson (Eds.), *Teaching in physical education* (pp. 46-56). Champaign, IL: Human Kinetics.

Siedentop, D. (1988). An ecological model for understanding teaching/learning in physical education. In, *New horizons of human movement: Proceedings of the 1988 Seoul Olympic Scientific Congress.* Seoul: SOSCOC.

Siedentop, D. (1994). *Sport education: Quality PE through positive sport experiences.* Champaign, IL: Human Kinetics.

Son, C.T. (1989). Descriptive analysis of task congruence in Korean middle school physical education classes (Doctoral dissertation, The Ohio State University, 1988). *Dissertation Abstracts International, 50*, 2379A.

Spradley, J.P. (1980). *Participant observation.* New York: Holt, Rinehart & Winston.

Tannehill, D., & Zakrajsek, D. (1993). Student attitudes towards physical education: A multicultural study. *Journal of Teaching in Physical Education, 13*, 78-84.

Tinning, R.I. & Siedentop, D. (1985). The characteristics of tasks and accountability in student teaching. *Journal of Teaching in Physical Education, 4*, 286-299.

Tousignant, M., & Siedentop, D. (1983). A qualitative analysis of task structures in required secondary physical education classes. *Journal of Teaching in Physical Education, 3*(1), 47-57.

Williams, J. (1986). The de-sissification of dance. *The British Journal of Physical Education, 17*, 149-150.

Woods. P. (1978). Relating to scholarship: Some pupil perceptions. *Educational Review, 80*, 167-175.

Peter A. Hastie is with the Department of Health and Human Performance at Auburn University, 2050 Beard Eaves Memorial Coliseum, Auburn University, AL 36849-5323.

Andrew Pickwell is with Ipswich Grammar School, Ipswich 4301, Australia.

QUESTIONS FOR DISCUSSION

1. Like the previous article, this article is a description of a research study. How are these two research reports alike? How are they different?

2. The study describes the social system in an Australian high school. How does their experience compare to your own experience in similar physical education classes? Did your high school require dance as a component of P.E.? Why or why not?

3. Discuss the student behavior that the researchers observed in their study. Would this behavior be typical of 11th graders in your high school?

4. Discuss the teacher behavior that the researchers observed in their study. Again, is this behavior typical of high school teachers, in your experience?

5. How would you describe the tone of this article? How are the researchers coming across through their writing? Why do you think they adopted the tone that they did?

6. In the discussion section, the researchers point to the "clear inequities in the treatment of the boys and girls." Is this a typical situation, in your experience? Have you observed teachers treating boys and girls unequally in high school classes? Do professors treat the men and women in their college classes differently?

7. The teacher in this study seemed content to allow the boys to be non-participants, as long as they didn't disrupt the class. What do you think about this teaching strategy?

8. Describe the social agenda apparent in one of the college classes you are currently taking. How is it alike and how different from the class described in this study?

Being a Grandmother in the Tewa World

Sue-Ellen Jacobs, University of Washington

This paper summarizes the descriptions of "grandmotherhood" provided to me by approximately 25 percent of women of various ages at San Juan Pueblo. It also includes observations I have recorded concerning use of kinship terms and other kin-based behaviors. In my attempts to understand the range of grandmotherhood, I use the concept of grandmother to denote both an achieved and an ascribed status: achieved by living long enough to raise a child healthy enough to have a child; ascribed by custom when a child of a child is born. One cannot change these biological facts. One can choose whether or not to engage in the behaviors expected of persons in this life stage.[1]

This paper is based on analysis of oral history materials I have collected; my reading of Doris Duke archival materials; formal interviews with a range of tribal members; and informal discussions and participant observations of more than three hundred members of a Tewa[2] extended family with whom I have worked annually for various lengths of time over the course of twenty-three years.[3] The full extended family represents approximately one-half of the Tewa who live at San Juan Pueblo.[4]

CULTURAL CONTEXT

The Tewa of San Juan Pueblo, New Mexico, are bilateral,[5] with dual organization consisting of two moieties:[6] Winter and Summer. In everyday language, people refer to the "side" they are born into, marry into, or are initiated into. Whether by birth, marriage or initiation, all Tewa are on either the Winter or the Summer side; they count, fulfill, recount, and transmit their ceremonial and everyday life obligations accordingly. Moiety membership is sometimes inherited through the mother but usually through the father. Moiety membership for females may not be fixed for life; women who marry outside their side customarily join their husband's side. When this happens, children belong to the side of both their father and mother. If the mother does not join the father's side, the children belong to their mother's side. In the process of fulfilling their many roles vis-a-vis

---

Reprinted from the *American Indian Culture and Research Journal*, vol. 19, number 2, by permission of the American Indian Studies Center, UCLA. © Regents of the University of California.

children, grandmothers must keep in mind the side to which each of their grandchildren belongs and carry out (especially) socialization and other childrearing activities accordingly.[7]

Formerly subsistence farmers, for the past fifty to sixty years most Tewa families have depended on wages received for work, on or off the reservation, to meet basic needs. Members of extended families consisting of three or four generations used to live in the same household or, if not under the same roof, in close proximity to one another, their residential units divided by walls in the classic "apartment" type of dwellings characteristic of Pueblo people until recently.[8] Modern homes tend to be more widely dispersed, built for and occupied by either nuclear or simple extended families.[9]

In daily life, great emphasis is placed on family structure and organization.[10] Childrearing is a common topic in everyday conversation and influences the organization of household as well as extradomestic work. From the birth of their own children to the ends of their lives, women (and most men) will be engaged in childrearing, along with other work and responsibilities. Thus, if one is to discuss grandmothers in this part of the Tewa world, one is drawn to focus on the work and roles women play in childrearing.

BIOLOGICAL AND CULTURAL CRITERIA AND LINGUISTIC MARKERS

If they have children and live long enough, most women at San Juan Pueblo achieve the status of grandmother. It is a biological, social, and ordinary eventuality of most women's lives. The English term grandmother used in the Tewa context denotes a kinship relationship and connotes the roles women play in the social reproduction of their extended families. The term is also used respectfully when addressing unrelated older women in the community.[11] The comparable English term of respect for old men is *grandfather*. *Grandmother* is not synonymous with female elder. The Tewa term for grandmother is *sa'yaa*; the term for grandfather is *thehtay*. When asked for the Tewa term for elder, several people have said it is *kwiyo*. When asked what this word means in English, they have said "old person." This is the same word used for "old woman" and "wife" (see table below). Red Clay Basket[12] (whom you will meet in subsequent paragraphs) says that *kwiyo* is used for old women and men and "for a lady, old or young; but if you really want to talk about an old man, you can say '*kwiyo sedo*'"[13] (an old woman's husband), which is also the term for old age.[14]

SUE-ELLEN JACOBS

Older Tewa women also occupy the role of tribal elder, but to consider Tewa women as elders, as opposed to grandmothers, requires a wider context for analysis. The status of grandmother is assigned when one's children have children; I have known grandmothers as young as thirty-six; for some women, the chronological age at which this occurred has been as young as thirty-two. Elders are all over fifty. The status of knowledgeable or respected elder is achieved by practicing traditions and sharing cultural knowledge and skills. Thus, although many Tewa grandmothers also achieve the status of elder, grandmother is not automatically synonymous with female elder.

Roles played by women elders in community organization include (but are not limited to) preparing and carrying out aspects of sodality (or "clan") and other tribal affairs they or their husbands and fathers engage in, and serving on advisory committees set up by the tribal council, the Senior Citizens Program and other community programs. Until one has achieved the status of old person, she is considered to be green (*p'oeseewi*), or unripened, meaning she does not know enough about traditions, language, and life in general to be involved in community decision-making. Notwithstanding the fact that, for most older women, the categories overlap, the focus of my paper is grandmotherhood, not elderhood.

At San Juan Pueblo, grandmothers are addressed as *T'saeya*h (older spelling), *Saya* (colloquial spelling), or *Sa'yaa*.[15] Sometimes children refer to specific grandmothers and great-grandmothers by adding the first names or nicknames of these individuals to *Sa'yaa* (e.g., Sayah Rita). The *San Juan Pueblo Tewa Dictionary* gives the following terms:

Tewa	English
yiya	mother
sa'yaa	grandmother
pahpaa sa'yaa	great-grandmother
yiya kwiyo	great, great-grandmother
ku'guu sa'yaa	great, great, great-grandmother
kwiyo	old woman, wife
sa'ya'ay	grandchild of a grandmother
ko'oe, nana	aunt

Esther Martinez, bilingual educator (and compiler and editor of the *San Juan Pueblo Tewa Dictionary*) at San Juan Pueblo says that most children use the word *sa'yaa* for all their grandmothers, even though they may know the terms that differentiate between degrees of grandmotherhood. I have observed that children who otherwise speak no Tewa most often address and refer to their grandparents using the Tewa terms *Sa'yaa* and *Thehtay* (grandfather). A woman elder may be addressed by any of the respect terms: *yiya* (mother), *sa'yaa* (grandmother), *yiya kwiyo* (literally, "mother old woman" or "mother wife"), or *ko'oe* (aunt).

The age range for grandmothers referred to in this paper is thirty-six to eighty-five. The average age at which women first acquire the status of grandmother in this community appears to be forty, the beginning of the final decade of their biological reproductive cycle—the age that marks the onset of what is now called "middle age." Many factors contribute to how they respond to this new status, but grandmothers whom I have come to know have all told me they were very happy when their "first grandchild came along." They say that each subsequent grandchild has "added to [their] happiness." They also say that sometimes these children have also added to their workload and consequently are "a mixed blessing."

SOME ROLES OF FOUR TEWA GRANDMOTHERS[20]

Red Clay Basket was born in 1900. She is an elder and a grandmother. Her own grandmother taught her how to cook and sew; how to identify and collect raw materials for making pottery and how to make the pottery itself; how to process the harvest of corn, squash, wheat, and other produce grown in the family fields; and how to identify and use various wild roots, berries, and leaves for cooking and medicine. These skills and knowledge were important for Red Clay Basket's future roles as wife of Sun Moving (who was later to become a sodality head), mother of five children, foster mother of six additional children (whom she raised after her sister died), grandmother of twenty-two, great-grandmother of twenty-seven, and great-great-grandmother of four.

After marriage and the birth of her first several children, Red Clay Basket periodically worked for wages as a housekeeper at the Los Alamos Scientific Laboratory, and she regularly made and sold pottery. The family depended in part on her cash income to meet the expenses of daily living. In the 1980s, her grandchildren (and she) benefited from her earlier years of employment at Los Alamos through the Social Security checks she and Sun Moving received.

Over the course of fourteen years, I have observed Red Clay Basket in her interactions with most of her grandchildren, great-grandchildren, and one great-great-grandchild. She says, "I have raised all my grandchildren," as a way of announcing that she has taken a major role in their early rearing. Her daughters, some of her nieces and nephews whom she took into her home when their mother died, and some of her grandchildren also say, "She raised all my children." The activities that I have observed include those that some scholars now refer to as "childminding" (called "babysitting" by Red Clay Basket). That is, children are left with their grandmother (or great-grandmother) for feeding and general care while the parents are engaged in work for wages. Sometimes, the parents of the child pay Red Clay Basket a fee for babysitting. Now, as part of a relatively new program, parents may apply to the tribe for child care subsidies that will be paid directly to the caretaker. In order to qualify as a recipient of the tribal funds, caretakers must have homes that meet federally defined minimal requirements of health and safety. Some older homes do not meet these requirements. In one instance, I noted that the denial of subsidy did not stop a mother from leaving her son with his greatgrandmother for care; Red Clay Basket was just paid less by the mother than she would have been by the tribal program.

Irrespective of the externally defined regulations regarding home safety standards for subsidized child care, everyone understands that part of the responsibility of child caregivers (babysitters or childminders) is to protect children from harm. Women who grew up in the older religious traditions explain that harm can come from spirit forces as well as from living forces. It is relatively easy to see and prevent harm from living forces, but spirit forces are not so easily seen. They might even approach on a gentle breeze and enter infants or young children who are not properly protected. An infant or young child in Red Clay Basket's care is never left unattended. If, for one reason or another, she must leave the child asleep and alone in a room, she places a protective sacred object on the blanket covering the sleeping child. At home, the children's parents do not always take these precautions. When I have asked the parents why not, I have been told that they "don't believe in those superstitious things." Yet, when the children become ill—for example, if they have digestive problems or a cold or need other health care—the parents often seek Red Clay Basket's advice before (and sometimes after) going to the health clinic.

Red Clay Basket is well known for her curing abilities. Sick children and infants are brought to her not only from San Juan but from other pueblos, too. Most frequently, however, it is her relatives who come to her for cures. If she decides that the solution to the health problem is beyond her knowledge and capabilities, she will provide preliminary treatment and then recommend that the child be taken to the medicine man; otherwise, she undertakes full curing, which usually requires four separate sessions.

Red Clay Basket employs a range of healing practices. She uses herbs, roots, ash, salt, soda, and other sources of medicine for a variety of adult and child afflictions. For example, she is often asked to help with care of an infant's drying umbilical cord. Using dust from the vigas (exposed round roof beams) in the kitchen, ash from the wood stove, salt and powder from crushed pottery sherds (if available), she makes a poultice and applies it to the umbilicus, which is then covered with an abdominal binding cloth. The mother or both parents of the infant will be instructed not to remove the covering for four days.

Parents of infants and young children call on Red Clay Basket's traditional knowledge for other purposes, too. For example, she has performed the naming ceremony for many of her greatgrandchildren, one great-great-grandchild, and some of her grandchildren. In previous times, the "naming mother" (customarily an elder who is a member of one of the parents' extended families) would perform the ceremony at dawn on the fourth day following birth. Most births now take place in hospitals. If all goes well, the mother and infant leave the hospital in time for the ceremony to take place on the fourth day; however, when this is not possible, the naming ceremony is performed at the earliest convenient time after the child is brought home to the pueblo.

Children and grandchildren depend on Red Clay Basket for advice and support in matters related to performance of traditional ceremonials. She will lend garments and jewelry from her store of these for her relatives' participation in ceremonies. On the day of these ceremonies, she often dresses her granddaughters and great-granddaughters and explains to them the attitudes they should have regarding the ceremony. She sometimes also describes the experiences she had when she took part in ceremonies in years past. Since most ceremonies also involve dance and song, she may also show the young women how the steps go and/or how the song is or used to be sung.

Children and grandchildren also call upon Red Clay Basket for economic support. Most of the time, she lends money to those who ask, but she warns them sternly that she must be repaid by a certain date or they will not be given further loans. Sometimes she has referred to herself as "the family banker." At other times, she provides work for the young people and pays them an agreed upon sum.

Red Clay Basket stopped working on pottery in about 1982. Prior to that time, she had taught her techniques to her daughters and some of her granddaughters. Two daughters became potters; no granddaughters have become potters. I have observed Red Clay Basket's grandchildren and great-grandchildren of both sexes forming pottery pieces while in their sa'yaa's care. When their pottery pieces were finished, they were included among the bowls, plates, and other items she either took to the Santa Fe Indian Market or sold to the traders who used to come to the house to buy pottery and carvings. The money was given to the children.

One daughter and several granddaughters have worked as domestics in Los Alamos. Now most granddaughters have fulltime employment commensurate with their level of education. Most of those who have children leave them in the care of their mothers or with Red Clay Basket until they are old enough for school. The school-age grandchildren come on the school bus to Red Clay Basket's house after school each weekday, where they have a snack, do some homework or watch television (but usually go outside to play), and wait for their parents to come home from work.

Rita (pseudonym), Red Clay Basket's youngest daughter, first became a grandmother at age thirty-six and now has six grandchildren. She has hosted baby showers for her daughter and daughters-in-law; has held feasts following the Catholic baptism of each grandchild and following the first Holy Communion of her first grandchild; and engages in other activities that will assure weekly contact with her grandchildren. Because she works full time at the Los Alamos Scientific Laboratory during the week and has an unmarried, school-age child still at home, she does not serve as a childminder for her children's children; but she provides financial and social support for them on a regular basis, and her oldest granddaughter (now twelve) occasionally spends the weekend with her.

Agnes (pseudonym), in her late fifties, is Red Clay Basket's daughter-in-law. When Agnes's husband retired from industry in the Midwest at age fifty-five, she resigned her job as a special education teacher, and they moved back to the reservation with four of their ten children. In the Midwest, Agnes had taken full responsibility for raising her first grandchild, who was incorporated into Agnes's home as a daughter. Subsequent children of children were incorporated as grandchildren. When Agnes and her husband moved west, all of these grandchildren stayed in the Midwest with their biological parents.

After settling into life in New Mexico, Agnes's husband began farming his parents' fields, and both he and Agnes became active in community affairs. They are members of the Senior Citizen Program advisory committee, serve on several church committees, and participate in tribal affairs. Agnes also began work as the tribal librarian, writing and administering grants for the development of a community lending library. The family's main sources of income are her husband's retirement money, Agnes's income from work as tribal librarian, and contributions to household expenses (food and utilities) made by the employed children who live at home. Over the past two years, Agnes's husband's farming has been yielding larger quantities of high-quality produce, stimulating an increased demand for it among local people. An expanded harvest requires a related increase in processing the harvest—a task that largely falls to Agnes, dramatically increasing her household chores during this season.

In a recent year, two new grandchildren were added to the family. Agnes held baby showers and then provided feasts to celebrate each infant's baptism. The mother of one lived with Agnes and her husband. She found it desirable to take a job when her child was about six months old. Agnes became her childminder while also working part-time at the library, writing grants, processing the harvest, serving on committees, and managing her household. Her husband could be called on to watch the baby when she needed to leave home to shop for groceries, pay bills, open the library for a limited number of hours, or engage in other necessary activities. Agnes and her husband have also assumed major responsibility for taking care of Red Clay Basket and Sun Moving, who live in a separate but nearby home.

Elsie (pseudonym), in her mid-fifties, is Red Clay Basket's other living daughter. Her husband works full-time, and she manages their home. They have two children and three grandchildren. Their first grandchild is being raised by their son's mother-in-law. Their daughter and her husband work full time. The daughter's children (a girl and a boy) were left with Elsie for care during their infancy. Over the years, the granddaughter has spent an increasing amount of time with her grandparents. Elsie has crippling arthritis and has become increasingly dependent on her granddaughter, who, by about the age of seven, had learned to cook, clean house, and help her grandmother with the laundry. Now, at age nine, the granddaughter rarely sleeps at her parents' home; occasionally, she spends the day with her mother's maternal grandmother (i.e., her great-grandmother, Red Clay Basket), who taught her how to make pottery when she was about four years old. Elsie and her husband provide their granddaughter with clothes, school supplies, toys, trips to the zoo in Albuquerque and other outings, and many other economic, social, and affective benefits. As with the other grandparents mentioned, Elsie and her husband express a great deal of love for this granddaughter and her brother.

All four grandmothers have described their feelings of love for their grandchildren, but Red Clay Basket warns that "it is dangerous to pet them too much" because "life is hard and they have to learn their lessons for when you are gone, when they are on their own." Still, she admits to having favorites among her grandchildren, those she "wishes to please." To these grandchildren she gives extra attention in the form of actual time and conversation, as well as money, clothing, jewelry, and other material goods.

SUE-ELLEN JACOBS

CHANGING ROLES OF GRANDMOTHERS THROUGH THE GENERATIONS

To be a grandmother in the Tewa world basically means that one has had children and has lived long enough to participate in the social education of one's children's children. The following overview of some childrearing activities of four grandmothers within one segment of a large, extended family may contribute to an understanding of the range of behaviors that can ensure a community's survival. For their children and grandchildren, these women

1. informally teach basic skills and knowledge; collaborate with parents in childrearing through daily care for limited or extended periods of time;
3. furnish ceremonial clothes, jewelry, and knowledge;
4. care for sick infants and children;
5. provide cash and material support in the form of loans, gifts, wages;
6. sponsor or conduct fourth-day naming ceremonies;
7. provision new parents who live within their households;
8. hold showers before, and baptism feasts after, the birth of a child, as rites of recognition and incorporation to which family and friends are invited; provide love, and
10. participate in other activities, as needed, for meeting family, moiety, and community responsibilities (e.g., helping with cooking for feast days and baking bread, pies, and cookies for weddings, feasts, and other events).

Being a grandmother in the Tewa world may mean doing all of these things for one's children and one's children's children and on down the generations; these activities, of course, add to the work a grandmother does and the responsibilities she holds for her own household and the community-at-large. For some women, when grandmotherhood includes direct involvement in child care, it means an increase in an already heavy workload, as in Agnes's case during harvest season. For others (such as Elsie, Rita, and Red Clay Basket), it has meant developing friendships across the generations, as well as (for Elsie and Red Clay Basket) resuming desirable primary care of young people in one's middle to later years.

Through their second-, third- and fourth-generation childrearing activities, most Tewa grandmothers have participated in the perpetuation and maintenance of their community's traditional values and customs. By providing child day care for working parents, they have also helped improve their children's economic conditions. Under these circumstances, cultural, social, and biological advantages seem to accrue to all generations in a family and to the whole community. But, as in other communities where emphasis has shifted to single-family households and wage labor economies, changes that have occurred over the generations, affecting the traditional socialization processes, may make this observation very conditional. These changes have to do with several things: first, an overall increase in life expectancy for members of the community; and second, an increase in secured wage labor by women, with retirement coming some twenty to thirty years (i.e., at age sixty-two to sixty-five) after an individual achieves the biological and cultural status of grandmother. Indeed, it is beginning to be clear that if one is going to depend on relatives for child care, one must hope for a great-grandmother, because she is the one most likely to be freed from the workforce and able (if she is willing) to make an investment in the rearing of her children's children's children.[22]

At the time of this writing, Red Clay Basket was eighty-five years old. In her generation, women first became grandmothers in their mid- to late thirties. Most women did not work off the reservation but rather remained in the domestic sphere of the pueblo, making pottery, tending to gardens, processing the harvests, and undertaking other tasks that allowed them to care for children simultaneously, including spending large portions of each day preparing and cooking food for all household members. They may have worked off the reservation sporadically; when they did, they left their children in the care of their mothers (if they were still alive) or other kin. People lived in close proximity to one another and shared in childrearing. With the birth of her first great-grandchild when she was about age fifty-five, Red Clay Basket began her involvement in rearing the third generation of her descendants. Her oldest daughter, Ellen (pseudonym), helped with the rearing of this child and then with others as they came along. Agnes, in her mid-fifties, has no great-grandchildren. She has engaged in childrearing with more than half of her grandchildren but not as intensively as Red Clay Basket did in raising her grandchildren. Rita has not been a childminder for any of her children, while Elsie has taken a major role in rearing her daughter's children. Gloria (pseudonym), Red Clay Basket's other daughter, had no children but assumed large financial and other responsibilities for Rita's sons. The diverse patterns found in the childrearing roles of these six women can be considered characteristic of those found throughout the reservation.

SUMMARY AND CONCLUSIONS

In the Tewa world, as in many other places, grandmotherhood is defined biologically. It is also defined culturally. Old women are addressed respectfully as *Sa'yaa* or Grandmother, irrespective of biological relatedness. When a woman becomes a grandmother, her status may change; she decides whether her familial and community roles will change at that time or later. Thus, becoming a grandmother is, at first, a biological event, occurring when a child of a child is born, then culturally and socially constructed. Three generations of biologically linked people are required for this new status to be achieved. Perceived biological change is another basis for becoming a grandmother, but in a fully sociocultural fashion (i.e., no biological link is required): A woman ages, and, whether she has grandchildren or not, when she is perceived to be "old," she will be called *Sa'yaa* (Grandmother) or *Kwiyo* (mother old woman)—highly respectful terms used for old women who are or are not related.[23]

Since grandmotherhood is a status defined at the outset in relationship to childbearing, it is not surprising that the expected associated roles include participation of grandmothers in rearing of their grandchildren. However, changes in work and living arrangements at San Juan Pueblo are leading to changes in role performance. Previously, grandmothers could care for grandchildren while doing their work, freeing mothers to have more children and to concentrate on nurturing the youngest children in turn. In Red Clay Basket's younger years, there were more extended family households than there are now, and childrearing tended to be a collective endeavor, with grandmothers taking a major role in socialization of their grandchildren. Now there are fewer grandmothers available for childrearing, as more mothers and grandmothers work off the reservation until the Social Security and union retirement age of sixty-two to sixty-five (or younger, if they have civil service jobs). This leaves the care of many young children to day care centers, professional babysitters, and other non-kin who are paid to mind small children during the day; others may be cared for by their great-grandmothers.

The Tewa definition of grandmother includes an expectation of significant socialization of grandchildren, which contemporary grandmothers strive to meet. Some grandmothers experience conflict, because their roles as household managers require them to provide all the domestic services (such as processing the harvest, in Agnes's case) once performed by younger adult women, who now must contribute to their own household economies by wage labor outside the home, often off the reservation. Those who cannot meet the socialization expectations themselves may provide monetary or other support for grandchildren, or they may encourage their children to avail themselves of the help their mothers can provide (i.e., the great-grandmothers become the primary childminders). Thus it appears that, with extended longevity, a specific "great-grandmother role" has developed, devoted to childminding as well as informal instruction in traditional culture (e.g., language, stories, pottery-making, cooking, and ceremonial matters). Many grandmothers now specialize in household management, tribal affairs, and full-time employment, while most mothers are expected to bear children and spend most of their working day in wage labor.[24] Today, being a grandmother in the Tewa world is much more complex (and involves less direct participation in the lives of grandchildren) than it used to be, but the status is aspired to by all the women I know at San Juan Pueblo.

ACKNOWLEDGMENTS

This paper is based on ethnohistorical research begun in 1970 and formal interviewing and participant observation begun in 1972. Research funds have been primarily out of my own pocket, supplemented by small grants from the Doris Duke Foundation (1972), the Melville and Elizabeth Jacobs Research Fund (1976, 1977), and the Graduate School Research Fund at the University of Washington (1978, 1979).

Two reading versions of this paper were presented at the eighty-fourth and eighty-fifth annual meetings of the American Anthropological Association in Washington, D.C., on 6 December 1985 and in Philadelphia on 5 December 1986, respectively, in the sessions entitled "American Indian Grandmothers," sponsored by the Association for Anthropology and Gerontology organized and chaired by Marjorie Schweitzer.

I am grateful to the following people for comments and suggestions on this paper: Alfonso Ortiz, Frances Quintana, Marianne Gullestad, members of the Seattle Women Anthropologists Group (Charlene J. Allison, Pamela Amoss, Joann Bromberg, Ronna Brown, Debra Boyer, Julie Ann Duncan, Lydia Kotchek and Sonja Solland), Marjorie Schweitzer, Joan Weibel-Orlando, my friends and colleagues at San Juan Pueblo, and two anonymous reviewers.

NOTES

1. This is an aspect of grandparenthood discussed by others who have studied lifecycling cross culturally; namely, that not all grandparents are willing or able to fulfill societal expectations. Joan Weibel-Orlando reports a similar finding from her research with South Dakota reservation and Los Angeles urban Siouan grandparents; however, her overall schemata of five grandparenting styles ("distanced grandparent," "ceremonial grandparent," "fictive grandparent," "custodial grandparent" and "cultural conservator grandparent") are not categories of persons found at San Juan Pueblo. Perhaps the five styles she reports are as clearly demarcated in the communities where she has lived, and her generalizations may fit other Plains societies as well. However, for this Pueblo world, in the practice of

SUE-ELLEN JACOBS

everyday life, sociocultural roles are seldom so easily categorized or clearly differentiated. At San Juan Pueblo, people may assume full cultural expectations for being grandmothers when it first happens to them, or they may wait until the have achieved elder status before meeting all objectives. This emphasis is made as a comparative issue in response to the suggestion of one of the anonymous readers of my paper. Although she did not cite my work, Weibel-Orlando had read a copy of the full version of my paper when she published "Grandparenting Styles: Native American Perspectives" in *The Cultural Context of Aging: Worldwide Perspectives*, ed. Jay Sokolovsky (New York: Bergin & Garvey Publishers, 1990, 109-125). Her discussion in that article provides an interesting parallel/contrasting point of view.

2. *Tewa* refers to the six linguistically related, yet autonomous, Rio Grande Indian pueblos located in north-central New Mexico, and their ancestors. In addition, it includes the language of the native peoples who reside in those pueblos. As with the terms Navajo, Apache, Cherokee, or American, it also refers to tribal or national identity and should therefore always be capitalized.

3. Members of the family, including the four grandmothers described and most of their female kin, have read this paper and have given permission for its publication.

4. This estimation takes into account all lineal and collateral consanguineal (blood) and affinal (in-law) relations. Senior family members estimated that "over a thousand of our relatives" attended a park honoring the oldest community elder on the occasion of his one-hundredth birthday. The 1986 total Tewa residential figures were projected by a tribal official to be "around 1,850," while the total tribal enrollment was projected to be "around 2,500" (which means that about 650 enrolled tribal members do not live on the reservation).

5. The term bilateral refers to the fact that people determine their kinship relationships through both their mother and their father.

6. The term moiety refers to the division of a society into two lineal kinship parts (or "sides"), each having specified responsibility for community social, political, economic, and religious organizations and functions. In the Tewa world, Winter people are responsible for these matters from approximately the autumnal equinox to the spring equinox; people on the Summer side have these responsibilities from approximately the spring equinox to the autumnal equinox. The above is a gross simplification of a very complex social order; for detailed information, see Alfonso Ortiz, *The Tewa World: Space, Time, Being and Becoming in a Pueblo Society* (Chicago: University of Chicago Press, 1969).

7. For details on differences between Winter and Summer people, their everyday and ceremonial obligations, and seasonal rounds, see Ortiz,

The Tewa World.

8. These complex housing structures, which were found throughout the American Southwest at the time of the Spanish arrival in 1540, have been retained in only a few locales. Old Taos Pueblo is probably the best known, since it is open to the public (for a fee) and often appears in tourist promotional photographs from New Mexico.

9. The adjective simple is the term anthropologists and other social scientists use to refer to small extended families, which usually consist of one grandparental generation, one set of parents and these parents' children. Anyone who has grown up in or has resided as a teenager or adult in such a household knows that they are by no means "simple" in terms of interpersonal relations, economics, and other aspects of managing everyday life.

10. This is noted in several ways: (a) In conversations, people frequently discuss aspects of affinal and consanguineal relationships and reciprocal obligations and privileges associated with these; and (b) in my observations, I note that people talk about and organize their work patterns in ways that allow them to meet familial responsibilities, e.g., taking off from work to bake bread, prepare the house, purchase the "give-away" or "basket" items, and attend to additional duties associated with special family or village feasts and other events.

11. Older women and men are sometimes also referred to as "senior citizens," a practice that came into being in the late 1970s as a result of the establishment of the Tribal Senior Citizen Program.

12. The names Red Clay Basket and Sun Moving are the ones approved for use by the elders before their deaths in 1990 and 1989, respectively. For this and subsequent papers, they preferred that I use the English translations of their Tewa names rather than initials for their English/Spanish names, as we had done in an earlier paper. It is inappropriate to use people's Tewa names without their explicit permission to do so. Other personal names that appear are pseudonyms I chose; these were subsequently approved (humorously) by the individuals to whom they refer.

13. The quote is from my 1986 field notes. The use of an inclusive, unmarked term for "old person" and "woman" is similar to Alfonso Ortiz's observation that *sa'aay*ing is inclusive of grandparents and grandmothers (personal communication, 1986). At the request of the anonymous Tewa reviewer of this paper, I asked a San Juan Pueblo native speaker and linguist, Blue Water, about current usage of *kwiyo* at San Juan Pueblo. She replied that *kwiyo* is still used as a formal term of respect when addressing certain elders; it can mean "old person" but is now rarely used in everyday conversational settings (personal communication, 1995).

14. *San Juan Pueblo Tewa Dictionary* (Portales, NM: Bishop Publishing Company, 1983).

15. This is the spelling used in the *San Juan Pueblo Tewa Dictionary*, op. cit., which is based on Summer Institute of Linguistics phonetics. In letters and notes I have seen written to grandmothers, I have never seen either the older spelling or the dictionary spelling; it has always been *Sayah*.

16. Also used as a term of respect.

17. Also used as a term of respect.

18. Also used as a term of respect.

19. Also used as a term of respect; "[i]n school[,] children address teachers and resource people as *ko'oe*...." Ibid., 66.

20. This paper was first written as a draft almost fifteen years ago. Ten years ago, the elders referred to in this and other papers were still able to respond to writings about them. They and their family members gave permission to publish materials submitted to them for approval. Red Clay Basket and Sun Moving were among the last elders who retained strict Tewa traditions within their home, while simultaneously enjoying improved material conditions (from indoor plumbing in 1970 to acquisition of their first telephone and first television in 1978, and a double hotplate for cooking instead of "always having to use our winter wood" for cooking, among others). Emphasis on Red Clay Basket in this article reflects the family's desire for my research to be on that generation whose members are now all deceased (1993). The biographies I am writing about these elders are done with the hope that their grandchildren and subsequent generations will appreciate the elders' lives and the changes they experienced. This article manifests a biographical focus on Red Clay Basket because she epitomizes her generation's style of "grandmothering." Her daughters and daughter-in-law are sketched briefly as representatives of "modern Tewa grandmothers." The emphasis on change is deliberately contrastive. This is the paper that, in 1988, we all agreed addressed the issues of "being a grandmother in the Tewa world."

21. This is the English term used for the woman elder who will give the child its first Tewa name. For details on the traditional naming ceremony, see Ortiz, *The Tewa World*, 30-31.

22. I am particularly indebted to Pamela Amoss for deducing this from information I presented in an early draft of this paper.

23. In 1984, some children who had called me *Ko'oe* (aunt) for as long as I had known them began tentatively addressing me as *Sa'yaa* (Grandmother). It had been a year since I had seen them, and my hair was grayer, my face, neck, and hands more wrinkled. They experimented with addressing me this way for several weeks, then resumed calling me *Ko'oe*, I am not sure why. I have noticed that *Ko'oe* is sometimes used to address

both old and young women, irrespective of biological relatedness.

24. I am particularly indebted to Pamela Amoss for deducing this from information I presented in an early draft of this paper.

Sue-Ellen Jacobs is an associate professor of women's studies and adjunct associate professor of anthropology and music at the University of Washington, Seattle.

QUESTIONS FOR DISCUSSION

1. Describe the relationship of the researcher to the subject she studied. How might her role have affected what she observed?

2. Compare the researchers' roles in the three research studies in this section of the book (Ballard & Coates, Hastie & Pickwell, and Jacobs). How are they alike, how are they different?

3. Describe what makes a grandmother in the Tewa world. How is this like being a grandmother in your culture?

4. Do grandmothers in your culture have specific social roles to play in the family? What kind of relationship do you currently have (or have you had in the past) with your own grandmother(s)?

5. The author describes how the roles of grandmothers have changed over the generations. Have you observed a similar change in your culture?

6. Notice the documentation style for this article. How would you describe it? What does this system of extensive notes accomplish that a references cited list does not accomplish?

Trading Arms for Hostages? How the Government and Print Media "Spin" Portrayals of the United States' Policy Toward Iran

William J. Brown, Regent University
Richard C. Vincent, U of Hawaii, Honolulu

The relationship between the United States and Iran has had an important influence on world affairs during the past two decades. Accordingly, the U.S. news media have an instrumental role in portraying U.S.-Iran relations to the public. The Iranian Revolution and hostage crisis of 1979-1981, the TWA hijacking of 1985, the Irangate controversy of 1986-1987, and the Persian Gulf War of 1990-1991 are examples of important media events that have impacted public opinion regarding U.S. policy toward Iran. This research analyzes government and print media portrayals of the Reagan administration's U.S.-Iran policy during Irangate. Results supported the prediction that the print media would fulfill their watchdog function by providing more critical portrayals of the United States' policy toward Iran than the Tower Commission Report, an investigative document published by President Reagan's Special Review Board. Among the three leading newspapers analyzed, there was significant diversity in the reporting of U.S.-Iran relations. Results indicate the Reagan administration's attempt to "spin" its version of Irangate did not successfully pressure the media to neglect their watchdog role. Although the Tower Commission Report was less critical of U.S. policy toward Iran than the print media, all four print media sources portrayed the Reagan administration's policy as a flawed approach that degenerated into trading arms for hostages. Implications of these findings for future research are discussed.

Key words: Irangate, press and foreign policy, press and White House, spin doctors, watchdog function

The U.S. news media's coverage of foreign policy and the U.S. government's attempts to garner support for its decisions are important research concerns of political communication scholars and public policy makers. The death in 1994 of former president Nixon, whose administration expended considerable effort battling the news media for control of its public image, has refocused attention on how the executive branch of government in the United States interacts with the news media. Although Nixon berated the news media, he also attempted to manipulate the media to accomplish his goals. Despite the devastating consequences of the Watergate Scandal, the Nixon administration successfully orchestrated media campaign coverage to promote its foreign policy actions and win support (Jamieson, 1984).

When considering foreign policy matters, the general public is especially dependent on the news media because very few people have access to first-hand information about U.S. foreign policy issues. The U.S. news media are instruments in creating, perpetuating, and modifying images of foreign nations and international leaders (Merrill, 1991). Media analysts often use a contemporary term called "spinning a story" to refer to attempts by an individual or organization to manipulate or control the media coverage of a specific issue. Government agencies and political parties commonly employ "spin doctors," professional communicators, and media strategists, who seek to influence the news media and generate public support to policy decisions.

Numerous studies indicate the electronic and print media help influence the public agenda (Barton & Gregg, 1982; Benton & Frazier, 1976; Carlsson, Dahlberg & Rosengren, 1981; Cook et al., 1983; Noelle-Neumann, 1974; Rikardsson, 1981 Roberts & Bachen, 1981) and mold public opinion of world events (Galtung & Ruge, 1965; Galtung & Vincent, 1992). Newspapers in particular have been identified as important information sources on which people base their opinions of international affairs (Arno & Dissanayake, 1984; Bennett, Gressett, & Halton, 1985 Dowling, 1989; Just & Crigler, 1989). Despite problems with accuracy and bias, leading newspapers play an important role in foreign policy agenda-setting, enabling citizens to become more informed about foreign policy decisions (Bennett & Edelman, 1985; Hopple, 1982; Kieh, 1990; Knight & Dean, 1982; Larson 1986).

Iran's strategic importance in the volatile oil-rich region of the Middle East has made U.S.-Iran relations an important foreign policy concern. News coverage of Iran has been the subject of a variety of scholarly studies, particularly coverage of the 1979-1981 American embassy hostage crisis (Altheide, 1985; Dowling, 1989, Harris, 1976; Meeske & Javaheri, 1982). This study examines portrayals of the United States' foreign policy toward Iran during the height of the Irangate controversy in late 1986 and early 1987. We expected that leading U.S. newspapers would portray a more negative image of the U.S. policy toward Iran during the controversy than would the Special Review Board appointed by President Reagan. Reagan formed the board to investigate the workings of the National Security Council, the government agency that interacted with Iranian officials.

A comparison of the print media's treatment of Irangate with that of the Reagan administration's Special Review Board is particularly relevant in the midst of controversy about the press's ability to fulfill a "watchdog function." The Tower Commission Report was intended to be critical of U.S.-Iran policy, but how critical it was compared to print news coverage of Irangate is not known. Thus the purpose of the present study is to analyze whether significant differences exist in the way President Reagan's Special Review Board "spun" an image of its Iran policy as compared with the image created by leading newspapers.

THEORY

Central to the study of news content is the recognition that American journalism is commonly thought to serve a watchdog function for society (Hutchins, 1947; Siga 1973). News reporters are often viewed as a potent force who keep the power of the government in check (Rivers, 1982). In the case of the executive branch, it very difficult for an administration to pressure news reporters to accept the scripted press coverage planned by White House media consultants (Gilmore, 1994; Rozell, 1992). Journalists have been regarded as neutral observers, participants, good citizens, and government adversaries. Journalists seek to neutralize the political "spin doctors" in government. A study of self-perceptions, for example, found that U.S. journalists frequently cited the investigation of government assertions and statements, analysis and interpretation of complicated issues, and a timely discussion of national policy as central professional goals (Johnstone, Slawski, & Bowman, 1976; Weaver & Wilhoit, 1986).

Ethical and moral considerations make it difficult for a privately owned press seeking to be profitable to balance its freedom and social responsibility. Picard refers to the notion of a socially responsible democratic press as the Democratic Socialist Theory (Picard, 1985), which Merrill (1991) calls a sixth theory of the press. In Picard's view, the media are not only intended to promote democracy and the free exchange of ideas and information but also to serve as a voice of the people controlled by the public rather than the interests of powerful elites. Thus a free and responsible press is seen as an essential institution that serves as a watchdog for society to protect democracy against the abuses of government.

Although there is some ambiguity regarding the definition of a responsible press, there is general agreement among media theorists that a free press should protect the masses from excessive powers of the elite (Altschull, 1984). During the past several decades the watchdog banner has been advanced most rigorously by non-elite print media such as the underground press, the alternative press, the advocacy press, and the investigative press. Altschull observed that the new journalism, another name for a vigorous watchdog press, became so prevalent during the 1960s that mainstream news reporters in Washington were accused of recklessly attacking the government.

However, following the Watergate years in which the Nixon administration attempted to outmaneuver investigative reporters, the view of a powerful watchdog press began to wane. An alternative view of the press emerged, highlighting the reasons why the press has difficulty fulfilling a watchdog role (Bennett, 1983). Media institutions receive pressure from governments and ruling elites to generate public support for their policy decisions (Brown & Facciola, 1991; Kieh, 1990; Dargolis & Mauser, 1989; Parenti, 1989; Qualter, 1962). For example, U.S. administrations have strategically used the news media to create public support for foreign policy by selectively providing the media with information that supports the government's viewpoint (Kieh, 1990; Parenti, 1989; Qualter, 1962). In such situations, news stories would be unlikely to publish content highly critical of U.S. policy.

A number of scholars claim that the executive branch not only influences the news media but also manipulates the media to control the portrayals of their policy decisions (Deakin, 1984; Denton & Woodward, 1985; Hertsgaard, 1988; Maltese, 1992; Streitmatter, 1988; Tebbel & Watts, 1985). Tebbel and Watts claim that the traditional watchdog function of the press was eroded by Theodore Roosevelt, who began using the press to mold public opinion. Maltese (1985) documented the great control the Nixon administration had of its press coverage until the Watergate scandal, and Smith (1988) contends that the Reagan administration also attempted to manipulate public opinion. Jensen (1993) charges the U.S. media with trading their traditional adversarial watchdog role for profits and deregulation during the Reagan-Bush era.

Intense criticism of the media coverage during the Gulf War provided further evidence to critics who believe that the press has lost much of its adversarial role (Hoover, 1993). The ability of White House spin doctors to manipulate the media for political propaganda has been documented by Jamieson's (1984) research on presidential campaigns. A recent analysis by Gilmore (1994) of David Gergen's role as a communication strategist for four U.S. presidents indicates that the executive branch can exert considerable influence on the news coverage of its policies and decisions.

Gans (1979) offered an explanation for the press's reluctance to oppose political powers. He observed that journalism is largely a middle-class occupation. As such, many journalists have an inherent loyalty to the status quo. In other words because media professionals have values in common with their employers, American journalists often perceive and decipher events in much the same way as the societal elites who really *do* have the power. While journalists may believe that they serve as watchdogs, in actuality they may not be the best equipped to do so. The result is that some journalists tend to avoid criticism of those in positions of power.

The tension between these two perspectives—the first being that the media is a powerful watchdog for society to keep government in check, and the second being that the government has a powerful influence over the media and can use the media to support its policies—is the primary focus of our research. A second important research concern is whether the government's ability to promote its own version of events may limit the diversity of opinions formed about its controversial foreign policy toward Iran. If the Reagan administration successfully put its spin on its policy toward Iran, then print media portrayals of that policy would be consistent and would support the administration. Thus, present theory provides two opposing viewpoints regarding the relationship between the news media and the executive branch of government. One set of expectations takes an executive bias perspective that accentuates the manipulative power of government to influence the press and promote conformity to the administration's viewpoint. An opposing set of expectations is based on a media bias perspective that emphasizes the watchdog function of the news media. This study addresses these two opposing expectations.

RESEARCH QUESTIONS AND HYPOTHESES

The two primary research concerns outlined earlier are examined by one four-part research question and three hypotheses. If government attempts to "spin" Irangate occurred in the case of print media coverage of U.S.-Iran relations, then leading newspapers would be expected to present a uniform portrayal of U.S.-Iran policy. Print news stories would generally be consistent with the Tower Commission's viewpoint. There is no theoretical or empirical basis for making specific predictions about the coverage of any individual print news source. Thus in the first set of analyses of print news coverage of U.S.-Iran relations, the following research question was examined:

> Does print news coverage of U.S. policy toward Iran in leading U.S. newspapers differ in: (a) the news content critical of U.S. policy, (b) the editorial content critical of U.S. policy, (c) the factual content regarding U.S. policy, and (d) the characterization of U.S. policy as "trading arms for hostages"?

The second set of analyses examined whether the U.S. print media fulfilled a watchdog function by presenting a more critical portrayal of U.S.-Iran policy than that of President Reagan's Special Review Board. There are several reasons why the press might be critical of the Reagan administration's policy toward Iran. First, journalists accused of going easy on Reagan during his presidency would have strong motivation to refute this criticism. Second, the opportunity to uncover the biggest presidential scandal since Watergate would create a media climate in which journalists and editors would be willing to take greater risks. Reagan was obviously wounded by the arms for hostages charge. When political blood is in the water, a journalists' "feeding frenzy" can ensue. Third, leading reporters were bitterly critical of Reagan's policy toward Iran (Emery & Emery, 1988). Fourth, initial analysis of print and television coverage of the Irangate story indicated harsh media criticism toward the Reagan administration's policy.

Therefore, our first hypothesis was:

> News stories published in leading representative U.S. newspapers would be more critical of the U.S. policy toward Iran than would the *Tower Commission Report*.

Although the purpose of the Tower Commission was to investigate problems that occurred through the activities of the National Security Council, we expected their report to consist more of factual content rather than evaluations. The Tower Commission had access to information sources not readily available to newspaper reporters. Therefore, we expected that the three newspapers would rely more on inferences and judgments and less on factual material than the Tower Commission.

Our second hypothesis was:

> The inferential and judgmental content of news stories of U.S.-Iran policy in leading representative U.S. newspapers would be greater than in the content of the *Tower Commission Report*.

Perhaps the most damaging accusation made against the Reagan administration was the contention that the United States was trading arms for hostages. President Reagan insisted that arms to Iran were sent initially as part of a diplomatic initiative to encourage better relations with Iran. He denied the charge that the United States traded arms for hostages with Iran and then used the profits of the arms sales to illegally fund the Contras in Central America. One of the tasks of the President's Special Review Board was to investigate U.S.-Iran diplomatic negotiations, which involved more than the consideration of American hostages and Iran's need for weapons against Iraq.

The Tower Commission claimed that it would not "cover up" a bad policy. However, the commission might have felt some pressure from the Reagan administration to offer a diplomatic explanation of U.S.-Iran policy to counter the press's allegations of trading arms for hostages. It was therefore uncertain whether the Tower Commission Report would downplay the arms for hostages linkage. If indeed the print media fulfilled their watchdog function, however, it would be expected that influential representative U.S. newspapers would focus more on the arms-for-hostages controversy than would the Tower Commission Report. Therefore, our third hypothesis was:

> News stories in leading representative U.S. newspapers would portray U.S. policy toward Iran as trading arms for hostages more than would the *Tower Commission Report*.

METHOD

The research questions and hypotheses were analyzed with data collected from four print sources: the *Los Angeles Times*, the *New York Times*, the *Washington Post*, and the *Tower Commission Report*. Articles that addressed U.S.-Iran relations in the three newspapers represented the print media's portrayal of the Reagan administration's policy, and the report published by President Reagan's Special Review Board represented the government's portrayal of the U.S. policy toward Iran.

The rationale for analyzing these media sources is based on four propositions. First, the print media are believed to affect public opinion of U.S. foreign policy (Bennett, 1983; McCombs & Shaw, 1972). The three newspapers chosen for analysis are all recognized as leading news sources: They are among the largest in circulation among U.S. prestige newspapers, they operate their own news services, and they have often been the object of foreign policy research (Barranco & Shyles, 1988; Chang, 1988; Daugherty & Warden, 1979; Myers, 1968, 1982). Second, the *Los Angeles Times, New York Times,* and *Washington Post* were leading papers in the investigative reporting of Irangate (Emery & Emery, 1988). Third, the American public had limited access to information about U.S.-Iran policy except through the news media. Print news stories provide much of the information that formulates public opinion about U.S. policy (Just & Crigler, 1989; McComb & Shaw, 1972). Fourth, the Irangate controversy stimulated the American public's interest in the *Tower Commission Report*. Reports of government policy are believed to have an important influence on public opinion (Margolis & Mauser 1989).

The print media sources analyzed in our study have been evaluated in several other studies of U.S.-Iran relations (Malek, 1988; Sadeghi, 1987; Tadayon, 1989) Dowling's (1989) study of the *New York Times, Time, Newsweek,* and the *Denver Post* revealed how the print media had a persuasive impact on the American public's beliefs about Iran. The release of the *Tower Commission Report*, which received extensive media coverage, provided another source of information about U.S.-Iran relations for the American public. In a previous study of media portrayals of Iran, Malek (1988) compared the content addressing U.S.-Iran relations in the *Department of State Bulletin* with the content found in the editorial page of the *New York Times*. The detailed narrative of the operations of the National Security Council contained in the *Tower Commission Report* and the extensive coverage of leading U.S. newspapers provide excellent sources for analyzing various portrayals of the United States' relationship with Iran. The *Los Angeles Times, the New York Times,* the *Washington Post,* and the *Tower Commission Report* furnished important information about U.S.-Iran relations as Irangate unfolded before the American public.

Content analysis was used to assess U.S. policy toward Iran in the four print media sources during a 4-month period from November 1986 through March 1987. This time period was chosen because the news that the United States was sending arms to Iran first became public in the United States during the end of November 1986, and received extensive print media coverage through March 1987. Meanwhile, the *Tower Commission Report* was being written by the President's Special Review Board and was publicly released at the end of February 1987. A comparison of the newspaper articles with the *Tower Commission Report* is appropriate because all four information sources were produced during the same time period. The two types of reports used many of the same information sources and each presented the American public with an image of U.S. foreign policy toward Iran.

A stratified random sample of newspaper articles was selected from the *Los Angeles Times, New York Times*, and *Washington Post* during the periods of November 24-30, 1986, and January 25-31 and February 27-March 5, 1987. During these time periods, 368 news articles, editorials, and public opinion pieces addressing U.S-Iran relations were identified in the three newspapers. These articles were first classified into four categories: straight news stories, editorials, special feature stories, and special opinion pieces (such as letters to the editor). The articles in each category were numbered and 25 percent of the articles were randomly selected for analysis. A total sample of 92 newspaper articles was content analyzed. A similar procedure was used to analyze the content of the *Tower Commission Report*. There are exactly 92 sections of the report, and 25 percent were randomly chosen for content analysis. Thus a total of 23 sections of the *Tower Commission Report* were analyzed.

Complete sentences were chosen as the unit of analysis, and each sentence was evaluated on three different dimensions. The first dimension identified sentences within one of three distinct topologies: a report, an inference, or a judgment. This classification system was developed by Hayakawa (1972) and has been used for content analyzing print news stories (Singhal, 1988). Sentences coded as reports were those that represented verifiable and reliable statements based on known facts. Inferences were statements about the unknown based on what is known (i.e., educated guesses, conjecture, or speculation). Sentences coded as judgments were statements that make positive or negative evaluations, such as whether something is good or bad, liked or disliked, accepted or rejected (opinions).

The second evaluation identified the thematic content of each media source. First, sentences were selected that specifically described the nature of U.S.-Iran relations. Then each sentence was coded to determine to what degree it portrayed U.S. policy toward Iran as (1) a diplomatic initiative to improve relations with Iran, (2) an attempt to gain the release of American hostages held in Lebanon, or (3) a dual policy encompassing both goals.

The third evaluation identified whether the content addressing U.S.-Iran policy was presented in a favorable, neutral, or unfavorable way, on the basis of a coding system developed by Janis and Fadner (1943). Intercoder reliability was established by using a second coder for 20 percent of the sample. Reliability was fairly high using both Holsti's (1969) coefficient of reliability (.924 by category; .947 by theme; .841 by dispositional analysis) and Scold's (1955) *pi* (.886 by category; .936 by theme; .788 by dispositional analysis).

RESULTS

The results were produced by calculating descriptive statistics and chi-square statistics with the use of SAS (1985) programs and are presented here in two sections.

RESEARCH QUESTION

The four-part research question examined the similarities and differences in how U.S. policy toward Iran was portrayed in the *Los Angeles Times*, *New York Times*, and *Washington Post*. The content analyses of the three papers indicate significant differences in the news reports critical of U.S. policy, $x^2(4, N=1,905) = 37.63$, $p < .001$. The contingency coefficient C, a non parametric measure of association for categorical data with more than two independent samples (Siegel, 1956), was .14 ($p < .001$). The *New York Times* was significantly more neutral than the other two newspapers; the *Los Angeles Times* had the highest percentage of critical content (33.5 percent). The *Washington Post* had the highest percentage of favorable content (6.3 percent). These results are shown in Figure 1.

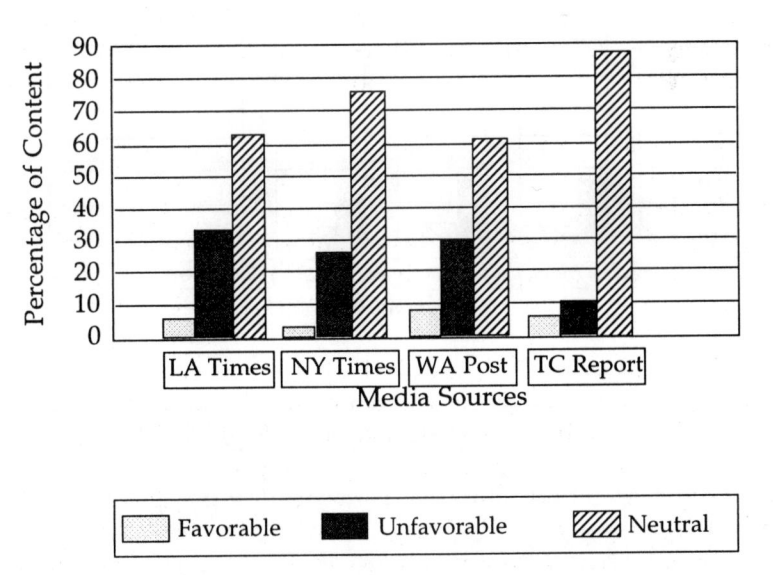

Figure 1. Percentage of content critical of U.S.-Iran policy, by media source.

Analysis of the newspaper editorials in the three papers also indicates significant differences, $x^2(4, N=681) = 13.28$, $p < .01$. The contingency coefficient C, which indicates the association between the favorable, unfavorable, and neutral content and the three newspapers was .15 ($p < .01$). The editorials published in the *Washington Post* were the most critical (64.5 percent of content was unfavorable). The *New York Times* was second most critical (50.5 percent of content was unfavorable), followed by the *Los Angeles Times* (45.7 percent of content was unfavorable).

Significant differences were also found in the factual, inferential, and judgmental content of the news stories in the three papers, $x^2(4, N-1,909) = 142.61$, $p < .001$. The contingency coefficient C was .26 ($p < .001$). Use of factual statements was highest in the *Washington Post* (87.4 percent of content), followed by the *New York Times* (81.3 percent of content) and the *Los Angeles Times* (81.2 percent of content). Use of judgmental statements by all three newspapers was very low, representing 2.3 percent of the content analyzed in the *New York Times*, 1.0 percent analyzed in the *Los Angeles Times*, and less than 1 percent in the *Washington Post*. These results are shown in Figure 2.

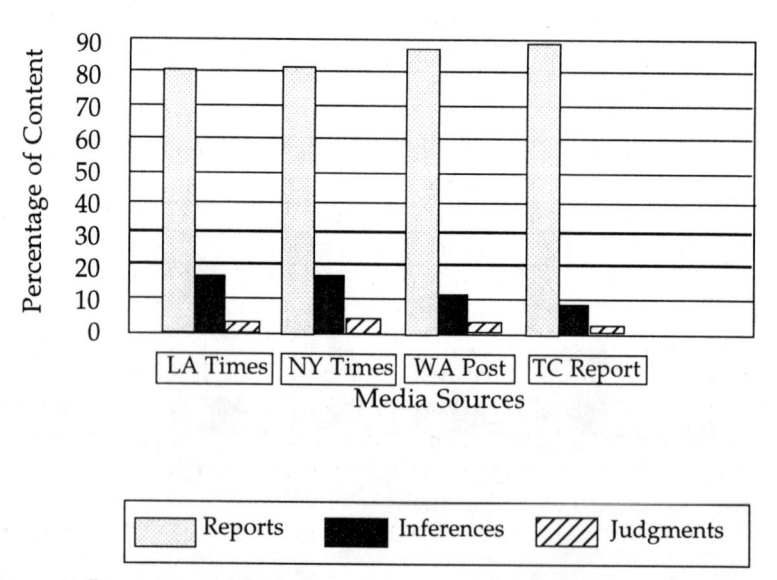

Figure 2. Percentage of factual content portraying U.S.-Iran policy, by media source.

Finally, significant differences were also found in how the three papers characterized the Reagan administration's policy toward Iran x^2(4, N - 94) - 16.62, p < .01. The contingency coefficient C was .39 (p < .01). The *Washington Post* (79.2 percent of content) and *New York Times* (73.7 percent of content) portrayed the Reagan administration's Iran policy as arms for hostages significantly more than the *Los Angeles Times* (25.0 percent of content). The *Washington Post* portrayed the Reagan administration's policy as a diplomatic initiative the least (10.4 percent of content) among the three papers, followed by the *Los Angeles Times* (12.5 percent of content) and *New York Times* (15.8 percent of content).

HYPOTHESES

The first hypothesis, which predicted that news stories published in the newspapers would be more critical of U.S. policy toward Iran than would the *Tower Commission Report*, is supported by our results. To compare the three newspapers with the *Tower Commission Report*, the number of favorable, unfavorable, and neutral statements were added together. The total news content analyzed in the three papers (N = 1,909 sentences) was significantly more critical of U.S. foreign policy toward Iran than was the content (N = 1,055 sentences) analyzed in the *Tower Commission Report* (x^2 = 166.68, df = 2, p < .001). The contingency coefficient C was .23 (p < .001). Results show that 29.8 percent of the content of the newspaper articles was unfavorable toward U.S. dealings with Iran. Only 9.1 percent of the content in the *Tower Commission Report* was unfavorable toward the Reagan administration's Iran policy.

The second hypothesis, which predicted that the number of factual, inferential and judgmental statements in the news content of the three newspapers would be significantly different from the content of the *Tower Commission Report*, was also supported (x^2 = 37.28, df = 2, p < .001). The contingency coefficient C indicating the relationship between the type of content and two media sources was 0.11 (p < .001). In each case, factual content was by far the largest category (83.6 percent for the newspapers, and 91.7 percent for the *Tower Commission Report*), followed by inferential content and judgmental content. Although the content in the papers was two times more judgmental than in the *Tower Commission Report*, judgmental statements only accounted for 1.2 percent of the content in the print news stories.

The third hypothesis, which predicted that news stories in the newspapers would portray U.S. policy toward Iran as "trading arms for hostages" more than would the *Tower Commission Report*, was not supported. Although the newspaper content (N = 94) did portray the Reagan administration's policy more as "arms for hostages" (72.3 percent) than did the *Tower Commission Report's* content (N = 157) that characterized U.S.-Iran policy (68.8 %), this difference was not significant (x^2 = 2.84, df = 2, p > .05). The contingency coefficient C is 0.11 (nonsignificant). However, 20.4 percent of the content in the *Tower Commission Report* that addressed the U.S.-Iran policy portrayed the policy as a diplomatic initiative, whereas only 12.8 percent of the newspaper content described the policy as a part of U.S attempts to improve diplomatic relations with Iran. Results of the analysis conducted for this third hypothesis are provided in Figure 3.

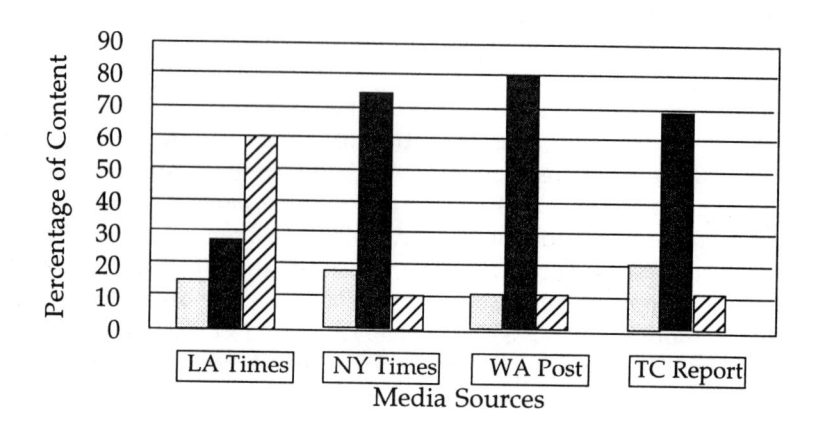

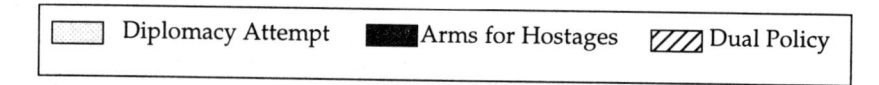

Figure 3. Thematic portrayals of U.S.-Iran policy, by media source.

DISCUSSION

Although the Tower Commission Report was found to be highly critical of Reagan administration's policy toward Iran, it was not as critical as the print media. Approximately 22 percent of the content of the combined articles published in the *Los Angeles Times, New York Times*, and *Washington Post* regarding U.S.-Iran relations was unfavorable, compared with only 9 percent of the content of the *Tower Commission Report*. Exposure to U.S. newspapers gave the public a more negative image of the Reagan administration's policy toward Iran than did the *Tower Commission Report*.

In addition, over one half of the content in the editorial sections of the three newspapers consisted of statements critical of U.S. policy toward Iran. There was very little difference in the critical nature of the editorial commentary in the *New York Times* and *Los Angeles Times*, but the *Washington Post* was found to be markedly more critical than the other papers. These results are contrary to those found in one study suggesting the *Washington Post* is pro-administration in its coverage of political controversies (Daugherty & Warden, 1979). Perhaps the subject of Daugherty and Warden's (1979) research, the Arab-Israeli conflict, reflected a foreign policy matter in which the *Post's* coverage better aligned with the Carter administration's sentiments at the time. In the case of Irangate, the *Post* did not hesitate to criticize the Reagan administration.

It is not surprising that the news stories we analyzed contained slightly more inferential and judgmental statements and less factual content than did the *Tower Commission Report*. The Tower Commission had the budget and resources to execute a thorough and aggressive investigation of U.S. foreign policy toward Iran. The commission composed a 200-page chronology of recent U.S. policy decisions toward Iran, a separate 200-page narrative of the events that followed these decisions, and an additional 200 pages of findings and recommendations (Barol, 1987). The commission also personally interviewed over 50 major figures involved in the implementation of U.S. foreign policy toward Iran, as well as former U.S. presidents and both U.S. and foreign government officials (Tower, Muskie, & Scowcroft, 1987).

Our results support the prediction that the print media fulfilled their watchdog function during Irangate. Each paper provided extensive print coverage that raised the question regarding the link between arms and hostages. About three-fourths of the content in the print news stories that addressed U.S.-Iran relations in the three newspapers portrayed the United States' Iran policy as an arms for hostages policy. Although this study cannot assess the effects of the *Los Angeles Times*, *New York Times*, and *Washington Post* on public opinion, polls taken at the time indicated President Reagan's job approval ratings dropped from 63 percent in late October to 47 percent in early November of 1986, the time period when U.S. interaction with Iran developed into a major controversy (Gallup, 1986).

If prior to Irangate the press had been lax during the Reagan administration in fulfilling its watchdog function, as some contend, perhaps this contention reinforces the view that the news media were strongly motivated to critique the Reagan administration Iran policy. The U.S. press withstood years of criticism regarding its inability to rebuff the "teflon President." When Irangate unfolded, the press probably reacted to the challenge that it had been "too easy" on Reagan. Despite the notion that the press may often serve the needs of the elite, the U.S. press also prides itself on serving as the public's watchdog. Our study indicates that concern for being a watchdog was greater than the pressure to support the Reagan administration's viewpoint of its foreign policy toward Iran.

Another important finding is that the print media could not be characterized as succumbing to the Reagan administration's "spin" on Irangate. Even the *Tower Commission Report* was critical of the administration's policy. Many government critics might be surprised that 69 percent of the applicable content of the *Tower Commission Report* portrayed the U.S. policy as essentially "trading arms for hostages" with Iranian officials.

A secret policy of "arms for hostages" is likely to be seen by the public as more scandalous than a policy of improving diplomatic relations with Iran as a means to pressure the Shiites in Lebanon to release American hostages. The report did give greater emphasis than newspapers to Reagan's claim that the initial policy with Iran was not the flawed "arms for hostages" exchange that it later became through the workings of the National Security Council. Reagan's Irangate was labeled by the print media as "arms for hostages" despite his public denials. The sparsity of print news content dealing with the U.S. diplomatic initiative is important vis-a-vis the public's assessment of the Reagan administration's Iran policy.

Whether former President Reagan will ever transcend the "arms for hostages" scandal attached to his presidency remains to be seen. Oliver North found it difficult to shake the extensive media coverage critical of him during and after the controversy, which was resurrected during his unsuccessful race for the Virginia Senate.

In summary, the *Tower Commission Report* presented more news on the U.S. diplomatic initiatives and less on the sale of arms for the release of hostages, and used less inferential and judgmental statements than the average for our test newspapers. As might be expected, the commission also made fewer unfavorable assertions about the Reagan administration's policies. Nevertheless, all four print media sources were unfavorable toward the Reagan administration's dealings with Iran, which were basically portrayed as a flawed foreign policy that degenerated in trading arms for hostages.

Future research should compare the effects of the various print media portrayals of foreign policy on public attitudes and beliefs. In this research, we examined how influential print media portrayed U.S.-Iran policy to the American public, but we do not know how the public was affected by these various portrayals. Such research questions as "Does the public believe the news media are effective watchdogs that formulate public opinion?" and "Do news editors and reporters succumb to pressure from White House spin doctors?" need further empirical analysis.

Future research is also needed to compare the similarities and differences between the U.S. government's and the print media's portrayals of foreign policy, and how these various portrayals influence the American public. Another topic that warrants further study is whether the ubiquitous presence of the news media and accelerated diffusion of news through new communication systems make it easier or more difficult for the government to control its foreign policy image with other nations. As in the case of Iran, the opportunity for a plurality of viewpoints to emerge and rapidly diffuse from both government officials and media watchdogs may protect against the government's attempts to "spin" stories to gain the support of public opinion for its policies.

REFERENCES

Altheide, David L. (1985). Impact of format and ideology on TV news coverage of Iran. *Journalism Quarterly, 62,* 347-351.

Altschull, J. Herbert. (1984). *Agents of power: The role of the news media in human affairs.* New York: Longman.

Arno, Andrew, & Dissanayake, Wilma. (1984). *The news media in national and international conflict.* Boulder, CO: Westview Press.

Parol, Bill. (1987, February 23). Under pressure, a marine loses control. *Newsweek,* pp. 22-24.

Barranco, Deborah A., & Shyles, Leonard. (1988). Arab vs. Israeli news coverage in the *New York Times,* 1976 and 1984. *Journalism Quarterly, 65,* 178-181, 225.

Barton, Richard L., & Gregg, Richard B. (1982). Middle East conflict as a TV news scenario: A formal analysis. *Journal of Communication, 32*(2), 172-185.

Bennett, W. Lance. (1983). *News, the politics of illusion.* New York: Longman.

Bennett, W. Lance, & Edelman, Murray. (1985). Toward a new political narrative. *Journal of Communication, 35*(4), 156-171.

Bennett, W. Lance, Gressett, Lynne A., & Halton, William. (1985). Repairing the news: A case study of the news paradigm. *Journal of Communication, 35*(2), 50-68.

Benton, Marc, & Frazier, P. Jean. (1976). The agenda-setting function of the mass media at three levels of information holding. *Communication Research, 3,* 261-274.

Brown, William J., & Facciola, Peter C. (1991). Effects of media coverage on public attitudes and beliefs of the Persian Gulf War. Paper presented at the 77th Annual Conference of the Speech Communication Association, October 31-November 3, Atlanta, Ga.

Carlsson, G., Dahlberg, A., & Rosengren, Karl. (1981). Mass media content, public opinion and social change. In Karl E. Rosengren (Ed.), *Advances in content analysis* (pp. 227-240). London: Sage.

Chang, Tsan-Kuo (1988). The news and U.S.-China policy: Symbols in the newspapers and documents. *Journalism Quarterly, 65*, 320-327.

Cook, Fay L., Tyler, Tom R., Goetz, Edward G., Gordon, Margaret T., Protess, David, Leff, Donna R., & Molotch, Harvey L. (1983). Media and agenda setting: Effects on the public, interest group leaders, policy makers, and policy. *Public Opinion Quarterly, 47*, 16-35.

Daugherty, David, & Warden, Michael. (1979). Prestige press editorial treatment of the Mideast during 11 crisis years. *Journalism Quarterly, 56*, 776-782.

Deakin, James (1984). *Straight stuff: The reporters, the White House, and the truth*. New York: William Morrow.

Denton, Robert E., Jr., & Woodward, Gary C. (1985). *Political communication in America*. New York: Praeger.

Dowling, Ralph E. (1989). Print journalism as political communication: The Iran hostage crisis. *Political Communication and Persuasion, 6*, 129-150.

Emery, Michael, & Emery, Edwin. (1988). *The press and America* (6th ed.). Englewood Cliffs, NJ: Prentice Hall.

Gallup, George, Jr. (1986). *The Gallup poll: Public opinion 1986*. Wilmington, DE: Scholarly Resources.

Galtung, Johan, & Ruge, Marl. (1965). The structure of foreign news. *Journal of Peace Research, 2*, 64-91.

Galtung, Johan, & Vincent, Richard C. (1992). *Global glasnost: Toward a new international information/communication order?* Cresskill, NJ: Hampton Press.

Gas, Herbert. (1979). *Deciding what's news*. New York: Vintage Books.

Gillmore, Kimberly D. (1994). *David Gergen: Communication, protection, and the presidency*. Unpublished master's thesis, Regent University, Virginia Beach, VA.

Harris, Phil. (1976). International news media authority and dependence. *Instant Research on Peace and Violence 4*, 148-159.

Hayakawa, Samuel I. (1972). *Language in thought and action* (3rd ed.). New York: Harcourt Brace Jovanovich.

Hertsgaard, Mark. (1988). *On bended knee: The press and the Reagan presidency*. New York: Farrar Straus Giroux.

Holsti, Ole R. (1969). *Content analysis for the social sciences and humanities*. Reading, MA: Addison-Wesley.

Hoover, Stewart M. (1993). Looking back at the Gulf War. *Media Development, 40*(2), 68-69.

Hopple, Gerald W. (1982). International news coverage in two elite newspapers. *Journal of Communication, 32*(1), 61-74.

Hutchins, Robert. (1947). Commission on freedom of the press. *A Free and Responsible Press.* Chicago, IL: University of Chicago Press.

Jamieson, Kathleen H. (1984). *Packaging the presidency: A history and criticism of presidential campaign advertising.* New York: Oxford University Press.

Janis, Irving L., & Fadner, Raymond. (1943). The coefficient of imbalance. In Harold Lasswell et al. (Eds.), *Language of politics: Studies in quantitative semantics* (pp. 153-169). Cornwall, NY: Cornwall Press.

Jensen, Carl. (1993). *Censored: The news that didn't make the news—and why.* Chapel Hill, NC: Shelburne Press.

Johnstone, John W. C., Slawski, Edward J., & Bowman, William W. (1976). *The net people: A sociological portrait of American journalists and their work.* Urbana, Il.: University of Illinois Press.

Just, Marion, & Crigler, Ann. (1989). Learning from the news: Experiments in media, modality, and reporting about Star Wars. *Political Communication and Persuasion, 6,* 109-128.

Kieh, George K. (1990). Propaganda and the United States foreign policy: The case Panama. *Political Communication and Persuasion, 7,* 61-72.

Knight, George, & Dean, Tony. (1982). Myth and the structure of the news. *Journal of Communication, 32*(2), 144-161.

Larson, James F. (1986). Television and U.S. foreign policy: The case of the Iran hostage crisis. *Journal of Communication, 36*(4), 108-130.

Malek, Abbas. (1988). New York Times' editorial position and the US foreign policy: The case of Iran. *Gazette, 42*(2), 105-119.

Maltese, John A. (1992). *Spin control: The White House office of communications and the management of personal news.* Chapel Hill, NC: University of North Carolina Press.

Margolis, Michael, & Mauser, Gary A. (1989). Public opinion as a dependent variable: A framework for analysis. *Political Communication and Persuasion, 6,* 87-108.

McCombs, Max E., & Shaw, Donald L. (1972). The agenda setting function of the mass media. *Public Opinion Quarterly, 36,* 176-187.

Meeske, Milan D., & Javaheri, Mohamad H. (1982). Network television coverage of the Iranian hostage crisis. *Journalism Quarterly, 59,* 641-645.

Merrill, John C. (Ed.). (1991). *Global journalism* (2nd ed.). New York: Longman.

Myers, David S. (1968). Editorials and foreign affairs in the 1964 presidential campaign. *Journalism Quarterly, 45,* 211-218.

Myers, David S. (1982). Editorials and foreign affairs in recent presidential campaigns. *Journalism Quarterly, 59,* 541-547.

Noelle-Neumann, Elizabeth. (1974). The spiral of silence: A theory of public opinion. *Journal of Communication, 24,* 43-51.

Parenti, Michael. (1989). *The dollar and the sword.* New York: St. Martin's Press.

Picard, Robert G. (1985). *The press and the decline of democracy: The democratic socialist response in public, policy.* Westport, CT: Greenwood Press.

Qualter, Terence H. (1962). *Propaganda and psychological warfare.* New York: Random House.

Rikardsson, Gunnel. (1981). Newspaper opinion and public opinion. In Karl E. Rosengren (Ed.), *Advances in content analysis* (pp. 215-226). London: Sage.

Rivers, William L. (1982). *The other government: Power and the Washington media.* New York: Universe Books.

Roberts, Donald F., & Bachen, C. M. (1981). Mass communication effects. *Annual of Psychology, 32,* 307-356.

Rozell, Mark J. (1992). *The press and the Ford presidency.* Ann Arbor, MI: University of Michigan Press.

Sadeghi, Menswear. (1987). *National differences and international crisis reporting: A gatekeeper study of the 1985 TWA hostage crisis.* Unpublished Ph.D. dissertation, University of Southern California, Los Angeles.

SAS. (1985). *SAS user's guide* (3rd ed.). Cary, NC: SAS Institute.

Scott, William A. (1955). Reliability and content analysis: The case of nominal scale coding. *Public Opinion Quarterly, 19,* 321-325.

Siegel, Sidney. (1956). *Nonparametric statistics: For the behavioral sciences.* New York: McGraw-Hill.

Sigal, Leon V. (1973). *Reporters and officials: The organization and politics of newsmaking.* Lexington, MA: D. C. Heath.

Singhal, Arvind. (1988, March-April). Indira Gandhi's assassination: A case study in international news reporting. *Vidura: The journal of the Indian Press Institute,* pp. 3-8.

Smith, Hedrick. (1988). *The power game: How Washington works.* New York: Random House.

Streitmatter, Rodger. (1988, Winter). The rise and triumph of the White House photo opportunity. *Journalism Quarterly, 65*(4), 981-985.

Tadayon, Mohamad. (1989). The image of Iran in the New York Times. *Gazette, 26,* 217-233.

Tebbel, John W., & Watts, Sarah M. (1985). *The press and the presidency: From George Washington to Ronald Reagan.* New York: Oxford University Press.

Tower, John, Muskie, Edmund, & Scowcroft, Brent. (1987). *Report of the President's special review board.* Washington, DC: Government Printing Office.

Weaver, David, & Wilhoit, G. Cleveland. (1986). *The American journalist.* Bloomington: Indiana University Press.

QUESTIONS FOR DISCUSSION

1. What were the central research questions posed by these authors? How did they turn these questions into hypotheses?

2. Which of their initial hypotheses were supported by the research, which were refuted? Does it make the research any less important when a hypothesis is not supported by the results?

3. The authors chose a text-analysis method for testing their hypothesis. Did this method seem appropriate for the questions posed?

4. They acknowledge at the end of the article that there are several related questions which this research was not able to answer. What were those questions?

5. In the results section, the authors use figures with bar graphs to represent their data. Were these figures helpful?

6. Who might be the prospective audience for this article? Who are the authors trying to convince?

7. The authors have included an extensive reference list. Does this list help to establish their credibility on the topic?

Doing Sociology: Connecting the Classroom Experience with a Multiethnic School District

Jose Calderon & Betty Farrell, Pitzer College

This article describes an innovative undergraduate sociology course in which college students helped develop and teach multicultural lesson plans to high school students in a district of metropolitan Los Angeles currently undergoing rapid demographic change. As a response to specific incidents of interethnic conflict in the public schools as well as to the call for more courses engaging students in sociological participant-observation research, this project provides one model of undergraduate education in which the classroom and the community are linked. The authors describe the origin and organization of the Pitzer College project in the Alhambra School District and address a number of structural and substantive challenges that emerge in teaching a community-based course of this kind.

Practical and applied courses in the college curriculum are becoming more prevalent (Neapolitan 1992; Schultz 1992). Some recent articles in *Teaching Sociology* have discussed how a rigorous academic curriculum in the classroom can be combined with theory and experiential learning, or "doing sociology" in the community (Bricher 1993; Miller 1990; Porter and Schwartz 1993; Schmid 1992). In the same context, other articles have focused on how the sociological perspective can go beyond the classroom to create "transformative action" and social change (Flint 1993; Schmid 1993).

Although these articles begin to discuss the relationship between theory and praxis, they offer few concrete cases in which experiential learning has led to structural change in the institutions involved. In this paper we describe a class at Pitzer College, "The Roots of Social Conflict in Schools and Communities," which connected coursework with experiential learning. In the process, it served as a catalyst for structural change in

From *Teaching Sociology* (1996, Vol. 24, pp. 46-53). Reprinted by permission of the authors and the American Sociological Association.

three high schools in our region that were undergoing rapid demographic and social changes. At the same time, we address the tension in finding a balance between theory and praxis, which many instructors and students face in experiential courses.

THE ALHAMBRA SCHOOL DISTRICT

The field setting for this class, the Alhambra School District, is located five miles east of downtown Los Angeles in a San Gabriel Valley suburb. This district is a particularly interesting field site because it is a microcosm of many of the larger demographic changes taking place throughout California. Currently the district serves a diverse student population of 20,526, of whom 51 percent are Asian, 39 percent are Latino, and 9 percent are "other," including Anglo/white, African American, and Native American. The Alhambra School District, which includes the city of Alhambra, part of San Gabriel, and almost all of the city of Monterey Park, now has the largest concentration of Chinese students anywhere in the United States.

The city of Monterey Park illustrates the larger changes occurring in the school district. Until 1960, Monterey Park's population was 85 percent Anglo, 12 percent Latino, and 3 percent Asian. By the time of the 1980 census, the population had changed to 40 percent Asian, 37 percent Latino, and 20 percent Anglo (U.S. Bureau of the Census 1980).[1] The demographic trends of the 1970s continued through the 1980s: the Asian population grew to 56 percent by 1990, Latinos held relatively steady at 31 percent, and the Anglo population declined further to 12 percent of the city's 62,000 residents (U.S. Bureau of the Census 1990). The neighboring city of Alhambra (population 71,000) has seen similar demographic changes, although the proportions of the three ethnic groups—36 percent Asian, 32 percent Latino, and 30 percent Anglo— were roughly equal by 1991.

As a result of these striking demographic changes in the two cities and in the school district, ethnic relations are characterized by both conflict and cooperation.[2] Alongside tensions at the city government level over urban development issues and the status of English as the "official" language, numerous racial incidents have involved Latino, Asian, and Anglo students in the schools. In 1986 one fight led to the stabbing of a Chinese youth at Mark Keppel High School in Monterey Park. In 1991 several fights broke out at San Gabriel High School between Latino and Chinese students and between Vietnamese and Anglo students. Differences in disciplinary actions following these incidents led to an escalation of tensions between Latino and Asian parents and to the formation of several ethnically based community coalitions.

In December 1991 a broader coalition—the Multi-Ethnic Task Force (later renamed the Multicultural Community Association)—was formed, uniting members around 10 different proposals to effect structural changes in the school district. These proposals included a review of disciplinary procedures, the application of conflict resolution programs, the implementation of a multicultural curriculum, sensitivity training for all school employees, and the involvement of parents, students, and teachers in the decision-making process. The first author, a resident of Monterey Park and a parent of children in this school district, was elected a chair of this new coalition, and thus provided an important link to crucial gatekeepers in the community and school system.

"THE ROOTS OF SOCIAL CONFLICT IN SCHOOLS AND COMMUNITIES": GOALS AND RESULTS OF THE COURSE

In this context, the course "The Roots of Social Conflict in Schools and Communities" was developed. In January 1993 Pitzer College received a competitive course development grant from the Ohio Campus Compact. This grant supported the development of courses that addressed the connections between service, participation in the political process, and public policy development. Over two semesters, we involved 40 students in participant-observation research in the three high schools of the Alhambra School District.[3]

We had several goals in designing this course. At the college level, it helped to implement a new educational objective promoting an understanding of "the ethical implications of knowledge and social action"—that is, enhancing a sense of social responsibility for students, especially in relation to work in surrounding communities. At the departmental level, it was part of a pilot program for a new sociology requirement that would allow majors to engage in the craft of "doing sociology." At the undergraduate course level, the class was designed to link an internship in the public schools with the academic study of communities and school systems that have been affected significantly by the demographic changes and subsequent interethnic conflicts in the Los Angeles metropolitan region.

In the first semester, 20 Pitzer College students, in teams of three or four, were admitted as observers in several classes in each school.[4] The selected classes represented all grade and ability-group levels. All of the students kept extensive field notes of their observations; these notes served as the basis of research papers that they prepared at the end of the semester. Following the standard guidelines of ethnographic research, the students were expected to record all observable data rather than focusing on predetermined questions or research areas.[5] Given the open-ended nature of their observation assignment and their placement sites, they tended to concentrate on the microcosm of classroom interaction. Through their initial observations, they were able to identify several patterns.

First, a number of observers from the college wrote that the classroom structure and the teachers' interaction styles made a difference in students' perceptions about school and in their achievement levels. Because Asian students tended to be tracked in the upper-level classes and Latino students in the lower-level classes in these high schools, differences in teachers' behavior, use of language, style of teaching, and expectations about students' abilities had the potential to reinforce group divisions and to perpetuate different achievement outcomes.

A second pattern observed by our students was the racial/ethnic segregation that shaped interaction inside and outside the classroom. Several observers noted, for example, that the voluntary seating arrangement in many classrooms tended to replicate the intraethnic friendship networks that appeared in the cafeteria and the schoolyard. One unintended consequence was that any collaborative work in the classroom tended to reinforce these networks because students who sat next to each other were often assigned to work together. Thus one significant opportunity to bring together different combinations of students for a common task was lost.

Finally, our students observed that the limited resources for the English as a Second Language (ESL) courses and the resulting "burn-out" among teachers lowered the morale in these courses. Because the recent wave of immigration to the San Gabriel Valley has contributed so substantially to the rapid demographic transition of this school district, ESL courses offer many first-generation students an especially important introduction to American society in general, and specifically to the culture of American high schools. Therefore these classes seemed to our student observers to offer an important but often missed opportunity to include significant multicultural education with the instruction in basic language skills.

Because educational reform was a topic of great concern to the newly formed Multicultural Community Association, and because the first author was co-chairing that group, all of these student observations were used to develop policy recommendations for the Alhambra School District. Coalition members, for example, began to question school district officials about the systematic grouping of Latino students at lower ability levels; they also began to address the effectiveness of disciplinary programs in the schools and to argue for the development of a more multiculturally-sensitive curriculum. These concerns became part of a district wide "goals action program," which was passed recently by the school board.

During the summer following the first phase of this project, the instructors met once again with Alhambra School District administrators and agreed that the second phase would focus on developing and implementing multicultural lesson plans. As a result, during the following fall semester, another 20 students were assigned to high school classes in psychology, world history, English, journalism, mathematics, art, and ESL with the goal of developing and teaching their own lesson plans. Encouraged by school district administrators, principals, and teachers to move from observers to active participants, sophomore- and junior-level college students worked closely with teachers, asking questions and exploring strategies to shift seating patterns, encourage cooperative learning, and open the curriculum to more multicultural approaches.

As they developed specific lesson plans, the students focused on introducing multicultural teaching strategies into the classroom. All the lesson plans actively involved the high school students through group discussions and writing exercises. In a lesson plan for a world history class, for example, students wrote down their initial reaction to images depicting people of different ethnicities as a means of starting a discussion on stereotyping. In an English class, students responded to "Dear Abby/Ann Landers" letters on issues of prejudice and discrimination. Members of another class compared themselves to characters on the TV show Beverly Hills 90210. A student teacher from the college even devised a multicultural lesson for a mathematics class by surveying the students on social issues relevant to their lives and then using the survey results to engage them in a lesson on circle graphs. The lesson ended with a discussion of the use and misuse of statistics.

At the college, the students participated in a weekly seminar organized around varied readings about the region, including educational stratification, demographic changes, and the Latino and Asian immigrant experiences. One book, *Always Running*, chronicled the experiences of writer Luis Rodriguez, who grew up in San Gabriel, attended Mark Keppel High School (one of our observation sites), and belonged to a local gang. The readings provoked lively discussions as the students related the materials to their own lives. The opportunity to draw connections between families, communities, and schools from their personal experiences, their fieldwork, and the course readings made this sociology seminar particularly engaging.

The Alhambra Schools Project culminated in a day-long conference at which our students shared their experiences as observers and teachers with an audience of high school teachers, school district administrators, and the press. Although some teachers and administrators initially had expressed reservations about the project, they now complimented the students on their energy and creativity.

Significant results continue to emerge. Teachers have reported that some of the high school students have formed new friendships in and out of class. The lesson plans still inspire new approaches among some of the teachers who participated, and they are being distributed to educators throughout the school district. Also, a number of our students have decided to make teaching their career choice. New opportunities for this type of experiential learning have opened up as other school districts contact us about developing a similar program in their schools. Finally, new types of coalitions—such as one formed recently between Pitzer College, the Alhambra School District, and the Southern California Edison Company, a corporation willing to support a multicultural education and conflict resolution program—have begun to change some of the institutional relationships in our region.

CONNECTING THEORY TO EXPERIENCE

One challenge—central to the sociological enterprise, but highlighted especially in this course—was to complement students' understanding of culture as a crucial variable of social interaction with the equally crucial but much less visible variable of social structure. In their high school classroom observations, for example, our undergraduates could readily identify the cultural barriers of language and custom that had led to specific instances of inter-ethnic conflict in the schools and to considerable general misunderstanding in the wider community. They were able to develop and teach lesson plans that effectively challenged racial/ethnic stereotypes and to engage high school students at all levels in a dialogue about the meanings and consequences of such cultural stereotyping. Yet when they were faced with dramatic data from these schools showing great divergences between Asian and Latino students' achievement levels and college preparatory tracks, our students were overwhelmed and dismayed by the implications of the same cultural explanations that they had earlier adopted rather uncritically to account for group differences.[6]

In logs recording their responses to readings on the high educational achievement levels of recent southeast Asian immigrants, the college students puzzled over the striking differences in the ethnic group patterns they had observed in their high schools. Thinking culturally, in this case, made our students uncomfortable because they anticipated that discussions about culturally based differences would only reinforce patterns of inequality. They were concerned that if cultural values were the source of these differential achievement levels, acknowledging and describing this phenomenon would only reify it as a justification for continued inequality. Wishing to celebrate diverse cultural values as the basis for group empowerment, they were dismayed that these same values might have harmful consequences for the social structure.

In our weekly seminar discussions, which focused on the history of racial/ethnic stratification in the United States and on the nature of structural discrimination, students began to question some of their own cultural assumptions in favor of more social structural and institutional analyses of group difference. Key sociological texts played an important role in raising these theoretical issues at various points throughout the semester.[7] Yet only by observing classroom interaction and by working directly with high school teachers and students did our students begin to discover the social consequences of concrete structural arrangements such as those in seating patterns, study group organizations, and the institutionalized tracking process through which students are channeled in the educational system. These insights were tentative, however; in the course of one semester they only began to challenge the primacy of the cultural explanations for behaviors that enjoy so much legitimacy today.

The challenge of making students understand the complex interplay between cultural values and social structural conditions is at the heart of experiential education. We believe that this understanding should become a central goal in teaching such courses. In this case, our students began to recognize that attributing ethnic inequality to cultural differences can lead to the tendency to blame the victim and can reinforce segregation and stereotyping. This discovery was rooted in their fieldwork experience, but it acquired greater depth and breadth when complemented by key supporting texts from the sociological literature. Through readings and experience that forced them to reconsider their initial single-causal explanations for differential group patterns in school achievement (e.g., "bad teachers," "an irrelevant curriculum," "cultural differences"), these undergraduates could begin to develop more complex structural and institutional explanations for the ways ethnic inequality can be perpetuated and maintained through the public school system—an institution in American society that has long been credited with offering meritocratic opportunities for social mobility.

A critique of an exclusively cultural analysis of group differences developed quite spontaneously in this class from the juxtaposition of readings with field experience. We now recognize many more opportunities to build the kind of creative tension between theoretical concepts and practical observation that this example illustrates by assigning more specifically contrasting perspectives in the readings and by organizing more in-class debates in future classes. Although there are many good reasons to use the seminar to process the fieldwork experience, we expect that students will benefit more in the long run by engaging in more critical dialogues involving theoretical ideas based on sociological readings and insights acquired in the field.

SOME DILEMMAS OF EXPERIENTIAL TEACHING

Although this course was highly successful from both the students' and the teachers' perspectives, we encountered some problems that may be generalizable to other experiential teaching situations. These problems are familiar to other qualitative researchers; they may be categorized generally as issues of establishing access and of developing continuity.

Establishing Access

Many immediate advantages accompanied the kind of direct access to a community coalition and to a school district allowed by the first author's position as chair of the Multicultural Community Association. The opportunity to introduce students into a community setting where serious educational issues are being debated and reform measures are proposed is invaluable. The first author's leadership position in the coalition provided leverage with the school district administrators, who otherwise might have been less willing to admit college students as observers during a period of heightened tensions in their schools. Yet because the students gained access to a field site through an activist coalition's political clout, it was also harder to separate the project of the college course from the coalition's agenda of educational reform. Administrators, who initially saw the project in terms of its potential to evaluate their programs, were quite reluctant to admit "untrained" undergraduate observers to their schools. In this case, some of their concerns were alleviated by the involvement of two faculty members in this course, only one of whom was identified with the community coalition, and by extensive discussions about the techniques and goals of participant observation research. By promising the school district administrators that our students would not give interviews to the press during their participant observation research, we also helped to moderate the concern that this project would become politicized. Thus, although we had more opportunities to gain access to this field site than many other college teachers, our channels of access were not always perceived as unbiased and interest-free.

Developing Continuity

A project of this kind requires much groundwork, not only with the school district administrators, who were the initial gatekeepers, but also with the participating high school teachers. In the first stages of the project we gave insufficient attention to the hierarchical structure of the urban public high school, and particularly to the frustration felt by many teachers when confronted with top-down decision making by their administrators. Several of the teachers initially chosen by their principals to participate in this project were less than enthusiastic about receiving our students in their classrooms. They saw few immediate benefits to working with college students, and they feared that field notes could be appropriated too readily for administrative review. In the face of such perceptions and potential opposition by important gatekeepers, the participant experience is seriously compromised.

In the future, we resolve to work more directly from the beginning with all teachers involved in this project. Although students benefit by learning to negotiate with a highly bureaucratic organization or to cope with the mistrust and anxiety of gatekeepers at all levels, we now recognize that we must play a more visible role as mediators between our students and the high school teachers. In many cases, these are teachers who feel besieged by the new demographic pressures, the political demands, and the economic constraints in their district.

Developing and maintaining a viable working relationship between our college and this public school district has also led us to consider our longer-term commitments more carefully now than at the beginning of the project. Recently we have faced the issue of how and what to give back to the high school students, teachers, and administrators who have worked with our students over the past year. We would like to challenge the perception that this project has primarily benefited the college students. Consequently we have begun to develop several ancillary projects that build on our relationship with the school district, including campus visits to introduce more "at-risk" students to a college environment and a one-on-one tutoring/mentoring program, located on our campus, for high school students. Supported by additional grant money, which was awarded because of the success of the initial course, we are establishing a resource center for conflict resolution studies on our college campus; this will allow us to gather materials and sponsor workshops on conflict resolution strategies and multicultural curricular development for local high school teachers. Our longer-term goal, with the support of our college administration, is to design college faculty internships with the local public school district, which will complement and enhance the program of students' experiential learning.

CONCLUSION

Our experience in co-teaching this course has been highly positive. The collaborative effort enriched our teaching experience; we also learned much about the culture and social structure of the American public school system from our students' field notes and discussions, as well as from our own negotiations with school administrators at all stages of the project. Occasionally we found ourselves caught in a mediating position between our student participant observers, who wanted to investigate the sources of ethnic conflict; the Alhambra School District administrators, who were concerned about possible negative publicity associated with "problems" discovered in their schools; and members of the community-based Multicultural Community Association, who were concerned with implementing policy for social change. As instructors, we sensed some competing forces in this project: concern with preserving an open and flexible learning environment for our students, on the one hand, and the constraints created by politically charged school and community issues, on the other.

A key lesson that we learned from this teaching experience is that it is often more demanding but also more rewarding to practice the craft of sociology both inside and outside the classroom, alongside our students and in local communities. In many ways this innovative teaching experience has brought us, as well as our students, back to the heart of the sociological enterprise, with its roots in praxis as well as in theory.

NOTES

1. Several external changes that deeply affected the city and the region in the 1970s help to account for this dramatic demographic shift. Briefly stated, these include the federal government's recognition of mainland China and the exclusion of Taiwan from official diplomatic status; the emergence of the Pacific Rim as an interrelated economy, along with more lenient U.S. immigration policies for this region; incoming immigrant Asian families' dissatisfaction with conditions in older ethnic neighborhoods in nearby Los Angeles; and the movement of middle-class Latino families from East Los Angeles to the San Gabriel Valley suburbs.

2. Some of the recent literature on the Monterey Park and Alhambra region includes Calderon (1989, 1990), Fong (1994), Morton (1989, 1992, 1995) Horton and Calderon (1990), Pardo (1990), Saito (1993), and Tseng (1994).

3. Pitzer College, with a student population of 730, is a four-year liberal arts college in the process of expanding its efforts to include

multicultural understanding and community outreach in its curriculum. As part of its educational objectives, the College is emphasizing the need for students to appreciate other cultures through direct involvement in institutions that advance the development of a multicultural world. These objectives have already produced results: numerous professors and students have taken up the challenge of involving themselves in communities that are microcosms of the larger demographic changes occurring in California.

4. Because we learned about the grant funding at the beginning of the spring semester, we had no time to develop a separate class to focus on the project. Consequently 20 students volunteered from four different classes that we were teaching. With very little time for pretraining, we met with students every two weeks and gave them introductory material from Lofland and Lofland's (1995) *Analyzing Social Settings: A Guide to Qualitative Observation and Analysis*. We reached an agreement with Alhambra School District administrators that our students would observe classrooms in the three high schools in the district. In return, we promised a final report outlining the students' findings.

5. It was crucial to explain to the district administrators, who generally had experience only with surveys and quantitative evaluation research, that qualitative researchers strive to develop concepts, insights, and understandings from patterns that emerge in their field notes. We stressed that the strength of this methodology is its flexibility and responsiveness to situations; ideally it allows the researcher to understand how social realities arise and operate, and how the various expectations and perceptions that people bring to particular settings shape individuals' behavior and organizations' responses.

6. A School Board report for the academic year 1990-1991, written by Assistant Superintendent of Pupil Services Diane Saurenman (1992), showed that Latinos have the highest dropout rate of any ethnic group in the three high schools. In the four years from 1989 to 1992, Latinos accounted for 50 to 55 percent of the dropouts, as compared with 32 to 46 percent of the Asian students at Alhambra High School. In those four years, Latinos made up 57 to 65 percent of the dropouts at San Gabriel High School, as compared with 24 to 36 percent for Asians. In 1990-1992, Latinos at all three high schools also ranked lowest of all ethnic groups in completing college preparatory requirements. At Alhambra High School, only 17 percent of Latino students completed these requirements, as compared with 38 percent of Asian students and 26 percent of all others; at Mark Keppel High School, only 3 percent of Latinos completed them, as compared with 29 percent of Asians and 12 percent of all others. These figures were also related to postgraduation aspirations by ethnicity. Between 1989

and 1992, surveys found that 80 percent of Asian graduating seniors at all three Alhambra District high schools aspired to attend four-year colleges; only 11 percent of Latinos had such plans. Instead, the great majority of Latinos at Alhambra High School indicated that they would opt to attend vocational/technical schools, enlist in the military, or enter the labor force following high school graduation.

7. As readings in this course, we also used Jonathan Kozol's (1991) *Savage Inequalities*, Mike Rose's (1989) *Lives on the Boundary*, Jeannie Oakes's (1985) *Keeping Track*, and Michael W. Apple's (1993) *Official Knowledge*. Each of these readings underscored the structural foundations of inequality in the educational system. Other books that could be used for this purpose are Ronald Takaki's (1993) *A Different Mirror*, Stephen Steinberg's (1981) *The Ethnic Myth*, and Michael Omi and Howard Winant's (1994) *Racial Formation in the United States*.

REFERENCES

Apple, Michael. 1993. *Official Knowledge: Democratic Education in a Conservative Age*. New York: Routledge.

Bricher, Marie R. 1992. "Teaching Introductory Sociology: Using Aspects of the Classroom as Sociological Events." *Teaching Sociology* 20:270-75.

Calderon, Jose. 1989. "How the English Only Initiative Passed in California." Pp. 93-109 in *Estudios Chicanos and the Politics of Community*, edited by Mary Romero and Cordelia Candelaria. Oakland: Cragmont Publications.

----------. 1990. "Latinos and Ethnic Conflict in Suburbia: The Case of Monterey Park." *Latino Studies Journal* 1(2):23-32.

Flint, William. 1993. "Ideological Contradiction and the Problem of Closure in the Sociology Capstone Course." *Teaching Sociology* 21:254-57.

Fong, Timothy P. 1994. *The First Suburban Chinatown: The Remaking of Monterey Park, California*. Philadelphia: Temple University Press.

Horton, John. 1989. "The Politics of Ethnic Change: Grass-Roots Responses to Economic and Demographic Restructuring in Monterey Park, California." *Urban Geography* 10:578-92.

----------. 1992. "The Politics of Diversity." Pp. 215-45 in *Shaping Diversity*, edited by Louise Lamphere. Chicago: University of Chicago Press.

Horton, John and Jose Calderon. 1990. "Language Struggles in a Changing California Community." Pp. 186-94 in *Language Loyalties*, edited by Jim Crawford. Chicago: University of Chicago Press.

Horton, John, with Jose Calderon, Mary Pardo, Leland Saito, Linda Shaw, and Yen-Fen Tseng. 1995. *The Politics of Diversity: Immigration, Resistance, and Change in Monterey Park, California*. Philadelphia: Temple University Press.

Kozol, Jonathan. 1991. *Savage Inequalities*. NewYork: Crown.

Lofland, John and Lyn H. Lofland. 1995. *Analyzing Social Settings: A Guide to Qualitative Observation and Analysis*. Belmont, CA: Wadsworth.

Miller, Wesley. 1990. "Internships, the Liberal Arts, and Participant Observation." *Teaching Sociology* 18:78-82.

Neapolitan, Jerry. 1992. "The Internship Experience and Clarification of Career Choice." *Teaching Sociology* 20:222-31.

Oakes, Jeannie. 1985. *Keeping Track: How Schools Structure Inequality*. New Haven: Yale University Press.

Omi, Michael and Howard Clamant. 1994. *Racial Formation in the United States*. New York: Routledge.

Pardo, Mary Santoli. 1990. "Identity and Resistance: Mexican American Women and Grassroots Activism in Two Los Angeles Communities." Doctoral dissertation, University of California, Los Angeles.

Porter, Judith R. and Lisa B. Schwartz. 1993. "Experiential Service-Based Learning: An Integrated HIV/AIDS Education Model for College Campuses." *Teaching Sociology* 21:409-15.

Rose, Mike. 1989. *Lives on the Boundary*. New York: Penguin.

Saito, Leland. 1993. "Asian Americans and Latinos in San Gabriel Valley, California: Ethnic Political Cooperation and Redistricting, 1990-92." *Amerasia Journal* 19(2):55-68.

Saurenman, Dianne. 1992. *Alhambra School Board Report According to Policy and Regulations 5113.2*, Alhambra, CA: Alhambra School District.

Schmid, Thomas J. 1992. "Classroom-Based Ethnography: A Research Pedagogy." *Teaching Sociology* 20: 28-35.

----------. 1993. "Bringing Sociology to Life: The Other Capstone Mandate." *Teaching Sociology* 21:219-22.

Schultz, Martin. 1992. "Internships in Sociology: Liability Issues and Risk Management Measures." *Teaching Sociology* 20:183-91.

Steinberg, Stephen. 1981. *The Ethnic Myth: Race, Class, and Ethnicity in America*. Boston: Beacon.

Takaki, Ronald. 1993. *A Different Mirror: A History of Multicultural America*. Boston: Little, Brown.

Tseng, Yen-Fen. 1994. "The Chinese Ethnic Economy: San Gabriel Valley, Los Angeles County." *Journal of Urban Affairs* 16:169-89.

U.S. Bureau of the Census. 1980. *Statistical Abstract*. Washington, DC: U.S. Government Printing Office.

----------. 1990. *Statistical Abstract.* Washington, DC: U.S. Government Printing Office.

Jose Calderon is an associate professor of sociology at Pitzer College. His scholarly research and community involvements focus on the multiethnic coalitions that have developed in Monterey Park, California, part of the Alhambra School District. In his courses on race and ethnic relations, stratification, and urban ethnic movements at Pitzer, he has involved students in a varied of community-based projects; e-mail: JOSE_CALDERON@EMAIL.PITZER.EDU.

Betty Farrell is an associate professor of sociology at Pitzer College with teaching and research interests in family, gender, and culture. Recently she has directed a grant-funded institutional project to develop more service-learning opportunities in the college curriculum. Address correspondence to the authors at Pitzer College, 1050 North Mills Ave., Claremont, CA 91711; e-mail: BETTY_FARRELL@EMAIL.PITZER.EDU.

QUESTIONS FOR DISCUSSION

1. This research is called "ethnographic" by the authors. How would you define ethnographic research, based on what these authors say about their study?

2. Compare the methods of this study to the methods of the other research studies in this chapter, e.g. Ballard & Coates, Hastie & Pickwell, or Brown & Vincent. The latter studies are called "quantitative" as opposed to "qualitative" research. How would you define the difference?

3. What kinds of insights does ethnographic (qualitative) research yield that can't be found in quantitative (statistical) research?

4. Does the fact that this study includes no statistical data make it less credible?

5. Summarize briefly the conclusions reached by the authors. What did they (and their students) learn about conflict in public schools?

6. What did the authors learn about this type of experiential teaching? Is the kind of internship experience described in this article something you would want to try yourself?

7. Can you think of other disciplines besides sociology which might benefit from experiential teaching? Have you ever been involved in anything similar?

8. The documentation style used by this journal differs slightly from APA style. What are the differences?

3

Readings from the Humanities and Arts

The humanities and arts have as an overall goal the exploration and explanation of the human experience. Writing formats and organizational patterns in the humanities tend to be less rigid and more widely varied than those followed by the sciences and social sciences. Typical patterns include problem/solution, question/answer, cause/effect, and comparison/contrast. Each of these organizational patterns helps the author to communicate his or her argument, generally stated in the form of a thesis, to the journal's readers.

Holland's article, taken from a philosophy journal, poses the question "What's wrong with telling the truth?" Through her extended analysis she argues that gossip is not frivolous or trivial, but rather a serious moral issue. Civello's article, from a literature journal, analyzes the novels of Stevie Smith for their anti-Semitic content. Like Holland, she argues that this anti-Semitic language can be morally harmful and that literary scholars need to bring these attitudes into public scrutiny. The next article, by Ambler, is less of a thesis-driven argument and more of a straightforward report. She informs readers of the history of Indian tribes and atomic weapons. She does imply that tribes have become more mature in their dealings with atomic issues, but largely the article reports various instances where tribes have interacted with government and industry.

Zilberg's article on Zimbabweans and country music, published in a popular culture journal, straddles the fence between social sciences and humanities. His is a research report, based on participant-observation, typical of the social sciences. But the subject matter, popular culture, is usually considered a subject for the humanities. Stinespring's article on multiculturalism is reminiscent of the curricular arguments found in the first two parts of this book. And finally, the Allen article from a music educator's journal is both informative and instructive.

Taken together, these articles show the enormous range of writing to be found in the humanities and arts. All of the articles included in Part Three are reproduced in their entirety from the journals in which they were originally published, by permission of the publisher and/or author(s).

What's Wrong with Telling the Truth? An Analysis of Gossip

Margaret G. Holland, U of Northern Iowa

Speech, which is the most pleasant and human of social ties, is made inhuman and unsocial by those who use it badly and wantonly ...
Plutarch[1]

Everyday conversation is not necessarily a morally neutral activity and certain ways of describing people can be corrupting and wrong.
Iris Murdoch[2]

The question of whether and under what conditions it is morally permissible to lie has received a good deal of attention, whereas questions concerning possible moral restrictions on truth-telling have been relatively neglected.[3] My concern here is to discuss one form of communication, gossip, and to examine the question of whether and why there may be moral objections to this type of truth-telling.[4]

There are a number of problems related either to gossip or truth-telling that I shall not address. For example, though gossip need not always involve telling the truth, I am not concerned with instances of gossip that involve lies or speculations. I also shall not discuss the question of whether or when one should "varnish the truth." Moreover, though in some circumstances lying is morally preferable to truth-telling, that issue does not fall within the purview of this paper.[5]

Closer to my concern are circumstances in which one doubts the moral wisdom of speaking the truth, circumstances in which silence may be preferable to either telling the truth or lying. The types of cases I have in mind include: testifying in court against one's spouse, becoming a political informant and denouncing members of one's community, outing closeted homosexuals, talking about persons in a manner which supports stereotypes and prejudice. Even if it were best to tell the truth in some cases which fall under these descriptions, there are surely cases in which truth-telling is not the best alternative.

In this essay I shall develop a provisional definition of gossip, discuss some motives, functions, and consequences of gossip, and con-

From the *American Philosophical Quarterly* (1996, Vol. 33.2, pp. 197-209).
Reprinted by permission of the author and publisher.

WHAT'S WRONG WITH TELLING THE TRUTH?

clude with an examination of its moral nature. I organize my discussion around the following set of questions: What is gossip? Why do we do it? How does gossip function? What are its consequences? and, What is the moral nature of gossip?

WHAT IS GOSSIP?

Gossip, you might say, . . . is candor at other people's expense.
Nikolai Aristides[6]

The dictionary defines the noun "gossip" as, "[a] person who habitually retails facts, rumors, or behind-the-scenes information of an intimate, personal, or sensational nature."[7] The verb is defined as, "to converse idly . . . about other persons."[8] "Gossip" originally comes from "godsib," meaning "one who has contracted spiritual affinity with another by acting as a sponsor at a baptism." In other words, what we would now call a godparent. It then came to refer to "a familiar acquaintance, friend, chum," and specifically was applied to "a woman's female friends [who were] invited to be present at a birth."[9]

The element of inclusion in the private lives of persons outside one's immediate family is present throughout the various permutations of the word. The notion of gossip as referring to discussions of the private lives of other persons may be traced to this access to the sphere of friends, as well as to notions about the sort of talk in which women engaged while gathered to await a birth.[10]

I understand the term to refer to certain sorts of communication (often conversation) about absent persons.[11] The absence of the person who is being discussed is not merely accidental; the conversation would change in tone, if not in substance, were its subject to enter. Most commonly, gossip concerns persons with whom the participants are familiar but to whom they are not deeply attached.[12] Topics of discussion in gossip are of a personal, though not necessarily a private, nature. Gossip may involve revealing confidential information, discussing new information, or commenting on public information of a personal nature. So, for example, gossip may involve telling a third party what a friend has confided in secret (but not telling state secrets), talking over the latest news about a colleague's new job offer (but not reading aloud published announcements of new appointments), discussing someone's style of dress or other aspects of physical appearance (but not describing this year's skirt lengths).

Though there are certain topics about which one cannot gossip (e.g. one may gossip about mathematicians but not about mathematics), there are many topics of discussion that may be gossip in certain circumstances,

143

but not in others. Without knowing the specific features of a particular conversation (including the motives and roles of the speakers), one cannot judge whether or not the conversation is an instance of gossip.[13] So, while certain topics are ruled out as gossip, knowing the topic is not sufficient for identifying an instance of gossip.

Gossip is usually evaluative.[14] Concerning the nature of the evaluations involved there is general, though not universal, agreement:

> It would be absurd for a gossip to retell to story of a son who behaved only with proper respect for his father . . .[15]
>
> Gossip contains a piece of news involving morally dubious if not outright reprehensible actions.[16]
>
> The very idea that purely complimentary remarks about a third party amounts to gossip is counterintuitive.[17]

To praise or compliment an absent person is not gossip. While some who write about gossip believe it always involves moral criticism (as can be inferred from the second quoted passage above), it is more common to hold (as I do) that the kind of evaluation involved in gossip is of a critical, but not necessarily a moral, nature. Gossip can concern style of dress, for example, without any suggestion that the style of dress is morally offensive.

The norms that gossip relies on for its evaluations are generally unstated. Gossip does not involve reflection on its assumptions.[18] Most commonly, the subject of gossip is viewed as failing to live up to the (assumed to be) relevant standards, and is directly or indirectly criticized for this failure. It is this feature of gossip that has led sociologists to claim that it serves to enforce social norms.

Most gossip is comparative in the sense that the speaker at least implicitly suggests that he or she is both unlike and superior to the person discussed. Gossip that conveys news may be comparative in the sense that the speaker presents him or herself as being more "in-the-know" than the person spoken to.

Of course, not all evaluative and comparative communication about the affairs of persons who are not privy to the communication is gossip. In addition to topics, evaluations, and comparisons, the motives and roles of the speakers are relevant in distinguishing gossip from other types of communication:

> The same information may be gossip or non-gossip depending on who gives it to whom; the communication that Mrs. A's child is illegitimate is not gossip if it is occurring between two social workers acting in that capacity, while it is gossip if Mrs. A's neighbors talk about it.[19]

It is possible for neighbors to discuss the birth of an "illegitimate" child without gossiping, since one or more of the other conditions may be absent. However, conversations between or among professionals who are concerned solely with their formal obligations to absent clients/patients are not instances of gossip, though the information discussed may be unambiguously personal.[20] Such professional communication differs from gossip in its motive and function, as well as in the role of the speakers and the nature of its evaluations. Most significantly, it is motivated by professional or institutional concerns; it functions within a formal setting; and its evaluations are guided by professional or institutional criteria.

As Aaron Ben-Ze'ev has indicated, *gossip* is not a concept that can be rigidly demarcated. In "The Vindication of Gossip" Ben-Ze'ev argues that gossip is a member of a prototypical, rather than a binary, category.

> Binary categories provide a clear criterion that constitutes the sufficient and necessary conditions for membership. It is an all or nothing category... Membership in a prototypical category... is determined by an item's degree of similarity to the best example in the category ...[21]

I agree with Ben-Ze'ev's claim that one cannot cite necessary and sufficient conditions in order to define gossip. However, one can describe what is typical of gossip. My discussion of what gossip is has taken its non-binary status into account by ruling out certain sorts of communication while not providing a precise definition.

Because gossip cannot be rigidly demarcated, there are, of course, borderline cases. Therefore, discussing its similarities to and differences from related concepts will help to specify further what is commonly meant by "gossip." Toward that end, I shall distinguish gossip from indiscretion, rumor, denunciation and chatter.

Indiscretion is often a matter of either communicating too much information or of communicating inappropriate information, though indiscretion may be expressed in conduct as well as communication. Indiscretion, unlike gossip, is not necessarily about persons; for example, business plans or military strategies may be the subject of indiscretion. When an indiscretion is about a person it does not necessarily occur behind

145

the subject's back; one may be indiscreet about oneself or be asked an indiscreet question about one's own affairs. Therefore, while gossip is often indiscreet, i.e. involves inappropriate disclosure, indiscretion is less likely to be gossip.

It is often difficult to draw a line between rumor and gossip, but the two may be contrasted by pointing out that the information rumor conveys is unsubstantiated, whereas the information gossip conveys is often known to be true. Moreover, the subject category of rumor is larger than that of gossip; events such as wars and stock-market collapses, as well as the lives of absent persons, may be the subject of rumor.[22]

Though the term "rumor" does not refer to instances of conveying accurate, complete, and well-founded information, it can refer to instances of communication in which the topic of discussion is of appropriate concern to the discussants. So, for example, though a possible plant closing is of proper concern to the plant's employees, it may be that they are not provided with adequate information, and rumors therefore may circulate within the plant. Gossip, on the other hand, is likely to involve topics which are not of proper concern to the speakers.

"Denounce" is often used to refer to the acts of informants who supply authorities with information about the activities of persons in their community.[23] The information may be of a political or personal nature, and it is conveyed behind the back of the person who is informed against, normally with the awareness that it is likely to cause damage. Gossip lacks the gravity of denunciation. In part, this is because denouncing someone usually has more destructive potential than gossiping does. It is also the case that the content that is conveyed through denunciation is likely to be substantive rather than trivial. So, for example, political activity rather than the value of a new engagement ring is a likely topic for denunciation. On the other hand, denouncing and gossiping are similar in that they both involve the secret sharing of information about a third party, often to the detriment of the subject.

Though in some instances chatter is very similar to gossip, the former may usefully be distinguished from the latter. I understand "chatter" to apply to conversation that is informal and casual, that takes as its subject matter topics which are of no great importance, and that is not directed toward a purpose beyond itself. Under *chatter* I include small-talk, catching-up talk, and telling-one's-day. "Telling-one's-day" is self-explanatory. By "catching-up talk" I mean conversation about what has been happening in the lives of friends, family members, and acquaintances. Certainly, in some instances it would be difficult to distinguish such conversations from gossip, but straightforward reports about vacations, jobs, moves, and graduations are generally not thought of as instances of gossip. Describing catching-up talk, Sabini and Silver write:

> It is distinguished from our prototype [of gossip] by: (1) we readily admit to this sort of talk; and (2) we wouldn't be embarrassed by the subject's overhearing us.[24]

Both these points may be extended to help distinguish not only catching-up talk, but also chatter, from gossip.

The following distinctions also apply. Chatter is always conversation, gossip is not. Chatter is not necessarily about persons or personal matters; it may, for example, be about the weather or the scenery. When chatter is about persons it does not necessarily exclude the person being discussed; one may chatter about one's own as well as others' vacation plans. Chatter is not especially evaluative or comparative. Chatter is talk that simply fills the time and has no purpose beyond itself. Gossip, on the other hand, "is not merely *idle* talk, but talk with a social purpose."[25]

In summary, there are a number of features which one may examine in order to distinguish gossip from related activities. Indiscretion, rumor, and chatter all have broader topic categories than does gossip. Moreover, when indiscretion and chatter involve communication about persons, they do not necessarily exclude the person being discussed. Indiscretion, rumor, and chatter are not especially evaluative or comparative. Denunciation is closest to gossip in that both concern persons, are evaluative, and occur behind the subject's back. The sort of activities which are reported by an informant are activities that fall outside the bounds of accepted norms, as is often the case with the activities discussed in gossip.

WHY DO WE GOSSIP? HOW DOES GOSSIP FUNCTION? WHAT ARE ITS CONSEQUENCES?

Sociologists and anthropologists have produced most of the scholarly writing on gossip. Their primary concern has been to describe its social function and, to a lesser extent, motives for gossiping. In this section I shall discuss some common motives for gossip, its social function, and its possible consequences.

Motives

Part of the universal attraction of gossip is the occasion it affords for comparing oneself with others, usually silently, while seeming to be speaking strictly about someone else.   Sissela Bok[26]

Gossip appears to be universal among cultures as well as among individuals. Most people find it entertaining, relaxing, and fun. It feeds curiosity about the lives of other persons, allows one (implicitly) to compare oneself favorably with others, provides the opportunity to display wit and humor, creates an intimate atmosphere, and fills time in a manner that is undemanding. Appearing to be "in-the-know" and being the first to tell interesting news provide part of the pleasure of, and motivation for, gossiping. Moreover, since gossip involves sharing personal information about other persons, one is able to use it as evidence of one's social connections. Gossip may, therefore, be used for social positioning as well as for enhancing prestige and power.

The intimate atmosphere created by gossip can contribute to establishing bonds among the participants and may serve as a step in forming friendships. Instead of indicating social ties and establishing intimacy, gossip may also serve to mask awkward social situations in which the participants find they have little in common and nothing of substance to say to each other.[27]

In addition to motives such as the desire for intimacy, the satisfaction of curiosity, the enhancement of social position, and the easing of awkward situations, gossip may also, of course, be motivated by anger or malice. For example, my dislike of someone or resentment about how he or she has treated me may be vented through gossiping. In addition to simply letting off steam, I may also use gossip to try to separate the person at whom I am angry from those to whom I speak, as well as from those to whom the story may be conveyed.

Sociologists who study gossip are correct, I believe, when they state that "gossip seems motivated primarily by ego and status needs."[28] Whether one gossips in order to appear entertaining and clever, to establish and exhibit social connections, or to satisfy anger or envy, in each case one makes an effort to improve one's image in one's own eyes and in the eyes of others.

It is the evaluative and comparative nature of gossip that allows it to be used as a vehicle for enhancing self-satisfaction. For example, in formulating an incisive description of someone's foibles, it is likely that I believe I appear to be more on top of things than the subject of my comments. When I make reference to my social connections, I indicate that I have access to interesting information. Finally, when I convey negative information about someone at whom I am angry, I gain the sense of having balanced the scales in my favor.

In discussing motives for gossip, I do not mean to suggest that one is necessarily conscious of any particular motive when one gossips, only that the motives I have mentioned are the sort that drive gossiping. For the most part, one simply enjoys gossiping and no more examines one's motives in doing so than one reflects upon the underlying norms on which gossip's evaluations are based.

Function

In *Discreet Indiscretions* Jorg Bergmann examines three current views of the social function of gossip: gossip as a means of social control, gossip as a mechanism for preserving social groups, and gossip as a technique of information management.[29] Bergmann describes this research as having found that gossip functions to preserve the status quo, particularly the norms and moral values conventional within a group. It is also thought to strengthen group identity and cohesion by providing a sense of belonging to a limited circle and by concealing conflicts. Moreover, sociologists claim that individuals use gossip to their advantage both in order to acquire useful information and to improve their standing by showing that they measure up favorably to accepted standards.[30]

In their discussions of gossip, sociologists and anthropologists speak, for the most part, in approving tones. Yet their work lacks reflective analysis. For example, the claim that gossip functions to preserve social groups does not take serious account of either the disharmony gossip may sow or the potentially corrosive effect of concealed conflicts. More importantly, these scholars appear to approve of gossip's reinforcement of conventional values, yet they express no awareness of the need to examine the moral nature of the reinforced norms prior to granting such approval. Surprisingly, Ben-Ze'ev, a philosopher, also seems to endorse conventional values uncritically. He writes:

> The violation of social norms presumably justifies the right of other people to speak about it, and in this sense, the object of gossip (as that of gloating) deserves the misfortune of having his or her intimate life be the topic of other people's conversations.[31]

Such uncritical acceptance of social norms is inexplicable. One need think only of the treatment of women who have varied in their actions from what was prescribed by gender roles, or of homosexuals in homophobic cultures, to realize that the violation of social norms provides no justification for having one's life taken as a topic for gossip.

Joel Feinberg discusses a similar issue in *Harmless Wrongdoing*. In his discussion of wrongful gain, Feinberg describes one of the categories of blackmail as follows:

> Threats to expose some innocent characteristic or activity that is not objectively discreditable but would in fact damage the victim's reputation in some benighted group if it were disclosed.[32]

Feinberg mentions homosexuality, the use of psychoanalysis, and having a black ancestor as examples of what he means by "innocent characteristic or activity." Such matters are the subject of both gossip and blackmail because they violate the social norms of certain groups. Discussing the right to reveal such information and demand money for silence Feinberg writes:

> There is then no plausible ground for positing a moral duty to disclose the embarrassing information. In fact there is good reason for affirming a moral duty not to make the disclosures, which is to say that one does not have a moral right to do so. Thus it would appear, morally speaking at least, that one may not in this way extract money by threatening to do what one has no right to do.[33]

Feinberg is correct; the violation of a social norm bestows no rights on third parties.[34]

While the empirical claim that gossip functions to bolster conventional values is plausible, to move from this observation to the normative position that views gossip as possessing positive value requires (at the very least) critical analysis of the norms gossip reinforces. Such analysis is missing from the sociological and anthropological work. Therefore, while I do not doubt that gossip may commonly function, as sociologists and anthropologists have suggested, to preserve the status quo, to strengthen group identity, or to help individuals acquire information, noting gossip's likely social functions does not inform one of its moral nature.

Consequences

In addition to its social function, gossip has consequences for individuals who gossip, those who hear gossip and those who are gossiped about. (Virtually everyone falls into all three categories.) Some of the moral concerns I shall address in the next section pertain to the consequences of gossip. Since a survey of all the likely consequences of gossip would be too wide ranging, in this section I shall focus primarily on the consequences for the person discussed; I begin, however, by mentioning possible positive consequences for the speakers.

Gossip may bring the participants closer together; it may, in the words of Patricia Meyer Spacks, "create and intensify human connection."[35] Sabini and Silver also suggest that gossip may make it easier for us to interact with someone with whom we are dissatisfied: "the most prudent way to insult someone and continue to do business with her is to insult her behind her back."[36] It even has been claimed that gossip contributes to a low crime-rate in rural communities. In an article on the crime-rate in Northern Ireland, an Ulster criminologist suggests that "a strong network of gossip" makes it difficult for criminals to "sneak into an area unnoticed."[37]

Though gossip may help develop intimate relationships among the participants, for the person being discussed it may damage relationships. For example, finding that a friend has gossiped about matters one thinks of as confidential can lead to a lost sense of security within the relationship (as well as more broadly), and to broken trust.[38] Gossip may damage relationships with persons who hear stories and may negatively affect the job security of the person gossiped about. Gossip may also serve to perpetuate the isolation of an outsider. In discussing a widow, Bergmann writes, "persons without family relations are the favorite subjects of gossip in all communities. They have no one whose presence would exercise an inhibitory effect on the emergence of gossip" (p. 52). Gossip may lead, then, to informal shunning, making it difficult for the individual gossiped about to become accepted as a member of the community. Sociological studies have shown that gossip may also result in teasing, mockery, and trick-playing.[39]

For the person discussed, gossip may bring about significant damaging consequences, it may cause a slight and temporary sense of alienation, or it may have no discernable consequences. There are, no doubt, instances of gossip in which the participants are aware that significant damage is likely to follow. However, while I do not want to slight the importance of harmful consequences for specific individuals, my analysis of the moral nature of gossip will concentrate on what I take to be more pervasive features.

WHAT IS THE MORAL NATURE OF GOSSIP?

Acting rightly toward another person does not necessarily, in fact more often does not, involve face-to-face encounters. Iris Murdoch[40]

Before discussing the more substantial aspects of gossip's moral nature, it is necessary to say a word about the common description and criticism of gossip as trivial or frivolous talk. In her book *Gossip* Patricia Meyer Spacks states that the "moral insufficiency of gossip" has been located accurately in its "frivolous modes" (p. 20). Spacks then proceeds to attempt to rescue gossip from "moral insufficiency" by claiming that there is a type of gossip that is serious as opposed to frivolous.

All things being equal, to say of something that it is frivolous or trivial is not to offer a moral criticism, any more than to say of something that it is serious is to offer moral praise. If Spacks is correct in her assumptions about the moral nature of the frivolous and the serious, it would follow that the life with the least frivolity is, morally speaking, better. Yet this is hardly a tenable position.

The relation of gossip to the frivolous/trivial and serious is as follows. Gossip often treats what is serious in a manner that is frivolous or trivial. Concerning this feature of gossip Gabriele Taylor writes:

> Gossip is often thought of as "trivial talk" and maybe it can be said to be trivial in this sense: it is not its subject matter that is trivial, but the manner in which it is handled. Gossipers trivialize experience by ignoring the impact with which the author of the experience will in some way have to cope. Thus they distort and belittle that person's experience.[41]

So, for example, gossip may involve casual and superficial talk about a third party's divorce.[42] Gossip is also likely to treat what is genuinely trivial in a serious manner. An instance of such gossip might involve sober discussions about the style of a third party's clothing, thus giving serious attention to matters of little importance.

It is characteristic, then, of gossip to fail to give matters their due regard; gossip often involves a mismatch between the tone and substance of the discussion. Such a mismatch may simply reveal superficiality or it may constitute a failure of empathy and moral understanding.

There are moral dimensions of gossip more serious than the mismatch between tone and substance. In my analysis of the moral nature of gossip, I shall focus on the impact of gossip on the social atmosphere, how one is treating others when one gossips about them, and the relation between gossip and moral character.

When I refer to the impact gossip has on the social atmosphere I have in mind Mill's concern in *On Liberty* with the despotism of custom exerted through the informal sanction of public opinion.[43] Mill is concerned that the freedom of the individual to think and live as she sees fit is significantly interfered with through mechanisms of informal censure. Since gossip is often concerned with what varies from the recognized norm, it lends itself to being used to create an atmosphere that inhibits and narrows the individual's freedom to live without unnecessary interference. That gossip is used in this manner is supported by the empirical research cited in my discussion of its function. Similarly, gossip has been described as a mechanism for policing the individual and community.[44] There is, then, reason to believe that gossip contributes to the culture of censure to which Mill so strongly objects.

Moreover, Mill's own experience of being the subject of gossip may well have influenced his recognition of how informal sanctions can thwart individual freedom. Gossip about his relationship with Harriet Taylor led them, during the twenty years of their friendship prior to their marriage, to hide their meetings, to withdraw from society, and to mislead people about their travel plans.[45] Though I am not going to pursue an approach informed by Mill's *On Liberty*, it is worth contemplating the moral nature of participating in informal sanctioning of the sort he discusses.

How are we treating others when we gossip about them? Certainly in some cases we are malicious, more often we are dismissive or intrusive. Generally, however, when gossiping, one is aware simply of the pleasure of sharing confidences, a pleasure by its nature voyeuristic and often titillating. Whichever of the myriad individual motives lies behind specific instances of gossip, virtually all gossip is experienced as pleasurable. What, then, about it is so commonly enjoyed? Gossip involves viewing others in a way which makes one feel better about oneself; it enhances self-satisfaction.[46] The link between the pleasure of gossip and self-satisfaction has been noted by a number of authors. George Herbert Mead in his discussion of the desire to feel oneself superior to others writes:

> There is a certain enjoyableness about the misfortunes of other people, especially those gathered about their personality. It finds its expression in what we term gossip, even mischievous gossip. We have to be on our guard against it.[47]

On the same topic, but writing more recently, Ben-Ze'ev suggests that:

> The immoral behavior of famous people, reported in gossip columns, enhances our self-respect. Celebrity gossip allows us to draw comfort from other people's misfortune.[48]

Later he notes that a person with a low self-image "may gain some respect by conveying information which is slightly damaging to others" (p. 19). Mead and Ben-Ze'ev agree that we tend to derive a sense of self-satisfaction from discussing others' misfortunes or inadequacies; Mead sees this enjoyment as morally troubling, Ben-Ze'ev does not.

Are there moral problems with deriving pleasure from communicating about the lives of others behind their backs so as to enhance one's self-satisfaction by (implicitly) comparing oneself favorably to their weaknesses, mistakes, etc? [49]

In order to reflect upon how one is treating the subject of gossip, it is helpful to consider an activity that shares with gossip the characteristic of occurring behind the subject's back: furtively observing someone for pleasure (that is, acting as a peeping Tom).

There is, as far as I am aware, no doubt that peeping Toms enjoy peeping. Moreover, there is little reason to believe that the person who is observed unawares suffers any consequences. Yet peeping is considered not only a moral, but a criminal, offense. Why is deriving pleasure from observing someone behind her back considered so much worse than deriving pleasure from talking behind her back?

The furtive voyeur circumvents the agency of the subject of his gaze; he conceals his activity in order to treat her as an object for his own gratification. Peeping is a breach of privacy for the purpose of the agent's pleasure; it is non-consensual. The following characteristics are shared by peeping and gossiping: they take as their objects persons rather than things, they occur behind the subject's back, they are not guided by concern for the subject, they would cease if the subject entered, they focus on personal features of the subject, and they are pleasurable for the agent. In both peeping and gossiping the person who is the subject of the activity is used to entertain or amuse the agent(s), and is not in a position to decline such use. Though relatively few of us take pleasure in peeping as opposed to gossiping, that alone cannot provide justification for the difference in how these two activities are understood. Yet, I am unable to discover a morally salient difference between the two that accounts for their being understood to be so morally dissimilar.[50]

When examining the question of how one is treating the subject of gossip it may be useful to think along Kantian lines. Specifically, one might ask whether one could wish to be treated in the same manner, whether one is treating the subject of gossip with respect, whether one is using that person merely as a means to one's own pleasure. It is unlikely that gossip could meet the requirements of either the first or second formulation of the categorical imperative. It is unlikely that the gossiper could will to be so treated, and it is also unlikely that the subject of gossip could be said to be treated as an end. While I am not suggesting that gossip is a grievous breach of the categorical imperative, it is doubtful that when gossiping one treats the subject of the discussion in a manner which he or she too could share.

Some of the arguments philosophers, including Kant, have given for the conclusion that lying is immoral may be used to argue that gossiping is immoral. Lying has been criticized for, among other things, undermining trust and confidence between friends, damaging human community, being driven by morally dubious motives, and expressing a failure to properly respect persons.[51] Gossip can be criticized for the same reasons. Gossip may undermine trust by placing in the hands of a third party what was meant to be kept in confidence between friends. It can damage community life by closing some persons out of the "charmed circle" and by serving as a substitute for forthright airing of disagreements and face-to-face discussions. Gossip, while it conveys true information, may have morally suspect motives ranging from maliciousness to jealousy to anger. Finally, even when its motives are more benign, gossip often involves a manner of discussing a person that falls short of respect. It may also express a smug and less than respectful attitude toward the listener.

In considering the relation between gossip and the moral character of the gossiper the following considerations are most salient: the significance of what one takes pleasure in as both a contributor to and indicator of the quality of moral character, and the impact of gossip on the clarity of both one's perception of other people and understanding of oneself.

Plato and Aristotle make note of what a powerful force pleasure is in directing the actions of human beings. Furthermore, they draw attention both to the importance of habituating oneself to derive pleasure and pain from the proper things, and to the relation between pleasure and virtue. Concerning the relation between pleasure and character Philippa Foot writes:

> Pleasure in the good fortune of others is, one thinks, the sign of a generous spirit; and small reactions of pleasure and displeasure often the surest sign of a man's moral disposition. [52]

What one derives pleasure from forms as well as reveals one's character. Deriving pleasure from talking behind someone's back in a manner that is intrusive, gloating, or dismissive runs contrary to the development and maintenance of the generous spirit that takes pleasure in others' good fortune.

Gossip can blunt one's understanding of one's own character as well as the character of others. Gossip can both increase the information one has available and diminish one's understanding. Part of the experience of gossiping is having a sense of insight into another person; one sees clearly that some aspect of his behavior or person is faulty. One has the impression of being an acute judge of character and conduct, and of not sharing the faults under discussion. Yet this sense of insight is deceptive. One is unaware, at least temporarily, of the person's strengths and the relation of his strengths and weaknesses to each other. One does not consider his character as a whole or the wider circumstances of his life. A sense of proportion is lost; news loom large. Moreover, one is nicely oblivious to one's own flaws and sharply aware of one's strengths. This may be very pleasant but it can hardly contribute to understanding, good judgment, perceptiveness or empathy.

In *Metaphysics as a Guide to Morals* Iris Murdoch writes:

> The person who regularly refrains from joining in spiteful gossip . . . lives "in a different world" and sees other people with a difference. The seen world . . . [strengthens] the more virtuous desires. . . . (p. 381)

Murdoch's point is that one's manner of speaking about other persons influences one's perception of them. Not only is the world one sees made different by habituating oneself to refrain from gossip and mockery (Murdoch's examples), but one's desires are also influenced for the better. Because empathy is often a matter of sharing another person's perspective, and because acting well towards someone (if it is not merely accidental) requires seeing her and her situation clearly, there is reason to avoid talk which may erect small preemptive barriers to discernment.

There is, then, good reason to believe that gossip contributes to a culture of censure, involves treating others in a manner which one would not want to be treated oneself, and coarsens one's perception. Enough doubt is thereby cast on its moral nature to show that it is preferable to avoid rather than indulge in this small pleasure.[53]

NOTES

1. Plutarch, *Moralia*, trans. W. C. Helmbold (Cambridge: Harvard University Press, 1939), vol. vi, 504, 6e.

2. Iris Murdoch, *The Sovereignty of Good* (New York: Schocken Books, 1971), pp. 32-33.

3. Exceptions to the neglect of this topic include: Joel Feinberg, *Harmless Wrongdoing* (New York: Oxford University Press, 1988), and Sissela Bok, *Secrets: On the Ethics of Concealment and Revelation* (New York: Vintage Books, 1984).

4. Gossip does not always involve truth-telling; it may involve speculation, exaggeration, falsehoods, or lies. I am interested in analyzing whether and why instances of gossip, which are also instances of truth-

telling, are morally problematic.

In *Secrets* Bok suggests that "gossip loses its interest when it is known to be false" (p. 96n). Bok is referring to the listener who is no longer engaged by gossip if there is reason to believe the speaker is lying. It is also the case that at least part of the purpose and the pleasure of gossip is lost for the gossiper if he or she knows that the information conveyed is false. This can be seen, for example, in cases in which the gossiper wants to show himself or herself to be "in-the-know." The pleasure of thinking of oneself as "in-the-know" is at least jeopardized if one is fabricating the story.

Though gossip may involve falsehoods or lies, typically those who engage in gossip believe that what they are saying and hearing is true. In this paper I am concerned with what is typical of gossip.

5. I have in mind special circumstances in which one must either lie or neglect a moral claim which is weightier than truth-telling.

6. Nikolai Aristides, "Entre Nous," *American Scholar* (1990), p. 11.

7. I have adopted the following conventions in order to distinguish between use and mention. When referring to the activity or phenomenon of gossip the word is unmarked. When referring to the concept the word is italicized. When referring to the word, term, or expression double quotes are used.

8. *Webster's Third New International Dictionary* (Springfield, MA: G. & C. Miriam Co., 1976).

9. *Oxford English Dictionary* (Glasgow: Oxford University Press, 1971).

10. The practice of gossiping is associated with women more often than with men. Some empirical studies have concluded that, in fact, there is no significant disparity in the extent to which women and men gossip. I find the definitions of gossip which are used in the empirical studies problematic. I do not hold a view on the question of whether women gossip more than men. However, it seems plausible to me that women have used gossip as a means to assert power in private life, and to compensate for the injury to self-esteem caused by being excluded from the public sphere.

11. I characterize gossip as a certain sort of communication because it occurs not only in conversation but also in the media and in letters. In this essay I am concerned primarily with conversational gossip, rather than the retailing of private lives in the media, or personal correspondence.

12. I do not mean to exclude gossip about celebrities who are strangers. Though famous strangers may be the subject of gossip, those who gossip about them must have enough information to be interested in them and to be able to discuss their lives.

For a discussion of the types of relationships which usually obtain between gossips and those about whom they speak, see Gabriele Taylor's

"Gossip as Moral Talk," in Robert F. Goodman and Aaron Ben-Ze'ev, eds. *Good Gossip (GG)* (Lawrence: Kansas University Press, 1994), pp.35-37.

13. Laurence Thomas and Gabriele Taylor make similar points in their discussions of the distinguishing features of gossip. Taylor writes: "It is not the subject matter that is decisive...but the participants' approach to these topics and their respective attitudes to what is under discussion that make the difference." See Taylor, "Gossip as Moral Talk," in *GG*, p.35; Thomas, "The Logic of Gossip," in *GG*, pp.49-50.

14. See John Sabini's and Maury Silver's discussion of the evaluative nature of gossip in *Moralities of Everyday Life (MEL)* (New York: Oxford University Press, 1982), p.91.

15. John Beard Haviland, *Gossip, Reputation and Knowledge in Zinacantan* (Chicago: University of Chicago Press, 1977), p.161.

16. Jorg R. Bergmann, *Discreet Indiscretions: The Social Organization of Gossip* (New York: Aldine De Grayter, 1993), Thomas Luckmann, Introduction, p. ix.

17. Thomas, "The Logic of Gossip" in *GG*, p. 48.

18. If a participant introduces questions, criticism or reflection concerning the assumed values and norms this is often perceived as an unfriendly interruption and gossiping will be suspended at least temporarily.

19. Ralph L. Rosnow and Gary Alan Fine, *Rumor and Gossip: The Social Psychology of Hearsay* (New York: Elsevier, 1976), p. 84, quoting U. Hannerz "Gossip, Networks and Culture in a Black American Ghetto," *Ethnos*, vol.32 (1967), pp.35-60.

20. See Sabini and Silver, *MEL*, p. 91.

21. Ben-Ze'ev, "The Vindication of Gossip" in *GG*, p.11.

22. See Bok, *Secrets*, pp.92-93.

23. I am concerned with "denounce" in the sense of inform against to the authorities, not in the sense of criticize forcefully or publicly.

24. Sabini and Silver, *MEL*, p. 97n.

25. See Rosnow and Fine, Rumor and Gossip, p. 91.

26. Bok, *Secrets*, p. 92.

27. See Sabini and Silver, *MEL*, p. 97.

28. Rosnow and Fine, *Rumor and Gossip*, p. 4.

29. Bergmann, *Discreet Indiscretions*, pp.140-49.

30. There is no reason to think that any of these functions serve as conscious motives in the minds of those who gossip. Furthermore, the fact that one neither reflects on how gossip functions in the social world nor examines one's own motives in gossiping, in no way affects how gossip functions or the advantages one gains from it.

31. Ben-Ze'ev, "The Vindication of Gossip," in *GG*, p. 22.

32. Feinberg, *Harmless Wrongdoing*, p. 249. I thank Clark Wolf for pointing out the relevance of Feinberg's work.

33. Feinberg, *Harmless Wrongdoing*, p. 250. See also Joel Feinberg, "Limits to the Free Expression of Opinion" in Joel Feinberg and Hyman Gross, ed. *Philosophy of Law* (Belmont, CA: Wadsworth Publishing Co., 1980), 2nd ed. Feinberg supports legal liability for "... all serious defamatory true statements except those that serve ... some beneficial social purpose" (p.195).

34. A distinction needs to be made between violating a social norm and violating a criminal code. All things being equal, I believe third parties do have a right (sometimes a duty) to disclose knowledge they have concerning the violation of a criminal code. I address this issue in a work-in-progress on morally problematic forms of truth-telling.

35. Patricia Meyer Spacks, *Gossip* (Chicago: University of Chicago Press, 1986), p.19.

36. Sabini and Silver, *MEL*, p. 104.

37. The Economist, October 22, 1994, p.70. I thank Arthur Madigan for bringing this article to my attention.

38. See Bok, *Secrets*, p. 87-88.

39. Bergmann, *Discreet Indiscretions*, p. 143.

40. Iris Murdoch, *Metaphysics as a Guide to Morals* (New York: Penguin, 1993), p.470.

41. Taylor, "Gossip as Moral Talk," in *GG*, p. 46.

42. Though, in such a case, the tone of the conversation implies that the matter under discussion is of a light rather than a serious nature, the statements made may be factual. Therefore, the mismatch between tone and substance does not alter the truth-value of the conversation.

43. I thank Carolyn Korsmeyer for pointing out the relevance of Mill's work.

44. Cathy Greenfeld and Peter Williams, "The Uses of Gossip: Women's Writing, Soaps and Everyday Exchange," *Hecate*, vol.17 (1991), p.130.

45. Phyllis Rose, *Parallel Lives: Five Victorian Marriages* (New York: Knopf, 1984), pp.116, 121. I thank Steve Nathanson for directing me to this book.

46. Though I believe that gossip is characteristically experienced as pleasurable, I do not claim that all persons who hear gossip always experience it as pleasurable. Feeling uncomfortable in the presence of gossip is certainly an experience which is familiar to many persons.

Several prominent discussions of gossip involve reference to gossip's role in what I refer to as "enhancing self-satisfaction." Various authors use different terms to discuss this characteristic of gossip. Their discussions include terms such as: "self-esteem" (*GG* p. 3), "boost the ego" (*GG* p. 17), "self-respect" (*GG* p. 17), "satisfaction" and "self-realization" (George Herbert Mead, *Mind, Self and Society* (Chicago: University of Chicago Press, 1934), p.205).

For a philosophical discussion of the conceptual differences and similarities between many of these terms see Robin S. Dillon, ed., *Dignity, Character and Self-Respect* (New York: Routledge, 1995). Since I believe that the self-satisfaction which is derived from gossip is morally suspect, I refrain from using the term "self-respect." I take "self-respect" to designate a "proper sense of personal dignity and worth." See Dillon, *Dignity, Character, and Self-Respect*, p. 7.

47. Mead, *Mind, Self and Society*, p. 206.

48. Ben-Ze'ev, "The Vindication of Gossip," in *GG*, p. 17.

49. The psychological benefits of gossip are not unlike some of the psychological benefits of racism and sexism. All three provide a sense of self-satisfaction, empowerment and enhanced self-respect. Such benefits do not justify the practices.

50. Peeping is always a violation of privacy, and rarely a violation of trust. Gossiping is sometimes a violation of privacy, sometimes a violation of trust, sometimes both, and sometimes neither a violation of privacy nor a violation of trust. Therefore, peeping and gossiping often have different relations to privacy and trust. However, even when peeping and gossiping have the same relation to privacy and trust, they are sorted differently morally and legally. The differences in moral evaluation can not be accounted for just by the usually different relations to privacy and trust. I thank an anonymous referee for this journal for comments which encouraged me to give this problem more thought.

51. See Immanuel Kant, *Lectures on Ethics* (Indianapolis: Hackett Publishing Co., 1963), p. 224; Sissela Bok, *Lying: Moral Choice in Public and Private Life* (New York: Vintage Books, 1989), pp. xvii, 50, 287.

52. Philippa Foot, *Virtues and Vices and Other Essays in Moral Philosophy* (Berkeley: University of California Press, 1978), p.5.

53. By criticizing the practice of gossiping I do not mean to criticize all conversation/communication critical of absent persons. I recognize that there are circumstances in which it is appropriate to impart information which is critical of, even damaging to, third parties. Determining the motive, purpose and role of the speakers is helpful in distinguishing legitimate critical communication from gossip.

Take, for example, a situation in which x is considering giving a personal loan to y, and I know that y habitually borrows and fails to repay money. Motivated by concern for x, I impart this information to her for the purpose of offering information relevant to the decision she is about to make. The news I convey may damage y's reputation as well as his chance of receiving a loan from x, and several of the distinguishing features of gossip are present (y is absent, the topic is of a personal nature, the discussion is informal, evaluative, and at least implicitly comparative). However, given the nature of my motive and purpose such a conversation has a good chance of not being an instance of gossip.

In practice it may be difficult to sort different cases into appropriate categories. However, in order to prevent the innocent from being harmed there are circumstances in which imparting damaging information about third parties is morally preferable to silence. See Joseph Butler, *Sermons by Joseph Butler, D. C. L.* (Oxford: Clarendon Press, 1897), pp.76-77, and Thomas, "The Logic of Gossip" in *GG*, p. 54.

I am grateful to Marina Barabas, Newton Garver, John Kronen, Laura Ruoff, and an anonymous reviewer for this journal for helpful comments on earlier versions of this paper, and I thank Ann Stokes for providing a wonderful place to work.

MARGARET G. HOLLAND

QUESTIONS FOR DISCUSSION

1. In the humanities, research questions differ quite markedly from those in the sciences and social sciences. How would you characterize the research question which this essay seeks to answer? How is this question different from those posed in the first two parts of this textbook?

2. This essay was published in a philosophy journal. What difference might that fact have made in the author's approach toward her subject? Who do you suppose is the audience for this journal? How might a sociology journal have handled the same topic?

3. At the bottom of page 142, the author gives her readers a preview of the information to be covered in the essay. Did you find this preview helpful?

4. Before each major section in the essay, the author includes quotes from famous writers. Why do you think she did this? Did you find these quotes interesting or useful?

5. The author defines gossip by comparing it to other related speech acts and actions, such as denouncing, chatting, indiscretion, or even peeping. How is gossip different, according to the author? Do you agree with her assessment?

6. Do you think defining by comparison, as this author has done, is a helpful way to understand the topic of gossip?

7. On page 149, the author criticizes other writers for not taking a moral stance in regard to gossip. Do you agree with the author "that the violation of social norms provides no justification for having one's life taken as a topic for gossip"?

8. Think about your own experiences with gossip. Do you and your friends engage routinely in gossip about others? Have you ever experienced negative results from gossip—either from being on the receiving or giving end?

9. The author has used extensive endnotes. What kinds of information are included in these notes? Did you find them helpful?

"Put a Pretty Face On It": Stevie Smith and Anti-Semitism [1]

Catherine A. Civello, U of Houston-Downtown

"What shall we do about anti-Semitism?" Sartre's question, asked in the waning years of World War II (147), retains cultural validity in the post-Cold War era, as strides toward geopolitical cohesion and global decency compete with neo-Nazis, the Ku Klux Klan, and other groups dedicated to ethnic annihilation. David Duke, ex-Nazi and Klan Grand Wizard, had this to say in 1986: "The Jews have developed a disease and given it to us already. It's called racial mixing, and they're being quite successful" (Applebome 17). One year earlier, he had denied that the Holocaust actually happened. Duke came close to winning the governor's office in Louisiana in the 1991 primaries. The next year, Jewish graves were wrecked in Berlin in conjunction with neo-Nazi rallies in other parts of Germany, turbulence so disturbing that Germany's Jewish leaders and the upper house of Parliament demanded that an official statement be issued on racism. On November 6, 1992, the Infas Institute of Bonn published a poll showing that one third of Germans surveyed thought that there were good points to the Nazi regime of Adolph Hitler and that 54% agreed that the Jews were partially at fault for the way they had been treated (Fritz 25). And, according to a survey by the Anti-Defamation League, 20% of Americans are strongly prejudiced against Jews, while 31% believe that Jews have "too much power" ("Twenty Percent").

Anti-Semitism is no less significant to feminist scholars than to heads of state. What shall *we* do about anti-Semitism when we encounter it in the novels, poems, articles, and letters of the same women writers who argue vehemently for women's rights? It is the purpose of this paper to confront and contextualize anti-Semitism in the writing of the English poet and novelist Stevie Smith. I grow less comfortable with the scholarly neglect of this undeniable dimension of Smith as her work attains a larger audience in both British and American journals and classrooms. [2] What shall we influence our students to do about anti-Semitism in the writing of Stevie Smith?

In addition to focusing on the anti-Semitic passages from Smith's writings and reinterpreting some of them in this light, I will show that Smith was not alone in her views among English women writers of the pre-

From *Re: Arts & Letters* (1996, 20.1, pp. 13-33). Reprinted by permission.

war period. Her friend Naomi Mitchison, as well as Nancy Mitford, Virginia Woolf, and Vita Sackville-West, joined her in bigotry. Another object of this essay is to place these authors' ideas in the historical context from which they emerged—the situation of Jews in Europe in the 1920s and 1930s. While questioning the general nature of prejudice, I will also examine the particular psychology and rhetoric of prejudice in the writing of these women.

Whereas Stevie Smith's anti-Semitism could pose as part of her political ideology, it often sank to the level of age-old stereotypes of Jews. In fact, Smith's first published work, *Novel on Yellow Paper*, opens in this way. On the second page of the novel, "I" (the narrator/protagonist Pompey Casmilus) "look at Leonie . . . a Jewess, but slim. . . . She is looking very elegant. . . . And who cares (NYP 10). The passage not only establishes Pompey's lack of interest in fashion, an important facet of the character, but also affirms her anti-Semitism albeit through an off-hand remark, "Jewess, but slim."

Novel on Yellow Paper teems with similar comments: "I was at that Jew party" (29); "I rang up some Jew-friends of mine out Charlottenburg way.... they were sound enough with a weather eye out for self-preservation" (99); "heaven help Deutschland when it kicks out the Jews, with their practical intelligence that might keep Germany from that dream darkness" (103); "oh how frightful if they [her Jewish friends] ever got coming to Germany nowadays, which they certainly wouldn't, having that practical common sense which is so the mark of their race" (109); "well I'll say it, [her friend] got married to a man who is a Jew, and the sort of Jew not like Herman or Bennie that has an artistic temperament working overtime on all cylinders, but just a plain ordinary safe businessman of a Jew with a whole hell of a lot of money" (119); and "he [the friend's husband] had chosen a Scotch name like they do, and his brother was there, and he had chosen a Scotch name too, like they do" (120).

While the narrator of a novel does not necessarily reflect the author's ideas, biographical evidence supports the view that, in the case of Stevie Smith, narrator/character and author work hand-in-glove.[3] Smith, moreover, seems perversely bent on conflating all three in her text as narratorial observations in the first person weave in and out of dialogue among characters, one of whom overlaps with the narrator herself. At the publication of *Novel on Yellow Paper* (1936) and its sequel *Over the Frontier* (1938), some of her friends became convinced of her anti-Semitism (Barbera, *Stevie* 56, 79, 82).[4] After reading *Novel*, the Jewish-American poet Naomi Replansky wrote to Smith: "When you talk about the practical common sense of the Jews I too (Jewish) can't help but wince slightly" (81). Finally, as Smith discusses her desire to change publishers in a letter to Naomi

Mitchison, she agrees with Mitchison's implication that the publishing industry is under Jewish control and concludes: "No no,—no Yiddisher would accept me I fear" (103).

Novel, then, can be read as an autobiographical palimpsest whose layers fall away to expose first Pompey's bigotry, then the narrator's, and finally Smith's itself. The seemingly casual "Jew-friends," instead of simply "friends," indicates the speaker's feeling that Jews are somehow different from the rest of her friends. "Eye out for self-preservation," "practical intelligence," "practical common sense," and "business-man of a Jew" refer to the stereotypical association of Jews and greed. The narrator further distances herself from Jews by locking them into such categories as "the mark of their race," "the sort of Jew," and "like they do"—the last repeated as if to transform the reader into a silent accomplice who acknowledges the charge.

Most of the above slurs could be attributed to persons of either sex, but the first—about Leonie being "slim" and "elegant"— more likely would originate from the pen of a woman.[5] In the course of the novel, Pompey goes shopping with two acquaintances, Jewish, who encourage her to try on clothes. She looks into the mirror and feels like "Christ crucified between thieves" (61). Then, in a passage that is prototypically Stevie Smith, she retreats into her own thoughts and spews out clause after clause of apparently incoherent, yet deeply meaningful, prose in the Modern tradition:

> I laughed and laughed, and looked to see the teeth showing through, and never shall I forget the fine picture that was. And my face was dark and brilliant and laughing, and Lottie's face was calculating, and then the calculations died, and the eyes were dead. . . . And I said: Blessed are they that are not offended. Oh how glad I am I am not Lottie Belt, and how glad I am I am not Rosa. . . . There are hazards enough in life and death. . . . (62-6)

Writing against the *mise en scene* of a ladies' dressing room in a clothing store creates a distinctly female milieu in this passage. Certainly, anti-Semitism was (and is) the domain of both men and women, but Smith's rhetoric here is clearly feminine. She transports her readers into a woman's domain on both a physical and a psychological level and merges the two until her prejudice and her gender become inseparable.

In *Over the Frontier*, the author maintains the level of bigotry that she attained in *Novel*. She describes a young actor as

> a blond Jew, it is rather fascinating, that so-racial bonework of the face, and the blond blond hair and blue-grey eyes. . . . I have a tendre for these blond Jew faces, they look so patient, so souffrant, so sicklied o'er, bleached, albinoed and depigmented. . . . (74)

The narrator, resting at a health spa in Germany, remembers attending a meeting at the publishing firm where she is secretary where "round that Board Room table sit Jew and Gentile, and hostility burns from empire blue eyes to the dark eyes of Israel, lord of the hidden rivers" (85). She goes on to assign motives, based on ethnicity, for the financial ambitions of the directors of the firm:

> In the mind of Empire-Blue-Eyes, the significance of gold is fury and pride and a great beacon of light and power. . . . And in the eyes of Israel what is the significance of Gold? Unity, flexibility, secrecy, control. Israel has lapped round that course already so many times, so many many times, and his eyelids are a little weary. O.K. Israel, keep it under your hat. (86)

It is difficult to determine whether Igor's "so-racial bonework" or the director's "eyes of Israel" fit more neatly into Pompey's predetermined notion of appearance. In any case, Smith's bigotry is showing again by her failure, as narrator, to subvert or undermine in any way the blatant observations on physical stereotypes that her character expresses while maintaining the secretarial silence expected of any woman who would have been allowed into that boardroom.

Pompey's stereotypes fail her, however: the Jewish actor and the Anglo-Saxon board member both have blue eyes. Moreover, her rhetoric—with its admitted "fascination" and "tendre" for the actor's physical attributes and the businessman's eyes—expresses feelings akin to female desire, a complicated vehicle for her bigotry. The entire scene, describing the actor and recalling the meeting, takes place in a bar. Smith has the narrator, musing on "fascism, communism, Italy, Germany," come to this conclusion: "There is nothing to be done about it, nothing at all, but nothing. So drink up my chicks and put a pretty face on it" (74).

The politics of the period, however, were not pretty. Historian Todd M. Endelman, in *Radical Assimilation In English Jewish History*, traces English anti-Semitism back to the thirteenth century, when Jews were not permitted to live in England; through the seventeenth, when Cromwell allowed Jews in London to stay and practice their religion; to the nineteenth, when intermarriage became common (9). Then Endelman focuses on the twentieth century, a time when Jewish prosperity rose in England while hostility against Jews increased proportionately (72-3). He records that, in the time immediately preceding World War I, anti-Semitism "assumed a sharper, more ideological focus than in the past and entered the arena of public discourse" (102). Of particular interest to students of English literature is the wording of the slogans that marred public places in the 1930s, the period between the wars: "The peace conference was a Jew conference." "All our troubles . . . Jews behind it every time." "Expel all Jews from the city" (192). This is the same rhetoric of so much of the literature of those years from Hilaire Belloc and Evelyn Waugh to Naomi Mitchison and Stevie Smith.

The turbulence of the inter-war years—"political agitation, social discrimination, street hooliganism" (Endelman 191)—culminated in the formation of the British Union of Fascists (BUF), an organization that promoted violence against Jewish persons and property such as synagogues and cemeteries. Endelman states that anti-Semitism "was common enough that few Jews could have avoided it altogether or been unaware of its existence" (194). He cites such examples as discrimination in clubs, jobs, schools, restaurants, hotels, and real estate, recalling that Jews were often denied car insurance because they "didn't have the same steady nerves as Englishmen; they were more excitable, easily losing their heads in dangerous situations" (196). By 1939, at the height of this anti-Semitic frenzy, 30,000 Jewish refugees had poured into England (Lipman 196). Even though these people, who had fled the nightmarish threat of genocide, constituted less than 1% of the total population, one *Sunday Pictorial* headline read: "Refugees get jobs—Britons get dole."

This distorted perception, that Foreigners were displacing "real Brits," perhaps contributed to the venom of much of Stevie Smith's fiction. The tea-table scene in *Over the Frontier*, for instance, closely resembles the historical record. "And the Jews?" asks a British colonel of Pompey, who has just pontificated on the danger of fighting for principle instead of for friends. At first she hesitates to answer: "I am in despair for the racial hatred that is running in me in a sudden swift current, in a swift tide of hatred, and Out out damned tooth, damned aching rotting tooth, rotten to the root" (158). Having begun her diatribe, Pompey seems unable to stem its flow:

> Would any but they have survived their persecutions?. . . 'None but the Jews would have survived their persecutions.' . . . But I have some very dear Jewish friends. Oh the final treachery of the smug goy. Do not all our persecutions of Israel follow upon this smiling sentence? (158)

167

Her newly found friend Tom, disallowing such ambivalence, pointedly asks her if she would fight with the Jews if it came to that:

> The virtue has gone out of me. Dully stupidly I bend my head. ... 'I will fight with my friends my true friends my real friends the people with whom I am happy.'
> 'And these are not Jews.'
> 'No.' (159)

It is no coincidence that, just a few pages later, Pompey dreams of going on an adventure in which she fights alongside Nazi-like forces "over the frontier." Smith had etched the hatred so deeply onto her fictional character that it had become imprinted on Pompey's unconscious, releasing itself in her dream. It is no wonder that, a few years later, Smith would say of the novel that it "was nothing to be proud of" (Barbera, *Me Again* 285).

Besides peppering her writing with egregious anti-Semitic stereotypes, Smith structures her novels around the complex political situation of the '30s. The beginning of *Novel on Yellow Paper* establishes Pompey as someone who sees herself as a "goy among jews" (11). She goes riding with her Jewish friend Leonie on page one; on page two, she proclaims, "Hurrah to be a goy!" It is superfluous dialogue, an uncalled-for digression unless Smith's motivation is less conscious than one of mimesis. After portraying Pompey as a London secretary who sees other people as satellites revolving around herself, Smith then sends her on a trip to Germany halfway through the book. Pompey muses about her previous German vacation, her then-boyfriend Karl, and her current guilt about Germany and the Jews:

> Ah that beloved Germany and my darling Karl. I too can see that idea of sleeping, dreaming, happily dreaming Germany, her music, her philosophy, her wide fields and broad rivers, her gentle women. But the dream changes, and how is it to-day, how is it today in this year of 1936, how is it to-day? (49)

In *Over the Frontier* Pompey's stay in Germany is considerably lengthier than in *Novel*; she is ill and in a dream she visits Aaronsen, a Jewish banker, in the line of her fantastic duties. He serves her a lavish tea and plays music for her before they transact their business. At one point, Pompey needs air and, as she walks outside his apartment, she observes a gang of students lying in wait, "and no doubt they had some catcalls ready for him" (201). Although she thinks of "what he and his race have brought upon their heads" and believes that "only a people hungry and ripe for persecution would have inspired and survived such a history" (198), Pompey's guilt returns and upsets those feelings. She asks herself, "Is it not to find in myself a little of this very barbarisms I so much should like to wipe out for all time from all people?" but she has to answer:

> No, I do not think this in me, and in those who feel as I do, is barbarisms, intolerance yes, but it is the sharp spear of defense against infamy that must bear for a sharp point the uttermost sharp point of a righteous pure intolerance. (197)

Only Stevie Smith knew the significance of distinguishing between "barbarisms" and ethnic "intolerance" in the context of the European political situation of the late '30s, but to a contemporary reader, the distinction seems absurd. Smith subtitled her first novel "Work it out for Yourself" and one can read the two Pompey novels as her own futile attempt to do so.

In 1936 Naomi Mitchison wrote her soon-to-be friend Stevie Smith a fan letter on the publication of *Novel on Yellow Paper*. After praising Smith's "craft" and "genius," Mitchison gushed: "I did so like separate things, the part about the Jews & about the Bacchae..." (Barbera, *Stevie* 90). In *All Change Here*, her first volume of memoirs published in 1975, Mitchison herself tells the story of her brother's friend, a Jew, whom her mother would not allow her to choose for games at parties: "I was confused, felt awful, not so much for him but for myself having been put into this position by some sort of net I didn't understand but which had caught us both, Clauser and me. Yet I didn't protest" (85). These memories of the period also contain her revealing comment that "anti-Semitism as such would definitely not have been approved."

Mitchison, like Smith, was denied a university education; instead, both became voracious readers and to a certain extent, autodidacts. Mitchison traces some of her ideas about political philosophy to her early reading of Plato and Hegel. She believed that Plato's admonition to sacrifice the individual for the good of the state led, in the twentieth century, to "The *fahrerpanzip*, the totalitarian state and the English public school" (41):

> But when the state itself goes bad? Somehow that thought had to be kept under. Thus *sittlichkeit*, product, via Hegel, of Plato, turned out to be a short, though as yet not obvious, step towards the theory of the Master Race.

Mitchison's wartime diary describes, not unsympathetically, fellow writer Storm Jameson, who was "extremely gloomy, owing to having dealt with refugees, especially Jews, since 1937 about, keeping alive people who would be better dead. Unable to see a tolerable new world" (Sheridan 184).

We Have Been Warned, Mitchison's pre-war novel, features a large cast that centers around an Oxford economics professor and his wife. The don, a Laborite, campaigns unsuccessfully for parliament; his dutiful wife devotes herself to his campaign. Two of his supporters, also members of the Labor party, are Reuben Goldberg and his wife. Mitchison ensures by the heavy-handedness of her naming that the reader is aware of the Goldbergs' ethnicity, though their Jewishness has virtually nothing to do with the plot of the novel. Finally, at the end of the arduous campaign and toward the end of the novel, the candidate's wife—bearing a strong resemblance to Mitchison who herself was the housebound wife of an Oxford don and MP and mother of six children—derives a strange solution to England's economic problems. Since her husband is too busy to listen to her, she ruminates in solitude on the connection between financial worth and intangible things, blaming Jews for what she considers the "modern" moral outlook:

> One can't get rid of these moral concepts, and what do they mean anyhow? They're all in terms of property. Value: that's a trader's idea, a Jew trader. Value: above rubies. And these commercial ideas have crept into all our morality, art and science. (441)

She continues in this vein, but tries to dissociate herself from charges of anti-Semitism by distinguishing between "Jews" and the English Jews who are her friends:

> She thought it was a very definitely anti-Semite idea, or rather perhaps anti-Eastern—for she felt it might be welcome to the kind of Jews whom she knew: the Jews who were sick of their traditional pattern. It was an idea opposed to all the bargaining of the East and the Mediterranean basin.... That was presumably what Jesus was after, but the East and the Mediterranean were too much for him, and, besides, he hadn't quite got rid of the idea of the Family Grocer; how could he with that racial inheritance and that education— even if he saw through the education very young? (443-44)

Just as Stevie Smith perpetuated the stereotypical view of Jews as uniquely materialistic, Naomi Mitchison associates them with "bargaining" and the "Family Grocer," traditionally women's concerns, and the character is a traditional woman. Her references to Jesus reveal her character's lack of intellectual sophistication, not unusual given women's educational history in that place and time. The naivete of the character forms a transparent filter through which Mitchison's opinions seep into the text much in the same way that Pompey functioned for Stevie Smith.

Anti-Semitism in English literature did not originate in the twentieth century and is not confined to female authors. Anne Aresty Naman traces it at least as far back as Chaucer's "Prioress's Tale": "Jewerye... [is] Sustened by a Lord of that contree/For foule usure and lucre of vileyne,/ Hateful to Crist and to his compaignye.... (11.490-92). Shakespeare and Spenser, moreover, reflect the anti-Semitism of the English Renaissance. Dickens has Sykes in *Oliver Twist* call Fagin "a covetous, avaricious, in-sa-ti-a-ble old fence" (Ch.13) and has the Jew Riah in *Our Mutual Friend* say "you must pay in full ... or you will be put to heavy charges.... Money, money, money" (Ch. 13). Trollope in *Phineas Finn* describes Madame Goesler as having "thick black hair ... eyes were large ... and she used them in a manner which is as yet hardly common with English women" (ch.40). And Walter Scott in *Ivanhoe* refers to "the obstinacy of the Jews" (Ch.6).

Attempting to define ethnic stereotyping, Gordon Allport states in his classic work that "much prejudice is a matter of blind conformity with prevailing folkways" (12). He sees fear, frustration, and guilt at the root. Allport concludes: "We may say that prejudiced people are those who have developed less frustration tolerance and therefore less skill in meeting their frustrations head on, rather than through infantile anger and displacement" (348). His analysis of the operation of prejudice parallels, to some extent, English women's psychological configuration in the first several decades of this century—fear and frustration resulting from limits put on social, educational, and career opportunities.[6] This frustration, coupled with not only "less skill" in confrontation but also outright behavioral injunctions against being straightforward, perhaps produced human beings vulnerable to the type of anger that Allport associates with the displacement that is prejudice. More recently, psychiatrist Jean Baker Miller has asserted that "within a framework of inequality the existence of conflict is denied and the means to engage openly in conflict are excluded.... For this hidden conflict, there are no acceptable social forms or guides because this conflict supposedly doesn't exist" (13). This explanation, of course, neither condones nor pardons the anti-Semitism of so many women writers in England during the inter-war period. Furthermore, it fails to account for men's anti-Semitism or that of non-English Europeans' but that is not within the aims or scope of this paper. Though their causes be different from women's, men's fears and frustrations lie at the source of their prejudice also. As Julia Kristeva wrote of Louis-Ferdinand Celine,

171

who was neither English nor female, "[His anti-Semitism] is a security blanket. A delirium, to be sure. . . ." (137).

Bryher—poet, novelist, life partner of H.D.—offers a less sociological key to female forms of prejudice than Allport. Bryher, like Stevie Smith who traveled to Germany and Naomi Mitchison who journeyed to Vienna, often stayed in Berlin. She reminisces:

> I fell in love with Berlin at once to my own amazement.
> ... We were conscious that we were standing near the center of a volcano, it was raw, dangerous, explosive.
> ... In Paris, people had used the classic phrases of me, 'She doesn't drink, she doesn't make love, what are her vices?' They guessed everything but the right one, it was danger....
> (247)

She also recalls that, as soon as the boat put out to sea, she would say, "in England you say don't to me always" (274).

Nancy Mitford's paternal grandfather likewise embraced Germany, but through the writings of Houston Stewart Chamberlain. Though English, Chamberlain wrote in German, became a German citizen, and eventually married Wagner's daughter. According to Jonathan Guinness, Mitford's nephew and biographer, Chamberlain was "an ideological inspirer of Nazis .. one of the theorists they had in mind when they glorified the German race and persecuted the Jews" (109) Guinness recalls his ancestor's admiration of Chamberlain's world, saying that "it was also permissible, and not unusual, to express dislike of the Jews" (111).

Although of a higher social station than either Stevie Smith or Naomi Mitchison, Nancy Mitford shared their resentment of being deprived of a university education while her brother attended Eton and became an attorney. Mitford married Peter Rodd and, "when he and Nancy were first engaged they even bought black shirts and went to some Fascist meetings" (Guinness 304). Her infamous sister Diana had fallen in love with Sir Oswald Mosley, the founder of the BUF, who believed that "the power of Jewish corruption must be destroyed in all countries before peace and justice can be successfully achieved in Europe" (336). According to Selina Hastings, a biographer who is not related to the family, Nancy wrote to her sister Diana about Mosley:

> [His] meeting was fascinating. . . . I think he is a wonderful speaker & of course I expect he is better still with a more interesting audience. . . . There were several fascinating fights, as he brought a few Neanderthal men with him & they

fell tooth & (literally) nail on anyone who shifted his chair or coughed. (96)

Nancy went even further in an article she authored about Mosley:

> We British Fascists [believe] . . . that our Leader, Sir Oswald Mosley, has the character, the brains, the courage and the determination to lift this city from the slough of despond in which it has for too long weltered, to an utopia. . . . Soon the streets will echo beneath the feet of the black battalions, soon we will show the world that the spirit of our forefathers is yet alive with us, soon we shall be united by the sacred creed striving as one man for the Greater Britain. (Hastings 96)

The Rodds stopped their public support of Mosley and the BUF only when Nancy's father-in-law, himself sympathetic to Fascism, implored them to cease for the sake of the effect that their known anti-Semitism would have on the family business (97).

In the late '30s, Nancy wrote a novel, considered humorous, in which she satirizes a number of contemporary political positions, Fascism among them. In a letter to Diana, she argues that "a book of this kind can't do your movement any harm. Honestly, if I thought it could set the leader [Mosley] back by so much as half an hour I would have scrapped it" (Hastings 103). *Wigs on the Green* centers around Eugenia, a thinly disguised version of Unity Mitford—the sister who committed herself to National Socialism so completely that she spent several years in Germany and became a friend of Hitler. Eugenia founds a local chapter of the Social Unionist Movement, the fictional equivalent of the BUF, with Captain Jack instead of Mosley as The Leader. Several other characters line up with members of the large cast of Mitford family and friends.

In a speech on the village green, Eugenia asserts that "under our regime . . . [women] will have husbands and great quantities of healthy Aryan children" (61). When someone asks her the meaning of "Aryan," a term she uses repeatedly in her speeches, she responds that "a non-Aryan is the missing link between man and beast. . . ." (195). Eugenia's headquarters burns to the ground, and she proclaims: "Wait until I have run them to earth, the brutal yellows [pacifists] financed by Jews too, no doubt" (173). Eugenia/Unity succeeds in bringing a few converts into the Fascist fold. One of them explains that "Germany and Italy have been saved by National Socialism; England might be saved by Social Unionism, who can tell? Therefore I say, 'Heil Hitler!'" (79). Eugenia herself concludes the novel with this image: "The [harassing poster] on Mr. Isaac's house promises that all Jews will be sent to live in Jerusalem the Golden with milk and blest. . . ." (209). While Mitford represents the pre-war fascist giddiness with some measure of accuracy, a post-Holocaust awareness of the fate of 16 million people gives this ending an irony to which, one might say, Nancy Mitford contributed.

Nancy Mitford died twenty years ago, but her sister Diana Mosley lives in Paris. In a recent interview, she reminisced about her and Nancy's girlhood, their grandfather's library (to which they had unlimited access), their French governesses, their love affairs, and their attraction to Fascism: "[The British] loved the Black Shirt because it had the double advantage of being very cheap and outside class distinctions. . . . Indeed the Black Shirt was so popular that an act of parliament was passed forbidding it to be worn" (Guppy 193-94). Sounding very much like a character in one of her sister's novels, she continued:

> If I had been given the choice for myself and my beloved children of being gassed or of being burnt to death in one of the firestorms created by Allied airmen in, for example Hamburg, I would have chosen the former. . . . Churchill said he hoped they [the Germans] would bleed and burn. Perhaps in Germany some said that the only good Jew was a dead Jew. I can't see that one proposition is different from the other. (198)

The interview concludes with Mitford's not entirely surprising statement: "Personally I was never anti-Semitic; so many of my close friends were Jewish . . ." (203).

If Diana Mosley's Jewish friends disqualified her from anti-Semitism, Virginia Woolf seemed to think that her Jewish husband gave her license to make the severest statements about him and his family. Her letters are replete with anti-Semitism. After Leonard proposes, Virginia writes him that "possibly, your being a Jew comes in also at this point. You seem so foreign" (I:496). She describes him in one letter as "a penniless Jew" (I:500) and, in another, says, "First he is a Jew: second he is 31" (I:502). To a friend, she describes the scene at tea when Leonard took her to meet his widowed mother and siblings:

> 'What? Ham sandwiches for ten?'
> 'Not Ham: potted meat. We don't eat Ham or bacon or Shellfish in this house.'

'Not Shellfish? Why not shellfish?'
'Because it says in the Scriptures . . .
It was queer. (I:502-3)

Seventeen years later, Woolf confides to Ethel Smyth: "How I hated marrying a Jew . . . their nasal voices, and their oriental jewellry, and their noses and their wattles—what a snob I was" (IV:195-96). As Todd Endelman reminds us, Leonard Woolf was a graduate of Cambridge and his family had lived for generations in England (100-01) but, in Virginia's own words, "First he is a Jew."

Virginia Woolf's friend and lover Vita Sackville-West shared her anti-Semitism. Her son, Nigel Nicholson, reveals in his biography of his parents that "his [father's] dislike of Jews and coloured people, the persistent 'bedint' prejudice, were characteristics he shared with Vita, and against which Ben and I later reacted" (255). Sackville-West's novel, *The Edwardians*, is a janus-faced mime of both that era (1900-10) and her own (1930s). The narratorial prejudice of the actual Moderns catalyzes the bigotry of the earlier, fictional Edwardians. Sylvia, a widow, considers marrying a Jewish businessman, a stereotype almost as heavy-handed as Naomi Mitchison's "Goldbergs." First she reflects that "it would be a comedown to marry a Jew, and physically Sir Adam was not appetizing, but then his millions were fabulous..." (25); then her son sees "the long nose of the Jew. A tip for the Stock Exchange! he thought" (34). Her friends would "ignore people like . . . Sir Adam, whom they dismissed as a Jew" (100). Finally, his grandmother tells Sylvia's son:

> King or no King, I don't like those Jews [who were Edward VII's friends]; I saw a lot of their horrid names today, when I was looking through the Visitors' Book. . . . They are no fit company for you. I dare say they've been putting ideas into your head—perhaps they want you to go into business with them? A name like yours would be the making of them. Don't you listen. (193)

Confirming Sackville-West's sense of history are the memoirs of her contemporary, the Countess of Warwick, who admitted that "we resented the introduction of the Jews into the social set of the Prince of Wales . . . because they had brains and understood finance" (43). So Vita Sackville-West assumes her place beside Stevie Smith, Naomi Mitchison, Nancy Mitford, and Virginia Woolf, not only for the content of her prejudice, but also for its form. Like the others, Sackville-West's fears and frustrations center around matters that were then considered a woman's area: physical attributes, family safety, and marital prospects.

Given recent outbreaks of ethnic violence from Brooklyn Heights to Bosnia to Berlin, worldwide concern over anti-Semitism is justified. But is it too late? Returning to Sartre, what shall we do about anti-Semitism? Sartre answered his own question: "Anti-Semitism does not fall within the category of ideas protected by the right of free opinions" (10). The applications to feminism are obvious; bigots should find no protection there. We should drag anti-Semitism out of the obscurity of footnotes and into the light of the text. We should address that dimension of an author's world view, if we find it, in conference presentations. We should include a writer's prejudices in class discussion. Above all, we should condemn bigotry. For, no matter how fine or how feminist the writer, our students—some of them for the first time—need to hear our condemnation of anti-Semitism as much as they need to read the works wherein it is too often found.

NOTES

1. My article benefitted from many conversations with Professor Lilian R. Furst to whom I am deeply indebted. I also wish to thank Dr. Molly Woods and the Organized Research Committee at the University of Houston-Downtown for their support. Dedication to C. Rossi Civello.[CAC]

2. Biographers Jack Barbera and William McBrien dismiss Smith's anti-Semitism as "the usual pre-war attitude of the English: not so much ethnic or religious hostility as a greater sense than people have today that Jews are 'different' or 'exotic'" (81).

3. Autobiographical parallels abound in Smith's first two novels: both she and the character Pompey grew up without fathers; both had ailing mothers; both worked as secretaries; both, as adults, lived with maiden aunts; both traveled to Germany; and neither was ever married. Smith, moreover, based many characters on her own friends. (See Barbera and McBrien.)

4. Although this paper focuses on Smith's first two novels, her third novel (*The Holiday*), written after the war, contains such anti-Semitic passages as this:

> It was better, I said, in the war. Now it is flat, and the heart has gone out of it, and there is no fighting now on the grand scale, but only the deadly puzzling post-war skirmishing, the flatness of Occupation, the sullen German people, the unreasonable Jews. (183)

5. Of course, many well-known English female authors of the period were not anti-Semitic—Bryber, Mary Renault, Elizabeth Bowen, Vera Brittain, Rosamond Lehmann among them.

6. Hitler said in 1932: "I can only confess that without the endurance and really loving devotion of women to the movement I could never have led the party to victory" (Thomas 28). Posters, at that time in Germany, were directed at women: "Come and bring your worries to Adolph Hitler—throw your burden on his shoulders." Goebbels waged a propaganda campaign to get women's votes, promising them a higher standard of living, a car, a refrigerator, a garden suburb, special marriage loans, and chances of promotion for married men. He cultivated the image of Hitler as a lonely bachelor, a teetotaller and non-smoker, who had gone to prison for his convictions. In the Third Reich, women were actually pushed out of politics, working in factories twelve hours per day. When they eventually saw through the propaganda, it was too late (31-37).

WORKS CITED

Allport, Gordon W. *The Nature of Prejudice*. Palo Alto: Addison-Wesley, 1954.

Applebome, Peter. "Duke: The Ex-Nazi Who Would Be Governor," *New York Times*. Nov. 10, 1991: 1 and 17.

Barbera, Jack and William McBrien, eds. *Me Again: The Uncollected Writings of Stevie Smith*. NY: Farrar, Straus, 1982.

Bryher. *The Heart to Artemis*. NY: Harcourt, 1962.

Countess of Warwick, Frances. *Discretions*. NY: Scribner's, 1931.

Endelman, Todd M. *Radical Assimilation in English Jewish History: 1656-1945*. Indiana, 1990.

Fritz, Mark. Hard-liners to Boycott German Anti-Racism Rally," *Dallas Morning News*. Nov. 7, 1992: 1 and 25.

Guinness, Jonathan and Catherine. *The House of Mitford*. NY: Viking, 1985.

Guppy, Shusha. *Looking Back*. NY: British American Pub., 1991.

Hastings, Selina. *Nancy Mitford*. London: Hamish Hamilton, 1985.

Kristeva, Julia. *Powers of Horror: An Essay on Abjection*. Trans. Leon S. Roudiez. Columbia, 1982. [1980]

Lipman, V.D. *A History of the Jews in Britain since 1858*. NY: Holmes & Meier, 1990.

Miller, Jean Baker M.D. *Toward a New Psychology of Women*. Boston: Beacon Press, 1986.

Mitchison, Naomi. *All Change Here*. London: The Bodley Head, 1975.

----------. *We Have Been Warned*. NY: Vanguard, 1936. [1935]

Mitford, Nancy. *Wigs on the Green*. NY: Popular Library, 1976.[1935]

Naman, Anne Haresty. *The Jew in the Victorian Novel.* NY: AMS Press, 1980.
Nicholson, Nigel. *Portrait of a Marriage.* NY: Atheneum, 1973.
Sackville-West, Vita. *The Edwardians.* NY: Doubleday, 1930.
Sartre, Jean-Paul. *Anti-Semite and Jew.* Trans. George J. Becker. NY: Schocken, 1948.
Sheridan, Dorothy, ed. *Among You Taking Notes: The Wartime Diary of Naomi Mitchison.* London: Gollancz, 1985.
Smith, Stevie. *Novel on Yellow Paper.* London: Virago, 1980. [1936]
----------. *Over the Frontier.* London: Virago, 1980. [1938]
----------. *The Holiday.* London: Virago, 1979. [1949]
Thomas, Katherine. *Women in Nazi Germany.* London: Gollancz, 1943.
"Twenty Percent Biased Against Jews," *New York Times.* Nov. 22, 1992: 1A.
Woolf, Virginia. *The Letters of Virginia Woolf.* Ed. Nigel Nicholson. 6 vols. London: Hogarth Press, 1975-79.

QUESTIONS FOR DISCUSSION

1. The author begins her piece by alluding to modern-day instances of anti-Semitism. How might such events have motivated her to write about anti-Semitism in the novels of Stevie Smith?

2. How would you describe the starting question or research question that this essay seeks to answer?

3. This essay is an example of literary criticism. How has the author woven in quotes and summaries from the novels into her own argument? Did she do this effectively?

4. Why does the author say it is important to bring anti-Semitism to light in literature?

5. Do you have any experience with being discriminated against? Or do you know others who have been discriminated against simply on the basis of race, class, gender, or sexual preference? How did it make you feel? What can we do to correct discrimination wherever we encounter it?

6. This author uses the MLA style of documentation. Why do you think it is important in literary criticism to use the author's name plus page numbers in the text citations rather than the author's name plus publication date as is customary in the sciences and social sciences?

Maturation of Tribal Governments During the Atomic Age

Marjane Ambler

For the most part, American Indian involvement in the major issues of the twentieth century has been ignored by historians and journalists. Indians have been part of the "dismissable terrain" to which Patricia Nelson Limerick refers. In discussions of the Atomic Age there have been oblique, ironic references to their names: Tewa and Zuni nuclear tests, the ship named Tecumseh, and the Sequoyah nuclear fuel processing plant. Recently major newspapers have carried stories about nuclear waste disposal proposals for reservations. By understanding the history of tribal involvement in the Atomic Age we can better understand such current controversies.

On April 2, 1980, I happened to be in Albuquerque, New Mexico, for one of the most moving encounters I have ever witnessed. I was traveling in the Southwest at that time to interview Indian uranium workers about their illnesses. As a member of the press, I was invited by an environmental group to a school gymnasium where a dozen Japanese were meeting with about the same number of Navajos, either ailing miners or the widows of miners. The Japanese radiation victims were there as part of a national tour, opposing nuclear weapons. The Navajo radiation victims were opposing uranium mining.

Their faces conveyed only recognition of their shared fate. They looked at each other and smiled silently, most of both the Japanese and the Navajo groups able to speak only their own language—not English and not one another's. Trying desperately to communicate, the Japanese bowed. So the Navajos bowed. The Navajos handed them signed posters opposing mining on their sacred mountain, Mount Taylor. In turn, the Japanese gave the Navajos origami birds, the symbol of their antinuclear movement. Before parting, they exchanged the few words they knew in English, saying, "thank you" and "good night" over and over.

It was a dramatic scene. Those who arranged it knew it would be and invited the press. We members of the press, of course, ate it up: monolingual Navajos, dying of cancer, fit neatly into a familiar stereotype. Not knowing English, they would not have been able to understand warnings about the dangers of uranium dust even if such warnings had been given. The meeting presented a black and white picture of two peoples bombed by technology. In this image, the Navajos represented the innocent

From *Halcyon* (1994, Vol. 16, pp. 59-70). Reprinted by permission.

victims of technology, an anachronistic people that would eventually be eliminated by the Modern Age.

THE REAL STORY

The real story is much more complicated than that, with more grey tones, as most real stories are. The suffering of the Navajo miners should not be downplayed; several later died from cancer caused by their work in the unventilated uranium mines. However, that snapshot omits as much as it tells. It implies that as Indians they were victimized more than the non-Indians in that area. In fact, the Navajos were not that much different from other residents of uranium-producing states at that time. They enjoyed the benefits of and suffered the effects of the Manhattan Project in much the same way, with two important exceptions, which will be discussed later. Both Indians and non-Indians received wages for their work. Both became sickened and died as a result of their work, and both Indian and non-Indian lands and waters became contaminated. The literature on the dangers of uranium mining was not available outside of medical libraries and used words such as microrems, microroentgens, and picocuries—language foreign to most people, Indian and non-Indian.

By including miners who worked primarily during the 1940s and 1950s, the snapshot from that gymnasium also represented a frozen moment of time. It omitted the growing sophistication of tribal governments between the 1950s and the 1980s and what they learned from the Atomic Age. It contributed to the stereotype of Indians as passive, helpless victims of economic development, never beneficiaries.

EXTENT OF INDIAN PARTICIPATION IN THE ATOMIC AGE

A few examples will illustrate the tribes' growing sophistication. First, however, we should outline how the Atomic Age has touched and continues to touch Indian people. Indian tribes and individuals have provided fuel for the front end of the nuclear cycle through mining and milling uranium. When reservations were established, no one knew of the value or even of the existence of uranium, of course. Although thought to be wastelands from an agricultural perspective in the late 1800s, some of the lands actually turned out to be rich in various minerals, including uranium. The Department of Energy estimates that more than one-third of the potential uranium reserves in the country lie beneath Indian lands, primarily on eight reservations.

During the 1950s, Indian mines on three reservations supplied uranium for the Atoms for Peace program: the Navajo Reservation in the

Southwest, the Spokane Reservation in Washington State, and Laguna Pueblo in New Mexico. The Laguna mine was the biggest open-pit mine in the world. Before the uranium bust of the 1960s, four uranium mills operated on Navajo lands and one within the boundaries of the Wind River Reservation in Wyoming. A sixth mill operated until the uranium bust of the 1980s on the Spokane Reservation.

Indian lands have also been involved in the waste end of the nuclear cycle. The Hanford Nuclear Reservation lies within the treaty area of three tribes: Yakimas, Umatillas, and Nez Perces. Other reservations lie close to nuclear power plants and uranium processing plants which now have de facto waste sites (for example, the Prairie Island Indian community in Minnesota and the Sequoyah processing plant near Cherokee lands in Oklahoma). Yucca Mountain, the site now being studied as a permanent repository, lies on land claimed by the Western Shoshone tribe in Nevada. In the latest approach to resolving the disposal of high-level nuclear wastes (monitored retrievable storage or MRS), half the current applicants (nine of eighteen on September 1, 1992) for study grants are Indian tribes. A total of fifteen tribes applied; six have since dropped out of the process or been rejected by the Department of Energy.

The third main arena in which tribes will be involved in the Atomic Age is transportation of wastes. Many reservations lie along major highways between waste generators and waste disposal sites (for example, near the Waste Isolation Pilot Project in New Mexico and the Idaho National Engineering Laboratory).

IMPACTS OF EARLY URANIUM DEVELOPMENT

In most cases during the early history of uranium mining in this country, private industries externalized their costs. As the sole purchaser of uranium from 1946 to the mid-1960s, the government accepted this practice. Because of the importance of uranium to defense, the federal government delayed implementing laws to protect workers and the environment. There are several examples of this. In fact, information that came out during the recent congressional hearings on the uranium miners' case against the government revealed that the Atomic Energy Commission made a conscious decision not to provide warnings on health effects and not to require better ventilation in the mines, which were little larger than dogholes at that time.

Lease contracts set before the 1970s did not require high enough bonds to reclaim mines or mills, and there were no federal laws to require reclamation of mines or mills on either Indian or public lands. When the government contracts began to be phased out, the companies walked away from the mills, leaving the mill wastes (tailings) piled high alongside streams. A U.S. Department of Health, Education, and Welfare report published in 1966 said twelve million tons of tailings had been stacked at seventeen sites along the Colorado River and its tributaries.

The mineral income to the federal, state, and tribal governments was not adequate to cover these costs. Nor were the wages adequate to cover the health effects for the miners. Thus uranium development came with a net cost to the governments and individuals, not a net benefit.

When the political climate shifted sufficiently, the tribes were at the vanguard, demanding changes and making changes. They had observed firsthand the heavy cost of past development of uranium and other minerals. Just as with other governments, they made mistakes and rarely had the resources they needed to fulfill their objectives. Nevertheless, through their efforts the tribes succeeded in helping to reduce the damage from past development and to assure that companies internalized more of the environmental and health costs. They employed several mechanisms for doing so, lobbying for national legislation, cooperating with state and federal environmental agencies, and adopting their own environmental programs. In some cases, tribal representatives first brought problems to the nation's attention. The experiences of the Navajos, the Laguna Pueblo, the Spokane tribe, and the Northern Arapaho and Shoshone tribes of the Wind River Reservation illustrate the tribes' growing environmental activism.

NAVAJO TRIBAL INITIATIVES

During the 1950s, tests of drinking water in Farmington, New Mexico, on the border of the Navajo Reservation, revealed high radium concentrations resulting from uranium mill tailings abandoned upstream. Soon after that, Colorado state and Navajo tribal officials discovered that the fine sands from the tailings piles had been used as construction material and even in children's sandboxes in the region. Later, both Colorado and the Navajo tribes began exerting pressure on the U.S. Environmental Protection Agency (EPA) to resolve the problem.

In the meantime, Harold Tso decided his Navajo people could not wait for the slow wheels of government to turn. A nuclear chemist and a native of Shiprock, New Mexico, he understood the danger. He used a tribal construction firm to start burying the tailings at Shiprock in 1973, the first large tailings decontamination effort in the country. As an indication of how much processed uranium had been accidentally released in the air when the mill operated, Tso said the crews found $100,000 worth of yellowcake between two layers of roofing in the uranium mill at Shiprock—dust that had settled on the old roof from the air before the new one was built.

Because of his concerns over uranium, oil spills, and air pollution, Tso helped establish the Navajo Environmental Protection Administration in 1974 and became the first director. After receiving training and equipment loaned by the EPA, the Navajo environmental staff went house to house on the reservation, testing for radiation. In one area, Red Valley, they found that thirty of the eighty homes had an anomaly, probably indicating that they had been built with tailings or mine wastes. Through the efforts of the Navajos and others, Congress in 1978 finally passed the Uranium Mill Tailings Radiation Control Act, which provided federal funds to clean up the twenty-two abandoned mills and tailings and homes built with those tailings across the country. The Navajo EPA has remained at the forefront of environmental regulation and cleanup in the past eighteen years, dealing, for example, with results of the nation's most serious radiation spill at Churchrock in 1979 and working with the tribal water department to adopt tribal water standards.

Why did the Navajo Tribe and others in the country devote so many resources to establishing their own environmental protection agencies? In the first place, states do not have environmental jurisdiction on Indian lands. Tribes prefer their own standards and regulations for the same reasons that states find their own better than federal ones. Congress, the courts, and the U.S. Environmental Protection Agency have confirmed the tribes' rights to use their own standards and regulations. Although both states' and tribes' environmental regulations must be at least as strong as the federal regulations, they can be stronger, depending upon local priorities. With one or two Navajos dying every month from radiation induced illnesses, the Navajo tribe considered strict controls over uranium development a high priority. In contrast to a distant federal environmental regulator, a tribal official would be less likely to write off the death of a neighbor or a clan brother as a "negative health effect." In addition, a staff person from the Navajo EPA once told me that when dealing with an elderly tribal member, it is very difficult to explain a lot of these matters in the Navajo language. It could be impossible in English. The poor roads on the Navajo Reservation, vast distances, and lack of telephones require an enormous commitment from environmental personnel, which federal agencies rarely could fulfill.

LAGUNA MINE RECLAMATION

In 1951, when Anaconda Copper Company geologists flew over

the Laguna Pueblo, most of the people below made their living raising crops and livestock. When the geologists met with tribal officials to lease the Pueblo's uranium, the tribal officials spoke only their native Keresan language and conducted business out of a trunk. They had no tribal offices.

Within a few years after Anaconda opened the Jackpile mine on those lands, it was considered the largest open-pit mine in the country. More than seven hundred workers, most of them Indians, worked at the mine, and the economy had largely been transformed from subsistence into a wage-earning economy. Miners made more money each year than they would have otherwise seen in a lifetime. During the thirty years that the mines operated, moreover, interest from uranium royalties provided tribal buildings and paid the salaries of the tribal staff.

Through their royalty investments, their experience providing government services to their people, their business dealings with Anaconda, and their contact with other mineral-owning tribes, the staff and elected officials became more experienced businessmen. With a donation from Anaconda, they started Laguna Industries, now a thriving company providing electronics and communications equipment to the Defense Department.

After Anaconda closed the mine in 1982, however, unemployment skyrocketed and now is about 70 percent. Although the Laguna miners working at the open-pit mines did not experience a cancer epidemic as the Navajo underground miners did, it is still unclear what health effects local residents may have suffered. During blasting, yellow dust fell on their dinner plates in the Laguna community of Paguate, one thousand feet away from the big mine, and the water was contaminated.

Because of the lax federal laws in effect during the 1950s, it was at first unclear whether the 2,600-acre open-pit mines and the underground mines would be reclaimed or to what standards. Other uranium companies encouraged Anaconda not to take responsibility for the mine because of the precedent it would set. No federal standards exist for uranium and metal mine reclamation, and the Jackpile-Paguate mines would be the first uranium mines reclaimed on Indian land. Companies had abandoned other uranium mines on Indian and federal lands.

The issue was critical to the continued existence of the Laguna Pueblo as a people. Russell Jim, a Yakima Indian well known for his efforts regarding nuclear waste, points out that relocation is not an option for Indian tribes. In this case, the Lagunas believe their ancestors have inhabited the area for thousands of years. Lagunas' family members, their traditions, and their religion are tied to their land. This is one significant way in which Indian people differ from non-Indians: the status of their lands.

Fortunately, Anaconda had posted a $45 million bond and also

MATURATION OF TRIBAL GOVERNMENTS

wanted to protect its corporate image. During reclamation negotiations, the tribe relied not just upon federal agencies but also on enlisted staff from an engineering firm specializing in uranium reclamation and from the Council of Energy Resource Tribes (CERT), a coalition of tribes based in Denver, Colorado.

The tribal negotiators found a unique solution. Anaconda signed over $43.6 million and the responsibility for reclamation to the tribe. Now Laguna Construction Company employs sixty people, most of them tribal members, and expects to complete the gigantic project by 1995; they have to move thirty-five million cubic yards of material. The Bureau of Indian Affairs has only an oversight role. The project engineer, Rudy Lorenzo, who grew up in Paguate at the rim of the pit, says his crew is very motivated and wants to do the job right. It's their land, not just bureaucratic requirements on a piece of paper. So far the work is going well. When they see that the contract requirements might have been inadequate, they change them, something industry might not have done. Laguna Construction has also begun work on other reclamation and construction projects in the area. It is hoped that the Laguna Pueblo will continue to succeed in using its boom/bust resource revenue to build the local economy.

SPOKANE AND WIND RIVER

The Spokane tribe's experiences with its two mines dramatically demonstrate the value of the lessons learned from early uranium development. The tribe's 1957 lease with Dawn Mining required a totally inadequate bond—fifteen thousand dollars for work later estimated to cost over ten million dollars. That agreement was written by the Bureau of Indian Affairs and given rubber stamp approval by the Spokane tribal leaders. As a result of their experience with Dawn, twenty years later the tribe demanded and received a bond much higher than BIA regulations required from Western Nuclear Corporation for the Sherwood mine and mill.

Now Dawn is threatening bankruptcy, and it is unclear who will take responsibility for the five hundred million gallons of acid mine wastes perched above a tributary to Franklin D. Roosevelt Reservoir. On the other hand, Western Nuclear's responsibility is clear, and the company plans to complete its work in 1994.

The Spokane tribe's experience also illustrates the hurdles to be overcome by small tribes. When the tribe was receiving uranium royalties, those royalties represented more than half of the tribal budget. With the end of those royalties and a drop in timber revenues, the tribe's budget plummeted and with it the tribe's capacity for monitoring their resources.

As political entities, tribes can exert some pressure on other governments and seek cooperation. For example, the Northern Arapaho and the Shoshone tribes of the Wind River Reservation were alarmed at the water contamination caused by tailings abandoned on their reservation in the 1960s. Since the old mill was located on private, non-Indian land within the reservation, the tribes had no official voice in the Department of Energy's decision making process. The DOE proposed stabilizing the tailings at the same location, and only the State of Wyoming had to agree. Despite the increased cost to the state, Wyoming eventually agreed with the tribes and convinced the DOE in 1984 to move the tailings off the reservation.

As the last example of utilizing tribal political clout and negotiating strength, Congress finally agreed in 1990 to help uranium miners and people affected by nuclear testing. Congress formally apologized to the Indian and non-Indian miners and downwinders and provided a hundred-million-dollar trust fund to partially compensate them. After the legislation passed, the Navajo tribe held a special ceremony honoring Stewart Udall for his twelve years of work for the compensation. (His experiences in this case will be discussed in his forthcoming book, tentatively called *Withered Legacy: The Lies, Illusions, and Unkept Promises of the Atomic Age*.)

SPIRITUAL TIES TO THE LAND

There is a second significant way in which Indians differ from their non-Indian neighbors on environmental and economic issues. Not only do they consider their reservations a permanent homeland, but they also have a spiritual relationship with their lands. In the past I have hesitated to discuss this because Indian religion has been misused so much by non-Indians. Some environmentalists and New Age practitioners have taken apart Indian shrines or philosophical frameworks and reconstructed them for their own purposes. It is a subject best addressed by Indian people themselves, such as Russell Jim.

The religious factor cannot be ignored, however. Although difficult for us to fully comprehend, it is critical to the motivation of many Indian people. Even when expressed in English, it is almost incomprehensible to the Western, European mind—like the barrier between the Japanese and the Navajo radiation victims. It is dangerous to generalize, since each tribe has its own traditions. We cannot say that their spiritual ties to the earth prevent any development of any kind. We can say that most tribal traditions require a different responsibility to the earth.

Rex Tilousi, a former vice chairman of the Havasupai tribe,

illustrates this point. The Havasupai Indians live under the rim of the Grand Canyon, just downstream from where intensive uranium mining has been proposed. Tilousi says, "We have a song to say that all people are sacred, each one of us. We say that everything we see is related to us. The springs that run through the canyon, the springs that we drink, it runs in our blood and nourishes the earth." He goes on, "We are the Grand Canyon. We were put here to protect her and to take care of this place. If the canyon is destroyed, then so is our meaning, our reason for being here."[1]

CONCLUSION

The story of Indian people in the Atomic Age is a story of fission and of fusion. It tells how splitting the atom separated them from their past innocence. At the same time, it is a story of working together—Navajos and Japanese, Indians and non-Indians—to control the effects of nuclear energy. Ultimately, it is a story of connections between humans and all elements of the earth.

NOTE

1. Cate Gilles, "Uranium Mining at the Grand Canyon," *The Workbook* 16, no. 1 (Spring 1991): 10.

BIBLIOGRAPHY

Ambler, Marjane. *Breaking the Iron Bonds: Indian Control of Energy Development*. Lawrence: University Press of Kansas, 1990.

Farrell, John Aloysius. "New Indian Wars." *Denver Post*, Nov. 1983 (reprint), pp. 20-27.

Jorgensen, Joseph G., ed. *Native Americans and Energy Development*. 2 vols. Boston: Anthropology Resource Center, 1978 and 1984.

Limerick, Patricia Nelson. *The Legacy of Conquest: The Unbroken Past of the American West*. New York: W. W. Norton, 1987.

Newmont Mining Corp. 1987 Annual Report. New York, April 1988.

Pearson, Jessica S. *A Sociological Analysis of the Reduction of Hazardous Radiation in Uranium Mines*. Prepared for the National Institute for Occupational Safety and Health, Public Health Service. Washington, D.C.: Government Printing Office, 1975.

Popkin, Roy. "Indians Act for a Cleaner Environment." *EPA Journal*, April 1987, pp. 28-31.

Reno, Philip. *Mother Earth, Father Sky, and Economic Development: Navajo Resources and Their Use*. Albuquerque: University of New Mexico Press, 1981.

Ruffing, Lorraine Turner. "Navajo Mineral Development." *American Indian Journal* (Vienna, Va.), Sept. 1978, pp. 2-15.

Shuey, Chris. "The Puerco River: Where Did the Water Go?" *The Workbook* (Albuquerque: Southwest Research and Information Center) 11: 1-10.

Taylor, Lynda."Uranium Legacy." *The Workbook* (Albuquerque: Southwest Research and Information Center) 8:192-207.

Tosan, Sandy. "Uranium Plagues the Navajos." *Sierra* (San Francisco: Sierra Club), Nov.-Dec. 1983, 55-60.

Government Documents
Interior agencies are abbreviated as follows:
BIA: Bureau of Indian Affairs
BLM: Bureau of Land Management
MMS: Minerals Management Service
OSMRE: Office of Surface Mining and Reclamation

Department of Energy. *Environmental Assessment of Remedial Action at the Riverton Uranium Mill Tailings Site, Riverton, Wyo.* Albuquerque, N.M.: DOE, June 1987.

Department of Energy. *Environmental Assessment of Remedial Action at the Shiprock Uranium Mill Tailings Site, Shiprock, N.M.* Albuquerque, N.M.: DOE, May 1984.

Environmental Protection Agency. *Potential Health and Environmental Hazards of Uranium Mine Wastes.* Washington, D.C.: EPA, June 1983.

Interior Department, Bureau of Indian Affairs. *Sherwood Uranium Project, Spokane Indian Reservation, Final Environmental Statement.* Portland, Ore.: BIA, 1976.

Interior Department, Bureau of Land Management. *Jackpile-Paguate Uranium Mine Reclamation Project Environmental Impact Statement.* Albuquerque, N.M.: BLM, Oct. 1986.

Interior Department, Bureau of Land Management. *Uranium Development in the San Juan Basin Region, Final Report.* Albuquerque, N.M.: BLM, 1980.

Office of Nuclear Waste Negotiator. "MRS Applicant List." Boise, Idaho, Sept. 1992.

Public Health Service, Health and Human Services Department, *Health Hazards Related to Nuclear Resource Development on Indian Land.* Washington, D.C.: Public Health Service, Nov. 1982.

Interviews with Author
Information is also based upon numerous interviews by the author with tribal, industry, and government officials between 1974 and 1992.

Mariane Ambler is a freelance writer living in Colorado, specializing in American Indian economic, environmental, and educational issues. She began traveling to Indian reservations in 1974 as an editor with *High Country News*, a natural resource biweekly newspaper now based in Paonia, Colorado. In 1980 the Alicia Patterson Foundation awarded her a fellowship to spend a year investigating Indian energy issues. The University Press of Kansas published her book, *Breaking the Iron Bonds: Indian Control of Energy Development*, in 1990.

QUESTIONS FOR DISCUSSION

1. How would you characterize the tone of this article? Is the author sympathetic to the Native Americans? Does she show any kind of bias against mining companies or the government?

2. After reading this account of tribal experiences with nuclear weapons, how would you characterize their "maturation"?

3. The author lists several instances of Native American encounters with the atomic age. Describe these encounters. How have they affected the tribes, for good or ill?

4. Did you find the organization of this article easy to follow? Would you characterize this article as an argument or a report? Why do you think so?

5. Notice that the author separated the works cited list into publications and government documents. Is this helpful to you as a reader?

6. The author is a freelance writer. Does this fact make her more or less believable on this topic?

Yes, It's True: Zimbabweans Love Dolly Parton

Jonathan Zilberg

Many Zimbabweans, old and young, rich and poor, urban and rural, love country western music. Though this might at first seem to be extraordinary, it is rather a commonplace experience in people's everyday lives. In fact, Dolly Parton, Jim Reeves, and Don Williams are amongst the most commonly sought-after records in the rural areas of Zimbabwe and have been for some time.[1] As an anthropologist I felt compelled to consider this popularity of American country music in Zimbabwe as this phenomenon has as of yet not received any attention in the extensive literature on Zimbabwe. During fieldwork, I found a ubiquitous and striking knowledge of country artists and their songs, for example of "Wild Flowers Don't Care Where They Grow" by Emmylou Harris, Dolly Parton's "Coat of Many Colors," Sissy Chapman's "Frontier Justice," and Slim Whitman's "Rosemary," to name a few of the more notable songs that I came to know whilst in Zimbabwe. While many Americans, particularly African-Americans in Northern rather than Southern cities, find this surprising, as they commonly associate country music in America with stereotypes of conservative, white Southern culture, country music, and Dolly Parton, in particular, are deeply inculcated in the multiplex Zimbabwean imagination.

The history of this affection for country music and world popular culture in general is eloquently captured in two provocative descriptions of urban life in what was then Rhodesia in the 1960s. In *Harvest of Thorns* Shimmer Chinodya, a local author, writes:

> Those were the days when there were loudspeakers at the centre of the township which were tuned to the radio station and you didn't have a radio in your home unless your father was a businessman or a fireman or, maybe, a teacher. Yes, those were the days of the mobile biscope, when the nights belonged to Mataka and Zuze and the Three Stooges and cinema was so alive you could smell gunpowder off the big white screen.

From the *Journal of Popular Culture* (1995, Vol. 21.9, pp. 111-125). Reprinted by permission.

> As we grew up, things changed, slowly. We had scorned the poverty we did not see in our ignorance of it, wearing our clothes till our bodies showed through, but we began to notice clothes that stole our souls. We saw bell-bottom trousers, 'Satan' denim jeans, platform shoes, bold, bright shirts with large, raised collars, checked jackets, massive belts. Dresses crept up woman's thighs and women were so much taller, suddenly; we heard of gogo shoes and hot pants.
>
> We were busy scavenging empty bottles and bones to get money for Chunkey Charlie Comics or to pay for Teen Time at the township halls. The Beatles came to us too—everybody sang "Don't let me die..." Jim Reeves and Elvis Presley and Dolly Parton came too from across the bridge to contend with our Harare Mambos, our Safirio Madzikatires and Spokes Machianes. Later Hendrix and Otis came, with 'feeling,' and many many many were to follow. With a swagger and a certain brashness of speech, young men took to rock and roll and refused to comb their hair. We heard of a new word, 'hippies.' Older men and women were seized by a passion for long coats, frilly swishing dresses and smooth long strides. On the radios we heard a flood of new foreign songs. S'manjenje from the South rushed in to the rescue, but mbakumba, shangara, m'chongoyo, ngquzu, and jerusarema [traditional dances] were dead before we knew them. (78-79)

Dambudzo Marechera gives us a similar report about popular culture and growing up in Rhodesia in the 1960s:

> I was a cowboy, an Indian, a GI, a 2nd World War British commando officer... [That was]... the sixties. Upheavals in politics, the surge of black nationalism, the banning of ZAPU, the early attempts at armed struggle. I was too young to know... The Beatles. The Rolling Stones. Cliff Richards, Elvis Presley. The Shadows. Every transistor radio seemed tuned up full blast. There was this small 'township' hall where we had bands playing smanjmanje, jazz, rockin'roll—one of them was called The Rocking Kids, all ghetto youths who had taught themselves to play guitars and drums and the saxophone. And every Friday there was a film show, Hoppalong Cassidy. Gene Autry. Tarzan. James Bond, Ronald Reagan, Fuzzy. Woody Woodpecker. And Wow! Charlie Chaplin...

[and] Batman. Spiderman. Super this, super that . . .Tarzan things and Tarzan thongs. (8)

For today in Zimbabwe, read Rambo and Arnold Schwarzenegger, Ninja Turtles, children running around screaming "Cowabunga," and teenagers rapping in New York Shona Zulu jive. Read *The Peter John's Show* "moving and grooving the nation," Michael Jackson and Madonna, Dynasty, Dallas, and Falcon Crest, and young girls singing along to Suzanne Vega.

Imagine, for example, listening to Tracy Chapman's latest songs as you wait in the check-out line of the supermarket, seeing Becky Hobbs and The Hearthrobs playing at the ZANU/PF (government) headquarters, or watching the World Wrestling Federation on Saturday afternoon and the 700 Club on Sunday morning. Yet rarely, in ethnographic and historical studies of Zimbabwe do we find analysis of such material, for academic studies typically do not take into account the role of radio and television in everyday life though anthropologists are increasingly turning their attention to the media (Abu-Lughod, Appadurai, Spitulaick, West and Fair).[2]

For Zimbabwe, besides the study of the state control of information during the Rhodesian regime (Windrich) and the review of the information system in 1977 by O'Callaghan, there are notable references to the effects of media in Kileff and Pendleton (133), Stopforth (34, 86) and Gwata (37), as well as an extended study of the role of the media in the marketing of commodities in Burke. For example, Gwata observed that in the 1970s, women and youth seemed to be more influenced by western media than working men at that time. Burke, studying the advertising of toiletries, notes that at this time 93 percent of the urban black population listened to radio at least once a week (267), and Stopforth found that 74 percent of his respondents had access to a radio at home, noting that media participation appeared to be high (34).

The 1990 value survey prepared for Zimbabwe Broadcasting Corporation by Probe Market Research provides a detailed survey of media exposure and shows that in general today a slightly higher percentage of men than women are listening to radio, watching television, reading newspapers and magazines, and visiting cinemas. In all categories, including the rural population, the media exposure is very extensive. For example, on any particular day, an estimated 71 percent of the estimated population listened to radio. Consequently, it could be assumed, as the below ethnographic data suggests, that the Sunday morning country music show, which I discuss, has a very large audience.

Generally speaking, anthropologists studying Zimbabwe, in particular, are missing important facets of contemporary culture. The way in which the youth grow up with radio and television, forming their identities

ZIMBABWEANS LOVE DOLLY PARTON

in great part through experiences with global popular culture, as many of their parents did, is a neglected area of study. This is a critical issue for understanding Zimbabwe today, as one high school student points out in the following interview in 1991:

> They [the younger generation] all want to be Westerners, they dance like Westerners, they dress like Westerners, they talk like Westerners... They're addicted to the radio... You'll find that people are glued onto the television...

Another, responding to the attacks on the westernization of the youth in the media as hypocritical, wrote this:

> Indeed, the youth have adopted Western norms and values, but what then did you expect? What did you teach us? And what did you raise us to be? ... Yes, indeed, we have taken Western values 'hook, line and sinker,' but can we really be blamed ... Our own culture remains a mystery to us ... The parents go to work everyday, the children go to school, and the rest of the day is spent watching Western-type television and/or listening to Western type radio ... Can I blame the disc jockeys? I don't think so. After all, they are only giving the listeners (not only youths) what they want. (Morisio Jays, *The Sunday Mail* 11 Nov. 1991)

Accordingly, we are missing interesting historical data on identity formation, for example in the role Zimbabwean disc jockeys such as Kudzi Marudza and Peter Johns play as popular artists with incredibly wide receptions. We have given very little attention to radio and television as part of ordinary daily life and thus history.

USING THE RADIO TO DEMONSTRATE A WIDESPREAD PASSION FOR DOLLY

Early every Saturday evening in Zimbabwe, much of the nation is glued to the television; they are watching the World Wrestling Federation and enjoying the show immensely, as much as they do the Country Music Show from nine to ten o'clock every Sunday morning. This experience with country music, particularly with Parton, is heightened for those watching the Dolly Parton Show, aired, in 1991, on TV1 every Wednesday evening after the eight o'clock news.

JONATHAN ZILBERG

For the remainder of this essay I will consider the affectivity of country music, and of Dolly Parton in particular. Through edited transcriptions of commentaries on Dolly Parton and her music made during some of those Sunday morning shows, as well as through a selection of the songs lyrics, I propose that the country music genre has been strongly incorporated into local subjectivities. In doing so, I consider the ways in which many Zimbabweans relate to Dolly Parton specifically, and to country music in general.[3]

Country music appears to be an affective component of people's lives in Zimbabwe, and consequently speaks in some way to the complex whole of the national imagination and local historical consciousness as I will tentatively explore below. Perhaps it is able to do so because it expresses everyday experiences (Horstman); it is, I propose, a meaningful and deeply integrated experience in their lives. For example, Admire Taderera, a famous Zimbabwean disc jockey, exclaimed the following one Sunday morning in response to Dolly Parton's "Oh What a Heartbreak": "that's how life is, isn't it!"

All over the world country music audiences relate particular songs and themes with specific country stars; "No knowledgeable country music fan for example, can hear Dolly Parton sing 'White Limozeen' about a Daisy-May-ingenue in Hollywood without thinking of the travails of Dolly's own rags to riches rise out of Sevier County, Tennessee poverty" (Peterson 6, Parton). Many Zimbabweans also know about her history and they relate to it in a very personal way as Admire Taderera, a disc jockey, explains:

> Her name is Dolly Parton. Believe it or not she was raised the fourth of a dozen children, in a very poor and unstable family, and that was in East Tennessee. She says that music was a constant source of pleasure and relaxation. She had the gift, went out, had the ability to sing, and she says she built that lovely voice from a church choir, and that was way back in time with a grand-dad who was a pastor in one church back in . . . (sigh) . . . way back when, in Tennessee.

So many Zimbabweans relate in the most basic ways to Dolly Parton, her music, and with the experiences she sings of. Her songs bring them pleasure, relaxation, and even strength and hope. Furthermore, they seem to relate to the Christian values and experience expressed in country music as well as with its potential to uplift one's spirits in difficult times, for example, with the song "One Day at a Time Sweet Jesus." In addition, there appeared to be an emphasis (both in disc jockeys' choices and in requests) on tragic love songs (Fabian for a similar phenomenon in Zaire).

For example, on another Sunday morning I recorded this:

> That's a beauty from Dolly Parton, from her new album, "Eagle When She Flies." It's called "What a Heartache". . . . I was just saying to myself, this lady knows how to sing those love songs, especially the ones that are very, very sorrowful. Well, if that made you cry, take a listen to this—have your box of tissues at arm's length, I hope you do . . .

Songs, such as "What A Heartache," remain huge hits in Zimbabwe. Take, for example, Dolly Parton's "Just Because I'm a Woman (my mistakes are no worse than yours)," the number "Before the Next Tear Drop Falls," "There Goes My Everything" (by Hank Williams), "Still Hold On" (from Kenny Roger's new album *Love Is What You Make It*) and "You Were the Wind Beneath My Wings" by Gary Morris. One hears these songs frequently on the radio which as I noted earlier is very much present in people's lives.

These country love songs may be deeply incorporated into local emotional experiences, ways of speaking and thinking about life. Furthermore, they are commonly used as a means for Zimbabweans to communicate over the radio with each other. For example, one Sunday morning, several minutes after playing "Before the Next Teardrop Falls," the disc jockey said this:

> Well it's good to know that a lot of people are enjoying the selection on the country scene this lovely Sunday morning. Just had a caller, her name she won't disclose, but she says she is missing her husband Jonathan Mandu and she says "Hey Jonathan, please call home before the next teardrop falls."

Later, in introducing the song "Darling If You Ever Leave Me," Taderera said, "as they say in Shona—'Benz, Ane Benzi Nderake' meaning 'Crazy, He's Crazy for Her.'" Comments like this indicate the degree to which country music has acquired a currency in the local imagination. There are any number of similar songs which constitute a deeply affective component of the most basic human experience and thus historical consciousness, for example, Slim Whitman's following song that many Zimbabweans know:

> Oh Rose, my Rosemary
> Oh Rosemary I love you
> I'm always thinking of you
> Oh Rose, my Rosemary

JONATHAN ZILBERG

The most popular of these songs are locally known as "country classics" and it is in part the intonation, the cadences, and the tunefulness of these songs that holds the listener, that makes them memorable and pleasurable. Often providing balanced perspectives on gender, in which both men and women are presented as victims of human frailty, these songs are emotionally empowering. Providing melancholic renditions of failed love, they assuage the tears in beers all over the world.

As I noted above, there appeared to be an emphasis on love songs among the predilection for songs with Christian themes, family values, as well as about the ways in which they help in overcoming the tragic circumstances in life. For example, one Sunday morning, Dolly Parton was singing a sorrowful number. It went,

> As I look around the little house, we were so happy in, I think of all the happy times we'll never see again. . . .
> . . .
> Daddy won't be home any more.

As the song ended, the disc jockey said:

> If you are in this position, don't worry too much, you're not the only one. This is one lady who sings so well about love and hate on record that a lot of people shed tears when they listen to her music. Dolly Parton, a track dedicated to some young people out there, 'Daddy Won't Be Home Anymore.' It's a fact. Got to live with it.

I am sure that a good number of people found the comment meaningful and, in cases, true to their lives.

Again, in addition to the bitter-sweet messages conveyed in country lyrics, it is the expressive way in which the songs are sung that makes them so popular. Deep sentiment is thus conveyed through the timbre of the voices and instruments and this is, to some extent, what makes this medium so appealing to Zimbabweans of all classes, ages, and linguistic backgrounds. Beyond the musical qualities of her songs, Zimbabweans who love country music relate in a basic and immediate sense, because as Admire Taderera said: "that's the way life is!" It moves them deeply: "some people even cry!"

APPROPRIATING COUNTRY MUSIC: THE SOOTHING OF DISCONTENT

Some aspects of the affectivity of country Western music to Zimbabweans are obvious. The songs are typically short stories, often about love, usually failed love (Rogers); or about Christian belief and traditional family values, of an idealized vision of rural life which, though poor, is seen as happy and never lonely (Peterson, Horstman). Peterson writes that the underlying message is commonly about the struggle to survive and not one with a revolutionary consciousness promising a better life to come. Many Zimbabweans know well the song that goes "Money can't buy happiness," and one of the most frequently played Parton songs that I heard on the radio was "Coat of Many Colors," a song about the way in which strong family ties and hard work helps one in overcoming the difficulties in life.

In *You Wrote My Life*, Peterson shows that there is a "class unconsciousness" in country music which asserts a working-class identity, and a recognition of exploitation which, "rather than being directed to a revolutionary consciousness...encourages pride in acknowledging one's own (past) poverty" (57). Peterson goes on to explain that lyrics such as those in Dolly Parton's "Chicken Every Sunday," "invite self-identification with hegemonic forms" (33) and foster a "Fatalistic state in which people bemoan their fate, yet accept it" (60). Despite this fatalism, however, through the choice of particular songs and their order in specific contexts, Zimbabwean disc jockeys are able to use this genre to comment on life and politics. For example, the first song to be played on Heroes Day 1991, without introduction and immediately after the unusually attenuated news, was "Your Cheating Heart" by Hank Williams. This is how it went for countless Zimbabweans scattered across the nation who were not at the annual celebration of the revolution held at Heroes Acre that morning. In light of the dissatisfaction widely expressed with "Heroes" at the time, it seems likely that there was a more than implicit satyrical political commentary at work in the choice of the first song and about what in life matters in those that followed.

> Your cheating heart will make you weep
> You try and try to get to sleep
> But sleep won't come the whole night through
> Your cheating heart will tell on you
> Praise the Lord
> The time will come when you'll be blue
> Your cheating heart will tell on you.

JONATHAN ZILBERG

The songs that followed were: "The Last Cowboy Song" (Country's Heroes) and "Heart" by Dean Rockwell. Then there was "One Day at a Time Sweet Jesus" and "Love Is a Beautiful Thing." These are the aspects of history that we anthropologists don't usually consider of any importance in our descriptions of the world.

Keeping this context and these examples in mind, I am proposing here that country music provides a certain healing function. The last example of recent Zimbabwean radio history that I use to support this relevance of country music are the lyrics to another popular Dolly Parton number and the disc jockey's witty response:

> When it's family you forgive them
> for they know not what they do
> You accept them because you have no choice but to
> ...
> When it's family you'll tolerate what you'd kill others for.
> Somehow you try to justify mistakes
> Try to find some better way to solve the problems day to day
> Because it's family.

The disc jockey playfully added, "When it's family, it's all right, but when it's somebody else's family, hey, then it's not. That's Dolly Parton. That's how life is, isn't it?" It would appear then that country music is an affective component of people's lives in Zimbabwe, that it speaks in some way to subjectivity and history, probably because, as a medium, it allows for the lyrical expression of everyday human experience, particularly in facing life's failures (Crafts, Cavicchi, Keil 161).

There appears to be both a generational and gender difference in this affectivity for Dolly Parton. It is interesting, that of the teenage Zimbabwean girls interviewed, all responded that they "loved" Dolly Parton, whereas the boys admitted that though it was indeed popular they were somewhat less enthusiastic. For example, one informant, laughing about this, said that he could not understand why his parents loved country music so much. Indeed, some Zimbabweans loath country music and Dolly Parton in particular (terming those who love Parton's music as the "Gusherettes"), yet the very intensity of their dislike signals the popularity of this form.

One interview with a teenage Zimbabwean girl (and six of her friends) clearly demonstrates this affection for Dolly Parton.

> Q. Do you like country music?
> A. I love it very much.

Q. You love it very much?
A. Mmmmm.
Q. Would you say most of your friends do as well?
A. Yes, they love it (six friends all laugh and nod their heads).
Q. Do you watch the Dolly Parton Show?
A. Yeah, I watched it every Wednesday evening (more laughter all round).

One male student gave a very different response to a set of similar questions.

Q. Do you like Dolly Parton?
A. No. No I don't.
Q. Did you watch the Dolly Parton Show?
A. No (laughter), in fact I avoided it every time.
Q. Did your parents like it?
A. Yeah. I don't know why.

(The interviewer, Daniel Soriano, notes, "there are six heads nodding furiously here.") Clearly then, Dolly Parton and country music are much loved in Zimbabwe.

Those Zimbabweans who do appreciate country music seem to relate in the most basic ways to Dolly Parton, her music, and the experiences she sings. While on the one hand this has much to do with shared working-class Christian values, i.e., an identification with the subject matter, as well as an appreciation for the musical qualities of the songs, on the other hand, it begs the question of whether some black Zimbabweans actually identify with Dolly Parton as a personal image, just as their daughters may do so with her or Whitney Houston, and their sons and brothers with local disc jockeys such as Peter Johns or American rappers such as Snoop Doggy Dog (Remes).

How can we theorize this identification with Dolly Parton (Schwichtenberg for the case of Madonna)? Could Dolly Parton, through her lyrics about love and survival, and her pleasure in performance, serve as a model/source of empowerment? Could her music provide a healing function? Could she be a certain source of sexual identification? Do women identify with her extravagance? During fieldwork I was struck, over and over again, by how much pleasure both black and white women, old and young, rich and poor, took in Parton's performances on radio and television. The identification seemed immediate and emotionally empowering, a recognition of similarities rather than differences. I am not proposing that these individuals are actively constructing themselves on Parton's image

199

(though it seems to be to some degree possible), but that they recognize something of value for themselves to which they can relate. One woman, who herself had experienced a rags-to-riches history, related to me that she loved Dolly Parton because "she is a good, happy success story, she is unashamed of her past, and she sings about our everyday life."

CONCLUSION

Just as country songs have been composed in Shona, Cewa, Ndebele, Kalanga, and Manyika among other dialects and languages by local musicians such as Phinias Tshawe (inspired by Jimmie Rogers) and Jordan Chataika amongst other Zimbabweans, country music has proven popular amongst Jamaicans and the Inuit (pers. comm. Lawrence Grossberg). But these are stories that have been, in the main, only recently related in studies of world popular music (Frith, Clark, Hamm, Nugent).[6]

Considering the extent of the Zimbabwean passion for country music, and similar phenomena that remain essentially undocumented, it is my most explicit hope, or challenge, that anthropologists and other social scientists studying Zimbabwe, in particular, take such popular culture seriously. Perhaps then, some day, we might find out about phenomena such as the emergence of the "Bhibho Brigade" (those Zimbabwean youths who conspicuously model themselves on images of urban African-Americans gained through the media). Then we could begin to understand how House, Hip Hop and Rap, radio and television are influencing Zimbabwean youth today and further understand the way in which their parents were influenced by American jazz, country music, and the mass media in general (Balantine, Burke, Clark, Coplan, Erlmann, Zeigler and Asante, and Zindi). In paying some attention to one little-studied aspect of everyday life in Africa, I have sought here, in a small way, to throw new light on Zimbabwean social history, and specifically to add to the call for interdisciplinary fertilization.

ACKNOWLEDGMENTS

I gratefully acknowledge the opportunity to pursue this line of research while a Zora Neale Hurston fellow at the Institute for the Advanced Study and Research in the African Humanities at Northwestern University. In particular, I thank Dr. Karin Barber, Dr. Paul Berliner, Dr. Ray Browne, Caleb Dube, Dr. Alma Gottlieb, Dr. Lawrence Grossberg, Dr. Veronica Kann, Patricia Sandier, Daniel Soriano, Dr. Karen Tranberg-Hansen, Dr. Ute Luig, Dr. James McGuire, Dr. Terence Ranger, Sipho Sepamla, Dr. Thomas Turino, and Alan Waters.

NOTES

1. Dave Smith, owner of Music Express, a record chain with stores throughout Zimbabwe, reports that some of the most sought-after records in the rural areas of Zimbabwe are those of Don Williams, Dolly Parton, and Jim Reeves, and have been for some time (pers. comm. Dr. Thomas Turino).

2. Anthropologists are however increasingly turning their attention to the mass media (Floyd, Fuglesang, Ginsburg, Hannerz, Michaels, and Turner, among others). For two very early and entertaining accounts of the history and reception of media in Zambia specifically concerning radio and film, see Powdermaker and Fraenkel. For accounts of the early days of television in Nigeria and the mass media in the Third World, see Olusala and Lent. For a wide-ranging review of the popular arts in African, see Barber. For the earliest, and by now classic studies of popular culture in the region, see Mitchell and Ranger.

3. Country music is very much a "story tellers' medium": "The chord structure is simple and predictable, the melodic range is slight, the rhythm is regular, the orchestration is sparse or at least clearly in the background so that the words can be understood... (Peterson and McLaurin 2; see Hamm 132 for a more detailed musicological description of stylistic features, and Fox for country music's narrative qualities). For a sophisticated anthropological analysis of the affectivity (or "affective salience" of country music, see Fox.

4. Most of the country songs on the radio were about love, usually sad songs about love such as "What a Heartache You Turned Out to Be" (by Dolly Parton), as were the teeny bopper dance songs, except for the one major difference between these genres which is that the latter heavily idealized the search for "true love" (Hayakawa).

5. For a collection of papers on the global influence of world popular music, see Mellers and Martin. There Frith challenges the notion of indigenous traditions as "pure" and the editors urge musicologists to give attention to the accelerated emergence of new musical traditions "spurred on by urbanization, immigration, international mass communications, and the availability of radios and recorders which allow more and more people, for the first time in history, to create their own musical environments" (ix). See Llorens, Turino, and Waterman amongst a rapidly emerging body of ethnomusicological literature on these new musical traditions. Furthermore, though I have not made any use of it here, there is in addition a very relevant body of literature on popular culture in sociology and cultural studies. For an extensive bibliography and overview of the latter field, see Grossberg, Nelson and Treichler. See Handler for an anthropologist's response to this literature.

WORKS CITED

Abu-Lughod, L. "Editorial Comment: On Screening Politics in a World of Nations." *Public Culture* 5.3 (1993): 465-68.

Appadurai, A. "Global Ethnoscapes: Notes and Queries for a Transnational Anthropology." *Recapturing Anthropology. Working in the Present.* Ed. Richard G. Fox. Santa Fe: School of American Research, 1992. 191-212.

Balantine, C. "Music and Emancipation: The Social Role of Black Jazz and Vaudeville in South Africa between the '70's and '40's." *Journal of Southern African Studies* 17.1 (1991): 129-52.

Barber, K. "Popular Arts in Africa." *African Studies Review* 30.3 (1987): 1-78.

Burke, T. "Lifebuoy Men, Lux Women: Commodification, Consumption and Cleanliness in Colonist Zimbabwe." Diss. John Hopkins U., 1993.

Chinodya, S. *Harvest of Thorns.* Harare: Boabab, 1989.

Clark, Leon. *From Tribe to Town: Problems of Adjustment*, Vol. 2 of *Through African Eyes: Cultures in Change.* New York: Praeger, 190.

Coplan, D. *In Township Tonight! South Africa's Black City Music and Theatre.* New York: Longman, 1985.

Crafts, S.D., D. Cavicchi, and C. Keil. *My Music.* Hanover: Wesleyan UP, 1993.

Dowmunt, T., ed. *Channels of Resistance. Global Television and Local Empowerment.* London: BFI, 1993.

Erlmann, V. *African Stars: Studies in Black South African Performance.* Chicago: U of Chicago P., 1991.

Fabian, J. "Popular Culture in Africa: Findings and Conjectures." *Africa* 48.4 (1978): 315-34.

Floyd, M.L. "Television, Culture and the State in Cote D'Ivoire: A Field Study of the Ivorien System." Diss. U of Texas at Austin, 1990.

Fox, A.A. "The Jukebox of History: Narratives of Loss and Desire in the Discourse of Country Music." *Popular Music* 11.1 (1992): 53-72.

Frankel, P. *Wayaleshi.* London: Weidenfeld and Nicholson, 1959.

Frith, S. "World Music, Politics and Social Change." *Papers from the International Association for the Study of Popular Music.* Manchester: Manchester UP, 1989.

Fuglesang, M. "Veils and Videos: Female Youth Culture on the Kenyan Coast." *Stockholm Studies in Social Anthropology* 32 (1994).

Ginsburg, F. "Aboriginal Media and the Australian Imagination." *Public Culture* 5.3: 557-78.

Grossberg, L., C. Nelson, and P. Treichler, eds. *Cultural Studies.* New York: Routledge, 1992.

Gwata, M.F. "Rhodesian African Cultural and Leisure Needs." Report commissioned by the National Arts Foundation of Rhodesia, Dept. of Sociology, U of Rhodesia, 1977.

Hamm, C. "The Fourth Audience." *Popular Music 1. Folk or Popular? Discontinuities, Influences, Continuities.* Ed. Richard Middleton and David Horn. Cambridge: Cambridge UP, 1981. 123-42.

Handler, R. "Anthropology Is Dead! Long Live Anthropology!" *American Anthropologist* 95.4 (1995): 991-99.

Hannertz, U. *Cultural Complexity: Studies in the Social Organization of Meaning.* New York: Columbia UP, 1992.

Horstman, D. *Sing Your Heart Out, Country Boy.* Nashville: Country Music Federation, 1986.

Kileff, C., and W.C. Pendleton, eds. *Urban Man in Southern Africa.* Harare: Mambo, 1975.

Lent, John. *Case Studies of Mass Media in the Third World.* Williamsburg, VA: Studies in Third World Societies, 1979.

Llorens, J.A. "Los 'Programas Folkloricos' En La Radiodifusion Limena" *Materiales Para La Communicacion Popular* 6 (1985): 2-15.

Marechera, D. "Dambudzo Marechera Interviews Himself." *Dambudzo Marechera.* 1952-1987. Ed. Flora Veit-Wild. Harare: Boabab, 1988.

Michaels, E. *The Aboriginal Invention of Television in Central Australia 1982-1986.* Canberra: Australian Institute of Aboriginal Studies, 1986.

Mitchell, J.D. *The Kaleh Dance: Aspects of Social Relationships among Urban Africans in Northern Rhodesia.* The Rhodes-Livingstone Papers No. 27. Manchester: Manchester UP, 1956.

Nugent, D. "Popular Musical Culture in Rural Chihuahua: Accommodation or Resistance?" *Workers' Expressions. Beyond Accommodation and Resistance.* Ed. John Calgione, Doris Francis, and Daniel Nugent. Albany: State U of New York P. 1992: 29-47.

O'Callaghan, M. "Information in Rhodesia." *Southern Rhodesia. The Effects of a Conquest Society on Education, Culture and Information.* Paris: Unesco, 1977. 275-90.

Olusola, S. "Television and the Arts: The African Experience 1959-1966." [Dakar] *1st World Festival of Negro Arts* Apr. 1966: 1-24.

Parton, D. *My Life and Other Unfinished Business.* New York: Harper and Collins, 1994.

Peterson, R.N. "Class Unconsciousness in Country Music." *You Wrote My Life: Lyrical Themes in Country Music.* Ed. Richard A. Peterson and Melton A. McLaurin. Philadelphia: Gordon and Breach Science, 1992.

Peterson, R.A., and M.A. Mclaurin, eds. "Introduction: Country Music Tells Stories." *You Wrote My Life: Lyrical Themes in Country Music.*

Cultural Perspectives on the American South Vol. 6. Philadelphia: Gordon and Breach Science, 1992: 1-14.

Powdermaker, H. *Copper Town: Changing Africa*. New York Harper and Row, 1962.

Probe Market Research Television Research Report. Value Survey, 1990. Viewers and Listeners under Examination. Electronic Media Monitoring Survey. No. 55/1089. Prepared for Zimbabwe Broadcasting Corporation. Habule, 1991.

Ranger, T.O. *Dance and Society in Eastern Africa 1890-1970: Thc Beni Ngorna*. London: Heinemann, 1975.

Remes, P. "Rapping: A Sociolinguistic Study of Oral Tradition in Black Urban Communities in the United States." *Journal of the Anthropological Society of Oxford* 12.1 (1991): 129-49.

Rogers, Jimmie. *The Country Music Message: Revisited*. Fayetteville: U of Arkansas P., 1989.

Schwichtenberg, C., ed. *The Madonna Connection. Representational Politics, Subcultural Identities, and Cultural Theory*. Boulder Westview, 1993.

Spitulaik, D. "Anthropology and Mass Media." *Annual Review of Anthropology* 22 (1993): 293-315.

Stopforth, P. "Two Aspects of Social Change. Highfield African Township, Salisbury. Department of Sociology." Occasional paper, No. 7, Institute for Social Research, U of Rhodesia. Salisbury: Bardwell, 1972.

Turino, T. *Moving Away from Silence: Music of the Peruvian Altiplano and the Experience of Urban Migration*. Chicago: U of Chicago P. 1993.

Turner, T. "Defiant Images: the Kayapo Appropriation of Video." *Anthropology Today* 8.6 (1992): 5-16.

Waterman, C. *Juju. A Social History and Ethnography of an African Popular Music*. Chicago: Chicago UP, 1990.

West, H., and J.E. Fair. "Development Communication and Popular Resistance in Africa: An Examination of the Struggle over Tradition and Modernity through Media" *African Studies Review* 36.1 (1993): 91-119.

Windrich, E. *The Mass Media in the Struggle for Zimbabwe: Censorship and Propaganda under Rhodesian Front Rule*. Gweru: Mambo, 1981.

Ziegler, D., and M. Asante. *Thunder and Silence: The Mass Media in Africa*. Trenton: Africa World, 1992.

Zindi, F. *Roots Rocking in Zimbabwe*. Harare: Mambo, 1985.

Jonathan Zilberg recently completed his doctoral thesis in the Department of Anthropology at the University of Illinois, Urbana-Champaign, IL.

QUESTIONS FOR DISCUSSION

1. The author states at the outset of the article that popular culture in African nations has not been adequately studied by sociologists or anthropologists. What question in particular does this author seek to answer through his research?

2. This article probably straddles the space between the humanities and the social sciences, as do many of the articles written about popular culture. What aspects of this article seem humanistic? What aspects seem social scientific?

3. How does this article help us to understand the people of Zimbabwe better?

4. The author uses several examples of song lyrics from Dolly Parton's music, as well as from other country western singers. Why does the author think that this music appeals to Zimbabweans?

5. In one interview, the researcher discovered that the girls (and women) liked Dolly Parton more than the boys (and men). Why do you think this was so? What explanation does the author provide?

6. What further research does the author think needs to be done in the realm of popular music and popular culture?

7. How do you think that mass media, such as radio and television, have influenced you or your generation?

8. Compare this article to the article by Ballard & Coates on the effects of music on mood. What similarities do you see between the articles? What differences?

Moving from First-Stage to Second-Stage Multiculturalism in the Art Classroom

John A. Stinespring, Texas Tech University

Art teachers are sensitive to calls for multicultural course content, but may be unclear about how to implement it. The most common approach has been to include examples in their instruction which show that representatives of previously excluded groups, such as minorities and women, can make art as good as that of traditionally accepted masters. This approach is certainly a constructive start, but an approach called second-stage multiculturalism is likely to lead to better understanding of human diversity and its impact on artistic expression. This approach is adopted from Frueh's (1991) discussion of feminist criticism.

Frueh identified three stages in recent feminist literary criticism. The first is "a resurrection of lost or ignored women writers and works" (p. 52). She characterized second-stage criticism as posing a separate "women's tradition either counter or related to the male literary tradition" (p. 52). Finally, she identified a third-stage feminism in which a more theoretical analysis examines "the interconnections among text or object, historical context, and culture" (p. 53).

FIRST-STAGE MULTICULTURALISM

This structure can be applied usefully to the entire subject of multiculturalism. First-stage multiculturalism seems to provide only that excluded "Others" share the canon of great artists and works. Vernon Minor (1994) explained that the concept of "The Other" is rooted in the cultural orientation where we refers to Western, meaning, "European, Anglo, and American white men and women, educated beyond the secondary level by the study of great books, great works of art, great scientific theories, great philosophical systems, great forms of government, great religions, and great social institutions" (p. 197).

The criticism of such a Eurocentric view is that it also represents false claims to ancient Egypt and Greece as being exclusively Western. It ignores the slavery of these societies and fails to recognize the contributions of Black Africa and the Arab world to the West. It is reluctant to claim the negative aspects of Western culture that are manifested in ethnocentrism,

From *Art Education* (1996, Vol. 49.4, pp. 49-53). Copyright 1996 by the National Art Education Association. Reprinted with permission.

racism, sexism, and homophobia. It dismisses as "primitive" the culture of non-Western societies. It has a one-sided perspective on basic concepts of progress, development, justice, and even such concepts as beauty and quality.

SECOND-STAGE MULTICULTURALISM

Frueh admitted that first-stage scholarship "has been important, by showing that women are a part of art history and thereby providing women artists with a sense of belonging" (1991, p. 52). But this level, she asserted, was flawed because it only reforms past tradition rather than providing the thorough revision that is needed. She objected to this level of scholarship on the grounds that it was still based on a traditional art historical point of view by attempting to admit selected women to the canon of great artists. In its place, she called for "a radical reform, if not a total Reconstruction of the present structure of the discipline . . . in order to arrive at a real understanding of the history of women and art." (Frueh, 1991, p. 52, quoting from R. Parker & G. Pollock *Old Mistresses: Women, Art, and Ideology*, 1981). Consequently, a second-stage multiculturalism would select artworks based on the uniqueness of the separate experiences of women, minorities, and other social entities. Such second-stage scholarship examines social class systems, sexism, and even basic assumptions about what constitutes "art." In the case of feminism, crafts such as quilting, normally done only by women, have been deemed low art while similar non-objective designs in paintings by Mondrian and Rothko are called high art.

Second-stage scholarship can serve to define the direction art curricula need to develop. While first-stage scholarship includes the previously excluded, those admitted must endure comparison in terms of criteria upon which the previously admitted had been recognized. While new and previously ignored works are being included among masterpieces, they may not always stand up to the narrowly defined standards of the past. As a result, they may seem to be second-rate because only those works which can be evaluated by traditional assumptions can be considered in the selection process. As a result, negative stereotypes might be reinforced rather than dispelled.

Frueh offered a rationale for new scholarship. She noted that, "Actually, feminists serve both art and art history: by seeking knowledge about the overlooked meanings of art by examining our own unacknowledged assumptions and biases and those of previous and contemporary art historians and critics; and by developing ways to write about art that will serve as new models for art critical discourse" (p. 50).

JOHN A. STINESPRING

FIRST EXAMPLE: ARTEMISIA GENTILESCHI

Let us consider an example to illustrate the paradigm. Artemisia Gentileschi (1593-1652/53), in 1616 the first woman to join the Accademia, the fraternity of painters in Florence, could be included in the standard list of Italian Baroque painters along with men of that time such as Annibale Carracci (1560-1609), Guido Reni (1575-1642), and Guercino (1591-1666). Gentileschi's paintings of *Judith and Maidservant with the Head of Holofernes* (c. 1625), *Susanna and the Elders* (1610), *The Penitent Magdalene* (c. 1619-20), *Portrait of a Condottierre* (1622), and *David and Bathsheba* (c. 1640-45), could stand comfortably beside Carracci's ceiling fresco in the gallery of the Farnese Palace (1597-1604), Reni's *Aurora* (1613), and Guercino's *Aurora* (1621-23) (Janson, 1977, pp. 484 -485). Mere appreciation of her artwork might be misinterpreted as suggesting that women and minorities can find their way to inclusion among the greats. While this may be partially true, it fails to recognize the struggles of the dispossessed, as well as their unique perspectives deriving from their life circumstances.

This level of inclusion alone fails to reveal what needs to be understood to appreciate Gentileschi's choice of strong women as subject matter. In actuality, Artemisia Gentileschi had to go through experiences unlike those of most male artists of her time. Although her father was included in contemporary biographies of artists, his more able daughter was all but ignored. As a woman, she was denied the usual training for artists: drawing antique casts, copying famous paintings, and drawing from nude male models. Her father studied with Caravaggio. To provide his daughter with art training, he hired Agostino Tassi to teach her perspective. The teacher raped her; her father took him to a court which tortured Artemesia with a thumbscrew as a kind of lie detector. Her forced testimony did result in his conviction and sentence to prison. However, after Tassi served only eight months in prison, he was acquitted. Artemesia was then branded as a sexually licentious woman. Yet, she has been declared "the first woman in the history of western art to make a significant and undeniably important contribution to the art of her time." (Harris & Nochlin, 1989, p. 118)

Her work has been admired for its Caravaggesque quality—still first-stage thinking—and full-scale figure compositions. At the same time her paintings are unique in their emphasis on psychological drama rather than the physical charms of the women portrayed. Second-stage scholarship gives the subjects of these works more meaning as uniquely feminine symbol systems. For example, a story from the Apocrypha tells how Judith saved Israel from Babylonian conquest by working her way into the enemy camp and then cutting off the head of Holofernes, leader of the Babylonian

MULTICULTURALISM IN ART

army. The army was so demoralized when the severed head was displayed the next morning that they were defeated. Or, in the case of Susanna, another Apocryphal heroine, we see a strong woman who refused to submit to sexual assault by two elders who then accused her of adultery. After an arduous trial, she was acquitted on the strength of her character and the elders were condemned. Another painting by Gentileschi featured Bathsheba, the mother of King Solomon, who was a strong woman and seemed to control events around herself. Heller (1987) characterized Gentileschi's work as portraying heroines "with a combination of vulnerability and strength" (p. 30).

SECOND EXAMPLE: EDMONIA LEWIS

Interpreting the experience of Edmonia Lewis, a sculptor born in New York in 1845, provides another illustration of the use of second-stage multiculturalism. Her father was an African American fugitive slave, her mother a Mississauga (Chippewa) Native American. They lived with the Mississauga until the Indians feared that allowing Blacks to marry tribe members would undermine their special rights on the reservation if the White society decided they were no longer Indians. When Edmonia was nine, her parents died and she went back to live with her Mississauga aunts. While in constant fear of being caught by slave hunters, she lived an Indian existence of wandering, fishing, swimming, and moccasin and basket making. Because her brother had gone to California and gained wealth in the gold rush, she was able to go to New York Central College, a Baptist abolitionist school. She found the English language and non-Indian rules about bedtime, dress, and meals difficult. The school was shut down in 1858 for admitting Black and female students. In 1859, her brother sent her to Oberlin College, a strong center of abolitionist thought. There she learned drawing.

The Oberlin College campus was upset by the arrest, trial, and hanging of anti-slavery agitator John Brown in 1859. Yet Edmonia became the victim of prejudice at that same institution when two female classmates accused her of poisoning them and caused her to be brutally beaten. Edmonia had difficulties getting along with the other students because of her Indian behaviors. Some people objected to having Blacks at Oberlin. While Edmonia was subsequently acquitted at the trial, the experience left her emotionally scarred and unable to trust anyone.

The next year, she was twice accused of stealing paint brushes and a picture frame. Even though the charges were dropped, Oberlin refused to let her register for the next semester. A sympathetic trustee gave the 18-year old woman a letter of introduction to use in finding a position in

Boston. She was able to make a living by making clay and plaster copies of popular figures such as John Brown. Nonetheless, even ardent abolitionists did not always believe Blacks had the intellectual capacity to do fine art. They saw her difficulties in speaking English and lack of traditionally refined manners as evidence of this inferiority. In spite of such obstacles, she established some reputation with a sculpture of an Oberlin classmate killed in the Civil War. She sold plaster copies of it, earning enough money to go to Italy to study sculpture in 1865.

In Italy in 1869, she produced a statue of Hagar, the biblical Egyptian who was cast out into the wilderness after bearing Abraham's child. An angel has just asked, "What aileth thee, Hagar?" Some art historians argue that Lewis identified her difficulties at Oberlin with Hagar's rejection by the Israelites. The production of the statue caused financial difficulties. She turned to John Jones, a successful African American in the tailoring and dry cleaning business, for support. He encouraged her to put the statue on exhibit. The resulting exhibit advertisement promoted the work as by "the young and gifted colored sculptress from Rome." She charged twenty-five cents for admission and, in 1870, was able to sell the piece for $6,000. Apparently many people came to see if it was possible for a woman, and a Black one at that, to make art (Bearden & Hendersen, 1993, p. 69).

Edmonia Lewis continued to make art that challenged concepts of style and subject master. Her work fluctuated between Naturalism and a commercially successful neoclassicism. Her sculpted faces tended to be Neoclassical generalizations while the garments, poses, and decorations are authentic Mississauga. This conflict can be seen in her sculpture, *Forever Free* (c. 1872), in which the man looks African American, but the woman is an idealized non-African.

Lewis' most talked about work was her 12-foot high, two-ton *Death of Cleopatra* (c. 1871-1875), selected to be included among the 673 sculptures exhibited at the 1876 Centennial Exposition. This is the same exhibit that rejected Thomas Eakins' *Gross Clinic* (1875) as not being art and placed it in the medical section instead. *Death of Cleopatra* was not without controversy itself because the pain she showed on Cleopatra's face departed from the Neoclassical tradition and offended Victorian ideas of idealized noble suffering. One source described Cleopatra as "the grandest statue in the exposition" (Helter, p. 87.) Unfortunately, the work has been lost.

While Edmonia Lewis may eventually have achieved some measure of success, it was a difficult path compounded by her gender and race. Her experiences probably influenced her selection of subject matter; her criteria of success for a work of art must have been at variance from the norms of the art establishment at the time. An evaluation of her work must consider what would speak artistically to one who was female, Black, and shared Native American ancestry. Further, the "realities" in the artwork can be assessed only in terms of understanding experiences of prejudice, discrimination and struggle. The established canon of "great artworks" may not have been broad enough to accommodate these perspectives.

THIRD EXAMPLE: ED WILSON

Whenever one examines the artistic experiences of any of the under-represented artiste for whom we have some sort of record, we almost invariably find unique experiences related to belonging to the under represented group. Of course, the selectivity of the art establishment may have relegated many artists of excellence to anonymity, or they may have been completely lost to the world, never to be recovered. But, while looking almost at random at the information that we do have about women and minority artists, we find evidence of struggles and unique experiences. Take the case of sculptor Ed Wilson (b.1925). Now rather well recognized for his commissioned works, such as the bronze relief patterns in the JFK Memorial Park (1969) in Binghamton, New York; *Second Genesis* (1969-71) in Baltimore's Lake Clifton High School; and *Jazz Musicians* (1982-84) at Baltimore's Douglass High School, he had much experience with prejudice and discrimination.

Wilson was drafted into the Air Force in World War II and fell under the command of a highly prejudiced officer who demeaned him and intentionally made life miserable while refusing his requests for a transfer. The bad military experience caused him to give up the idea of becoming an architect, but he was able to use the GI Bill to attend the University of Iowa to study art. After completing his master's degree in 1953, he began to teach art at North Carolina College (now North Carolina Central University) in Durham, a traditionally all Black institution. His anger made him want to "destroy the system that had brought about all that inhumanity" (Bearden & Hendersen, 1993, pp. 454-455). He was furious with African Americans who, having achieved some success, were reluctant to challenge discrimination. His outspoken behavior caused him to be perceived as subversive, radical, or rebellious. He was often torn between his desire to be a civil-rights activist and his drive to be a productive artist.

CONCLUSION

The cases of Gendleschi, Lewis, and Wilson are illustrations of movement beyond first-stage to the second stage of multiculturalism. It is not enough to select good works and only identify the race, ethnicity, and/

or gender of the artist as examples are presented in the classroom. The lesson needs to include experiences of hardship, discrimination, and the unique perspective that other persons in the same circumstances may develop, as well as explanations of socio-cultural context in order to help the student to better appreciate the subject matter of an artwork. Often the same forces and circumstances that caused exclusion or under representation in the art world have caused discrimination and neglect in other aspects of society. The same barriers to full citizenship, equality of opportunity, and economic stability were at work in the arts.

A teacher's task is further complicated by the need to go beyond the already diverse population of the United States to recognize the existence of additional varieties of cultural traditions and experiences that have made an impact on the world of art. Suddenly, art teachers are being exhorted to make inclusion a major theme in their curricula. The bewildering array of available choices makes the job appear insurmountable. It can seem all too easy to give up and return to what one has been doing all along.

Rather than give up, teachers need to find some examples of artists and artworks that go beyond the traditional list. Rather than adopting a these-artists-were-good-too approach (firststage multiculturalism), some information about the uniqueness of the female, minority, or international artist's experience and world-view should be provided along with examples of their artwork and opportunities for formal analysis. Equitable coverage of all of the world's diversity is challenging for an individual teacher, if, indeed, such an ideal would be ever possible for anyone. But exposure to some examples of diversity can help move students to a second-stage of multiculturalism. Sources of information are improving (see Bearden & Hendersen, 1993; Harris & Nochlin, 1989; Heller, 1987.) Diversity is, after all, a concept with some universality. Learning that we are not all alike, but that we can each be respected and, to some extent, understood, is an important idea which can be advanced very successfully in the art classroom.

REFERENCES

Bearden, R. & Hendersen, H. (1993). *A history of African-American artists. From 1792 to the present.* New York: Pantheon.

Frueh, J. (1991). Towards a feminist theory of art criticism. In H. Smagula (Ed.), *Revisions: New perspectives of art criticism* (pp.50-64). Englewood Cliffs, NJ: Prentice Hall.

Harris, A. S., & Nochlin, L (1989). *Women artists: 1550-1950.* New York: Alfred A. Knopf.

Heller, N. G. (1987). *Women artists: An illustrated history* (rev. ed.). New York: Abbeville Press.

Janson, H. W. (1977). *History of art* (2nd Ed.). Englewood Cliffs, NJ: Prentice Hall.

Minor, V. H. (1994). *Art history's history.* Englewood Cliffs, NJ: Prentice Hall.

Editor's Note: Since this article was written, the statue has been found.

John A. Stinespring is associate professor of art in the Department of Art at Texas Tech University in Lubbock.

QUESTIONS FOR DISCUSSION

1. What do we mean by the term "multiculturalism"? Why does the author begin the article by saying that most art teachers are sensitive to calls for "multicultural course content"?

2. The author says that typically we are slow to claim the negative about Western culture, including "ethnocentrism, racism, sexism, and homophobia." What do these terms mean and why are they problems in Western culture?

3. What does the author mean by second-stage multiculturalism and how does it differ from first-stage?

4. The author provides three examples of artists who have historically been under-represented. How do these artists illustrated second-stage multiculturalism?

5. Why does the author think that it is important for us to study art from such a multicultural perspective? Do you agree with his argument?

6. Look closely at the documentation style in the references list. What is the style and why do you think this journal uses it?

213

Playing It Safe

Britt Allen

Every day, performers around the world experience pain as they practice their art. You may know of some who have had to terminate their careers, not due to a lack of commitment but because injuries made performance impossible. A new medical field, performing arts medicine, has developed over the past fifteen years to serve the needs of performers and to treat their injuries and illnesses. It is equivalent to the athlete's sports medicine.

Music teachers and performers realize that playing musical instruments can result in some aches and pains. Many, however, may not be aware of the range of these injuries, either in terms of frequency or severity (see the *Music Educators Journal*'s special focus issue on music education and medicine, January 1991). Some instrumentalists choose to ignore their injuries because they feel responsible for their symptoms.

The most common performance related injuries include muscle spasms, tendinitis, and nerve impingements. These injuries occur because performers place abnormal stress on their musculo-skeletal systems—the human hand was not designed to hold a violin bow or achieve a four-mallet technique. Performance-related injuries can result from several factors: overuse, misuse, and the repetitive stress involved in prolonged practice. Faulty techniques, poor physical conditioning, stressful postural positioning, and extreme schedules increase the risk of injury. A congenital defect may also contribute to physical problems.

Although there is no guarantee that performance-related injuries can be avoided during the career of a musician, the risk of injury can be decreased by using a few preventive techniques. First, adjust your instrument to maintain correct posture during practice and concert performance. For example, saxophonists should keep neck straps at a comfortable height, trombonists should not rest the bell of their horn on their knee, and violinists must never twist their necks to fit their instrument. Incorrect posture, besides restricting your breathing, also increases tension in the body and makes you tire more easily. If you're a pianist who slouches over the keyboard, you may find you can only practice for an hour. But, if you maintain good posture and sit up straight, your level of endurance increases substantially.

From *Teaching Music* (1996, Vol. 4.1, pp. 30-31). Copyright 1996 by Music Educators National Conference. Reprinted with permission.

PLAYING IT SAFE

Musicians should not experience any tension when performing. If you play woodwinds, be aware of jaw tension. A small amount of cushioning tape placed on the top of a mouthpiece can help alleviate the "lockjaw" syndrome. If you're a string player, remember to keep your left hand relaxed. Fast fingerings cannot be executed if the hand is rigid. All percussionists have to use relaxed strokes, even hand drummers. A good slap on a *djembe* (an African drum) will never be achieved with tension in the hands. Relaxation is the key for all instrumentalists. A performance routine combining stretches, warm-ups, and cool-downs decreases the risk of injury. Think like an athlete. You would never run a marathon without stretching, warming up, and cooling down—a marching band rehearsal is just as demanding

Time management is essential for painless practice. It is better to practice for short periods of time regularly, rather than perform a long practice session every few days. If practice must continue for an extended period of time, alternate short periods of practice with rest. At one time or another, everyone has to cram for a lesson or performance, but such extreme practice habits place abnormal stress on the body and can lead to injury.

The fatigue that results from poor performance habits is a major cause of performance-related injuries. As fatigue sets in, postures begin to alter, requiring adaptive movement patterns. Pain develops, technical execution suffers, and a vicious cycle is created.

Percussionists are fortunate to have more than one instrument. By practicing one hour on a variety of instruments (marimba, timpani, snare drum, etc.), they use different muscle groups. By doing so, the amount of repetitive stress placed on one area of the body is less than if practice occurred on, for instance, only marimba for several hours.

All musicians can discover ways to minimize practice time. Visualization can reduce the amount of time spent at an instrument. Mentally playing music will improve memorization skills. You may discover phrases you need to practice physically through the use of imagery. If an area of the composition is "foggy" or difficult to picture, you may not know the section well.

As teachers, you play a pivotal role in the musical health of your students. You are, in fact, the first line of defense against performance-related injuries. Always consider your students' physical characteristics when training them as instrumentalists. Make sure the instrument is the correct size and height for natural body positioning. For example, a small student should not have to overstretch to play a full-size cello. Also, the size of the student's embouchure should be taken into account when choosing a suitable wind instrument. Most important, it is your responsibility to

215

instill correct technique and safe practice habits. Although musicians do not consider themselves athletes, physicians find that the injuries sustained are similar. The instrumentalist should develop the same qualities of strength, flexibility, agility, coordination, and endurance in certain muscle groups that athletes develop overall (see Raoul Tubiana and Philippe Chamagne's article, "Functional Anatomy of the Hand," in *Medical Problems of Performing Artists,* January 1991). Physicians specializing in performing arts medicine have discovered a correlation between physical fitness and musical health (see Alice G. Brandfonbrener's article, "Performing Arts Medicine: An Evolving Specialty," in the January 1991 *MEJ*). A healthy balance of performance, exercise, diet, and sleep strengthens resistance to performance-related injuries. A study of yoga and natural movement techniques, for example, the Alexander Technique, may help develop an awareness of one's body that is invaluable to the musician.

What should you do if you or your students experience pain while playing? First, stop playing. Temporarily rest and evaluate your technique. The worse response is to "play through the pain." Pain will worsen as performance increases. Some players have been known to increase their practice sessions because they believed the pain came from insufficient practice. Remind students to come to you for help in discovering the source of any pain they may have. You may observe problems in technique that have been overlooked. If the problems with pain are not solved, suggest that the student consult a medical professional. Physicians specializing in Performing Arts medicine can be found in major cities throughout the United States and abroad. Physical therapists, yoga instructors, massage therapists, chiropractors, and other alternative health care providers also have a high level of proven success.

Dedicated musicians, both professional and amateur, are susceptible to performance-related injuries. The attitude of "the show must go on" compounds the problem. Remind your students that some musicians take better care of their instruments than they do of themselves. Advise them that they can always buy a new clarinet or violin, but their true instrument—the body—cannot be replaced.

By **Britt Allen**, DMA candidate, Division of Music, College of Creative Arts, West Virginia University, Morgantown.

QUESTIONS FOR DISCUSSION

1. What is the central argument of this article? According to the author, why is it important to pay attention to the physical as well as the musical?

2. Who is the audience for this piece? Does the audience change throughout the article? Is there more than one audience? Is the "you" at the top of page 215 ("if *you*'re a string player") the same as the "you" at the bottom of the same page ("*You* are, in fact, the first line of defense")?

3. How is musical medicine like sports medicine? How is it different? Do you think comparing music to athletics is a fair or effective comparison?

4. Why does the author say that a musician should not play through the pain? Does this same rule of thumb apply to athletes?

5. Have you had any experience with either music-related or sports-related injury? Or do you know someone else who has? Describe that experience and related it to this article.

6. Describe the tone of the article. Do you think it is effective, given the author's audience and purpose?

7. There is not a formal works cited listing for this article. Would it have been better for the author to include such a list? How effective is it to list sources right in the text itself as this author has done?